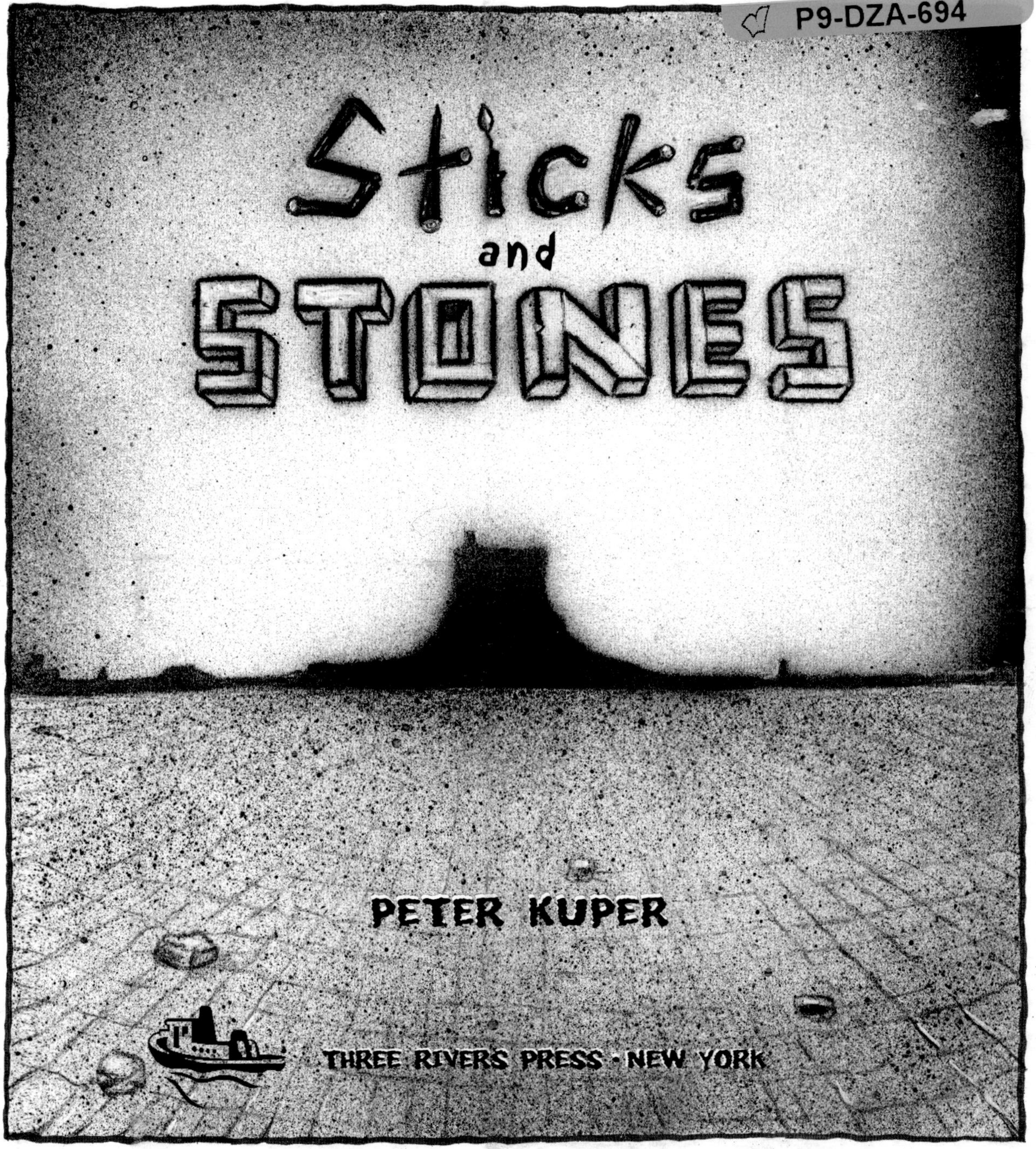
Sticks
and
STONES
PETER KUPER
THREE RIVERS PRESS · NEW YORK

Dedicated to
Walt and Nancy

Published by Three Rivers Press, New York, New York.
Member of the Crown Publishing Group,
a division of Random House, Inc.
www.crownpublishing.com
THREE RIVERS PRESS and the Tugboat design are registered trademarks of Random House, Inc.
Printed in China
Design by Peter Kuper
Production Assistance by Ryan Inzana

Library of Congress Cataloging—in—Publication Data
Kuper, Peter, 1958-
Sticks and stones: an epic in pictures / Peter Kuper.—1st ed.
1. Stories without words. I. Title.
PN6727.K67S75 2004
741.5'973—dc22 2004045969

ISBN 1-4000-5257-2
10 9 8 7 6 5 4 3 2 1
First Edition

Thanks to the inspiring work of Andy Goldsworthy;
for suggestions and critiques, Chris Jackson, Scott Cunningham,
Jim Rasenberger, John Thomas, and Seth Tobocman;
for stencil cutting and much more, Ryan Inzana;
for moral support, Betty Russell, Emily Russell,
Emily Kuper, Tony Stonier, and Steve Ross.

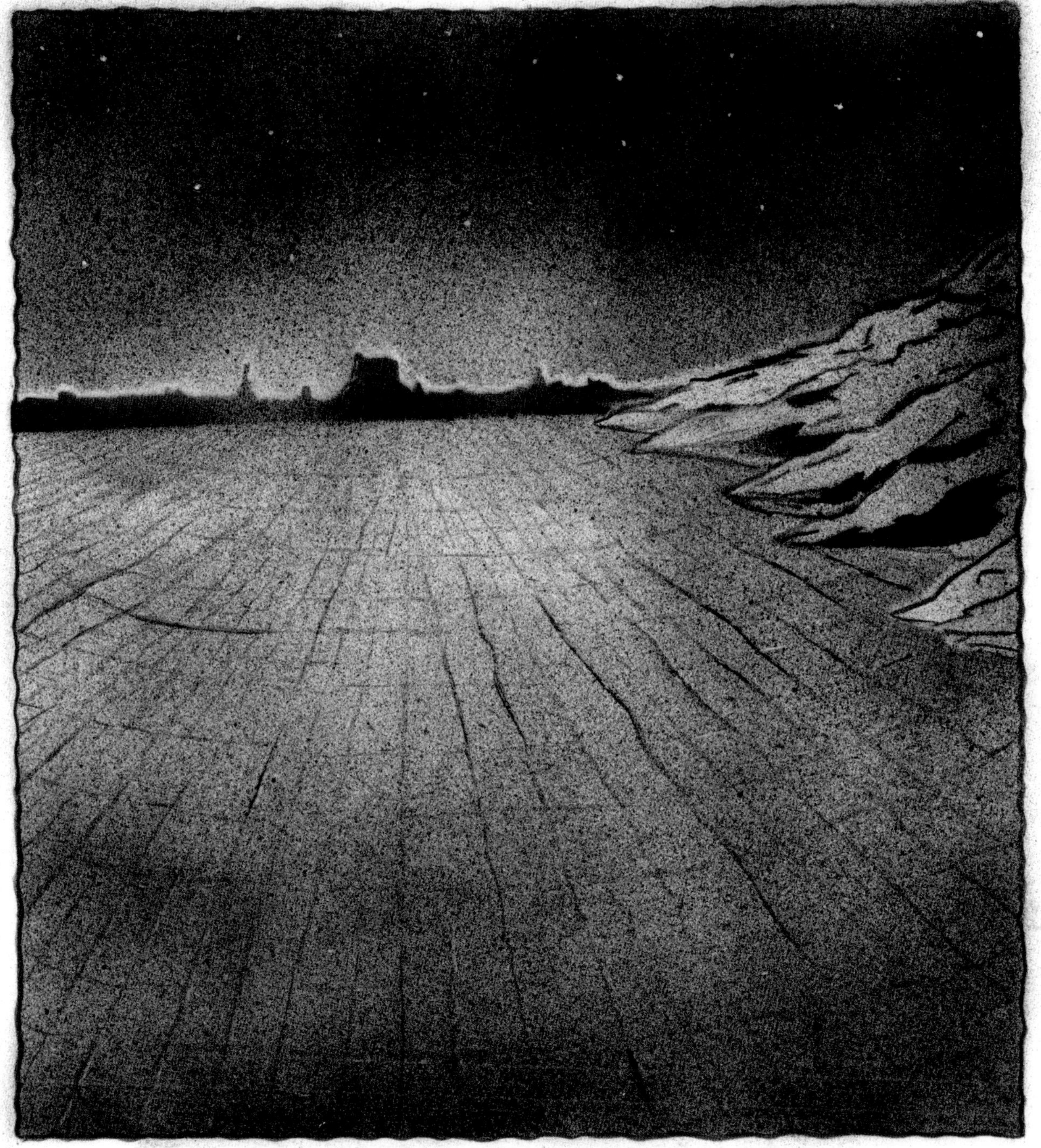

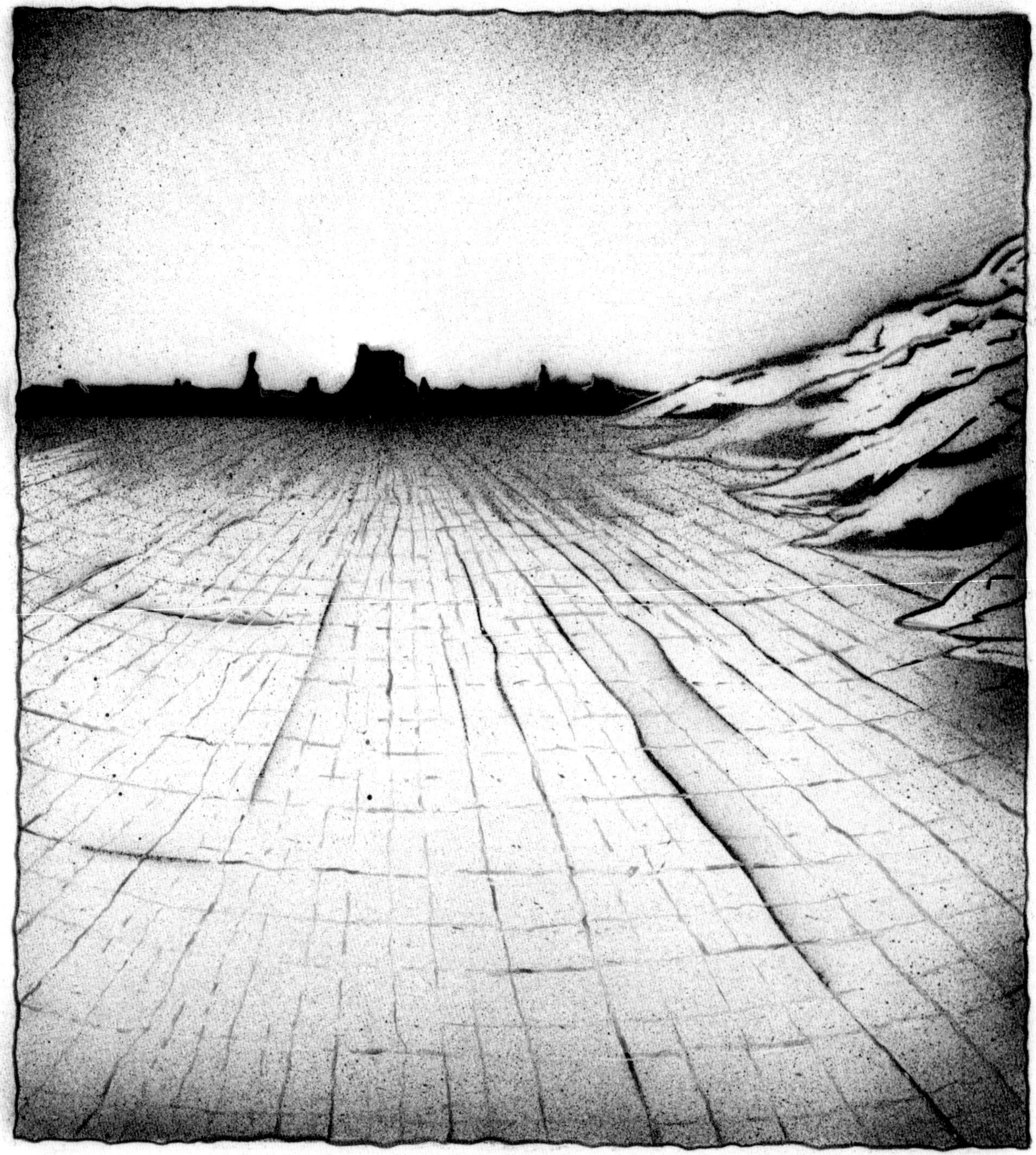

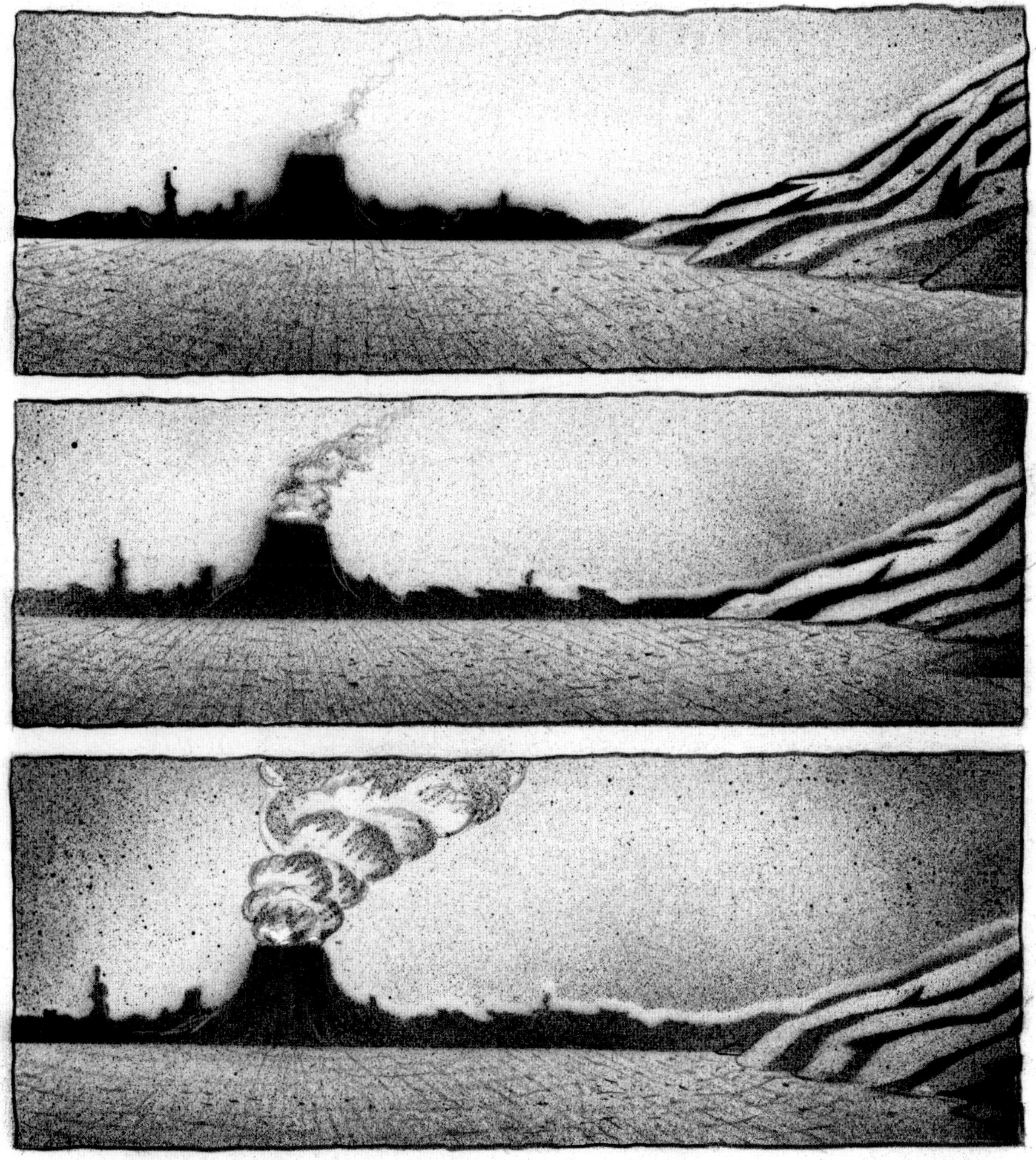

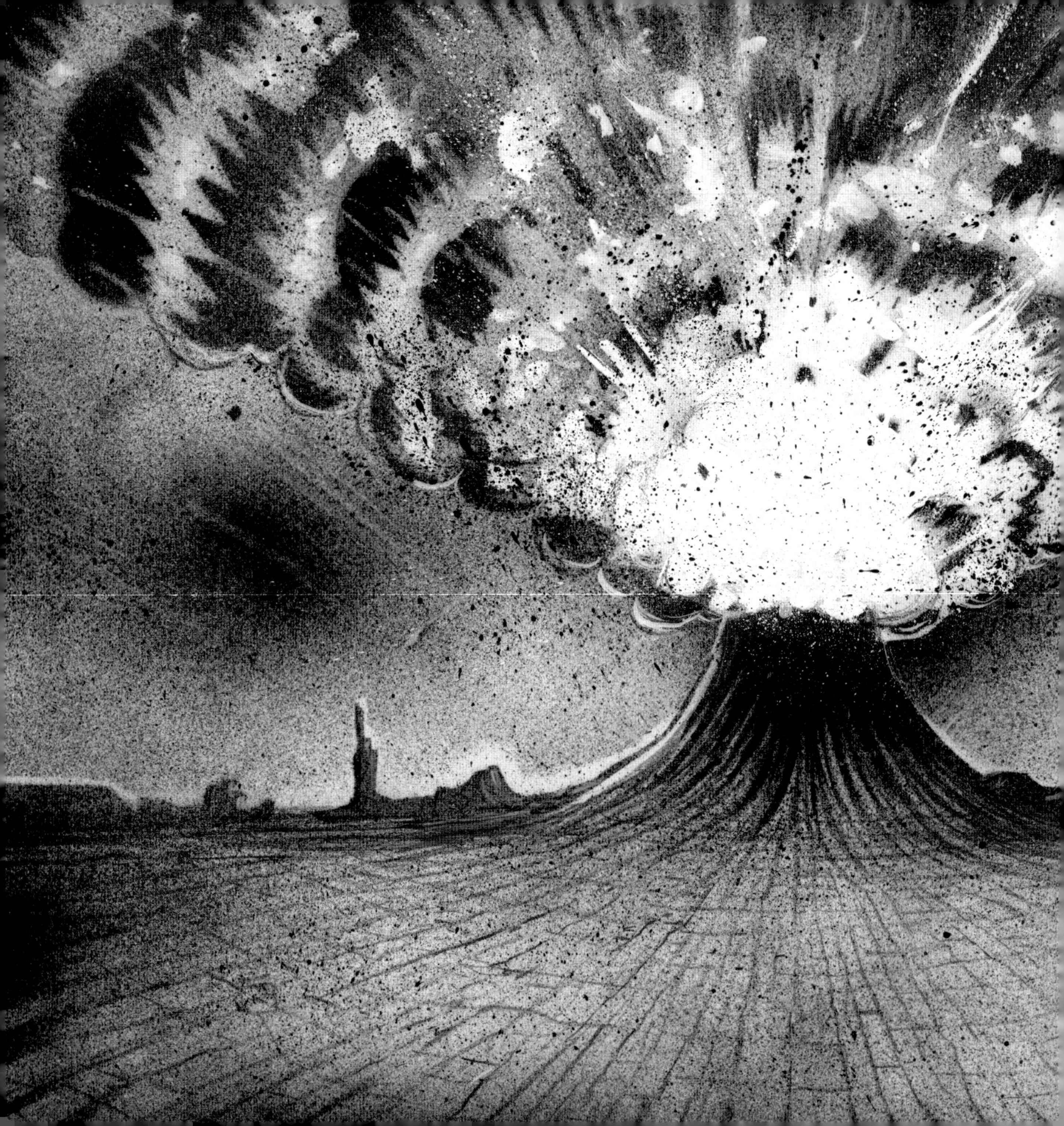

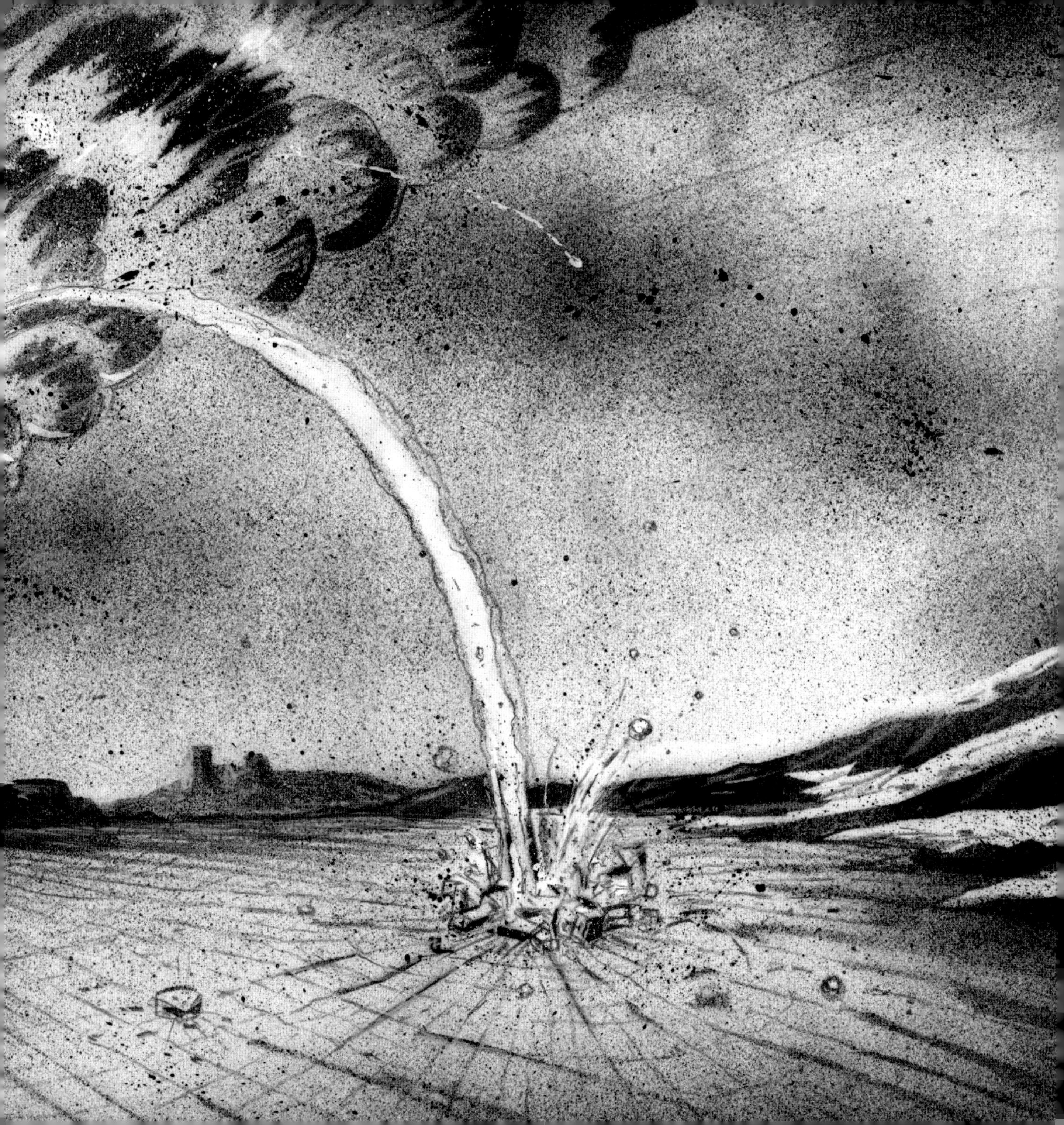

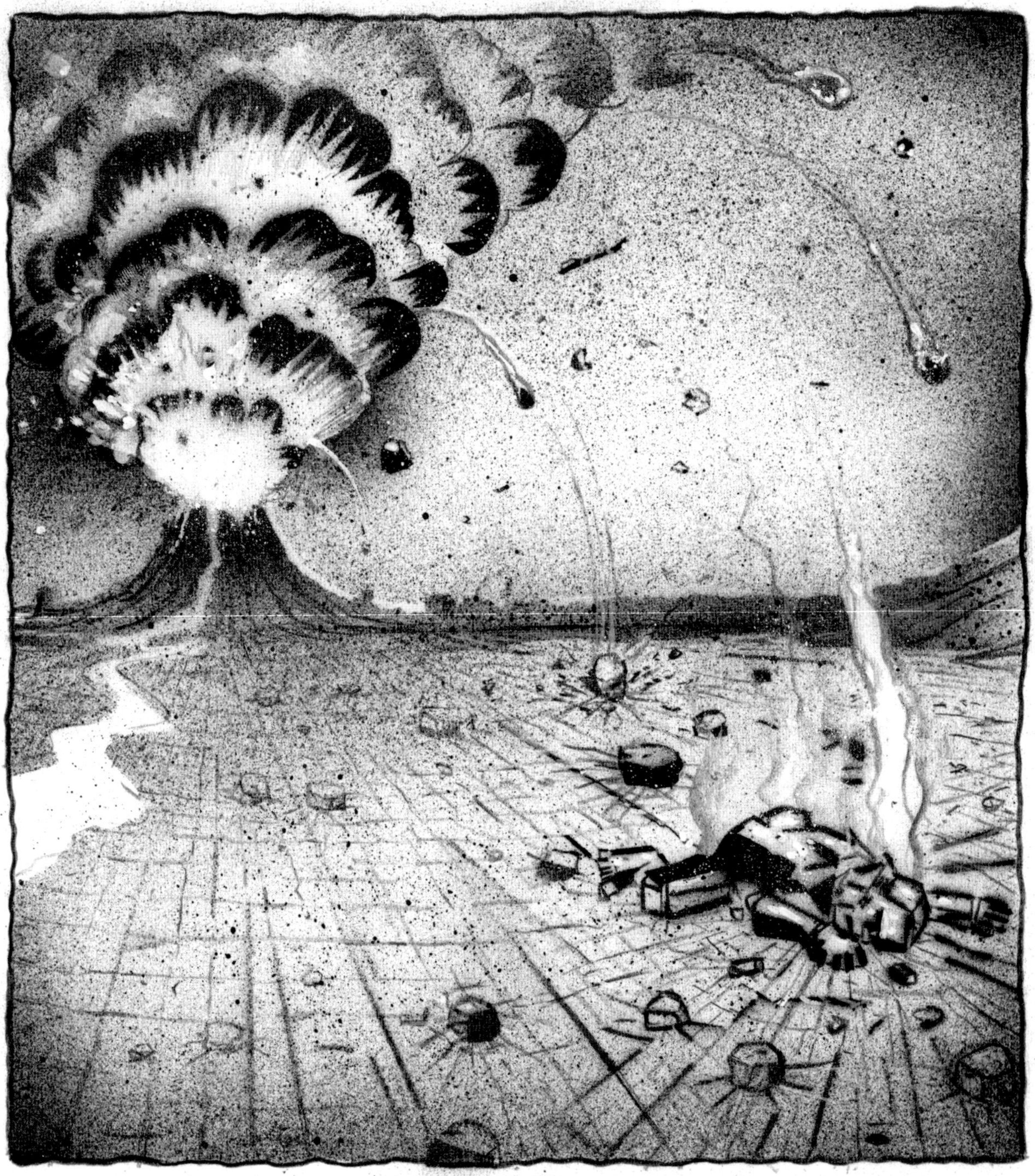

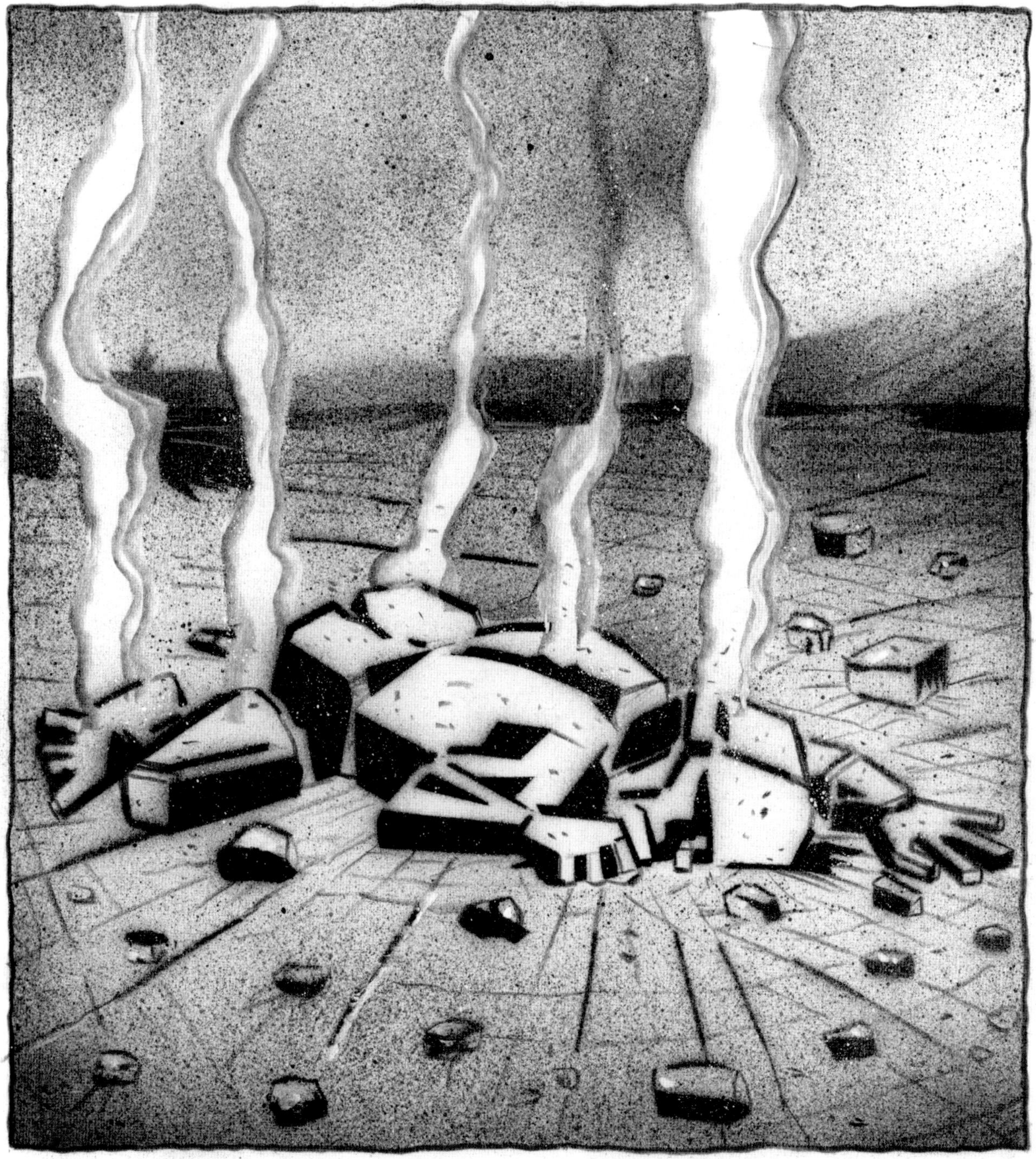

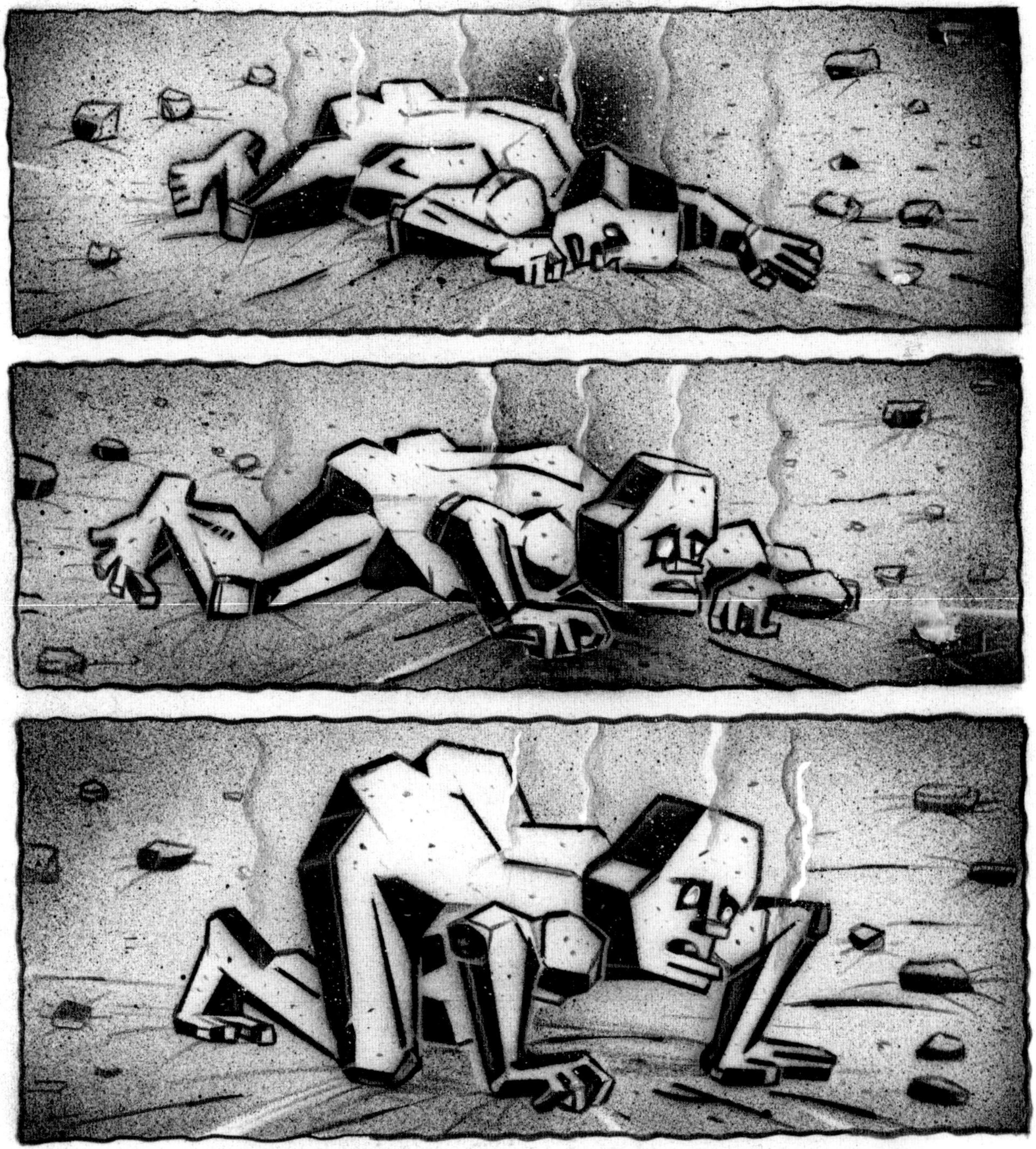

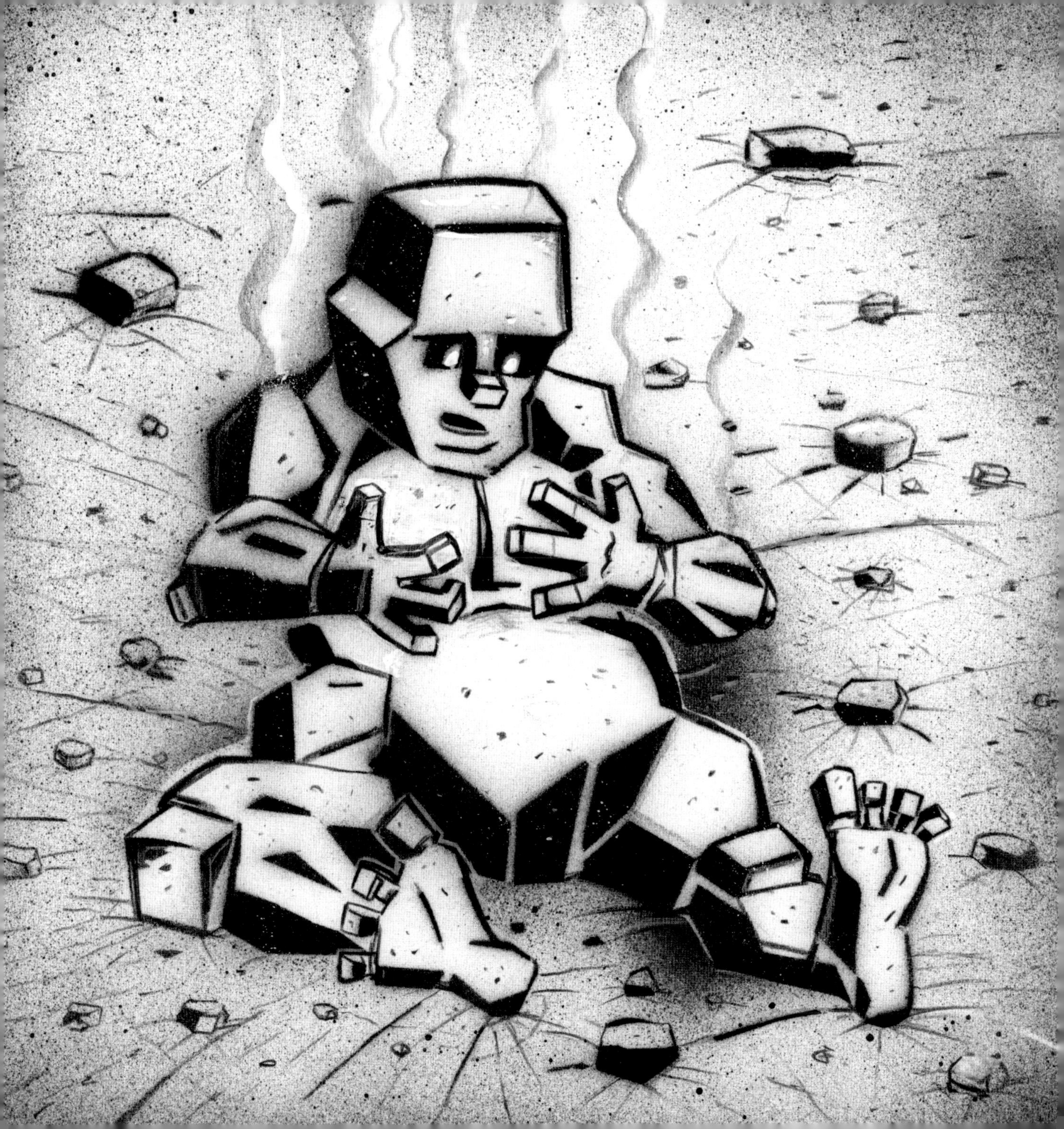

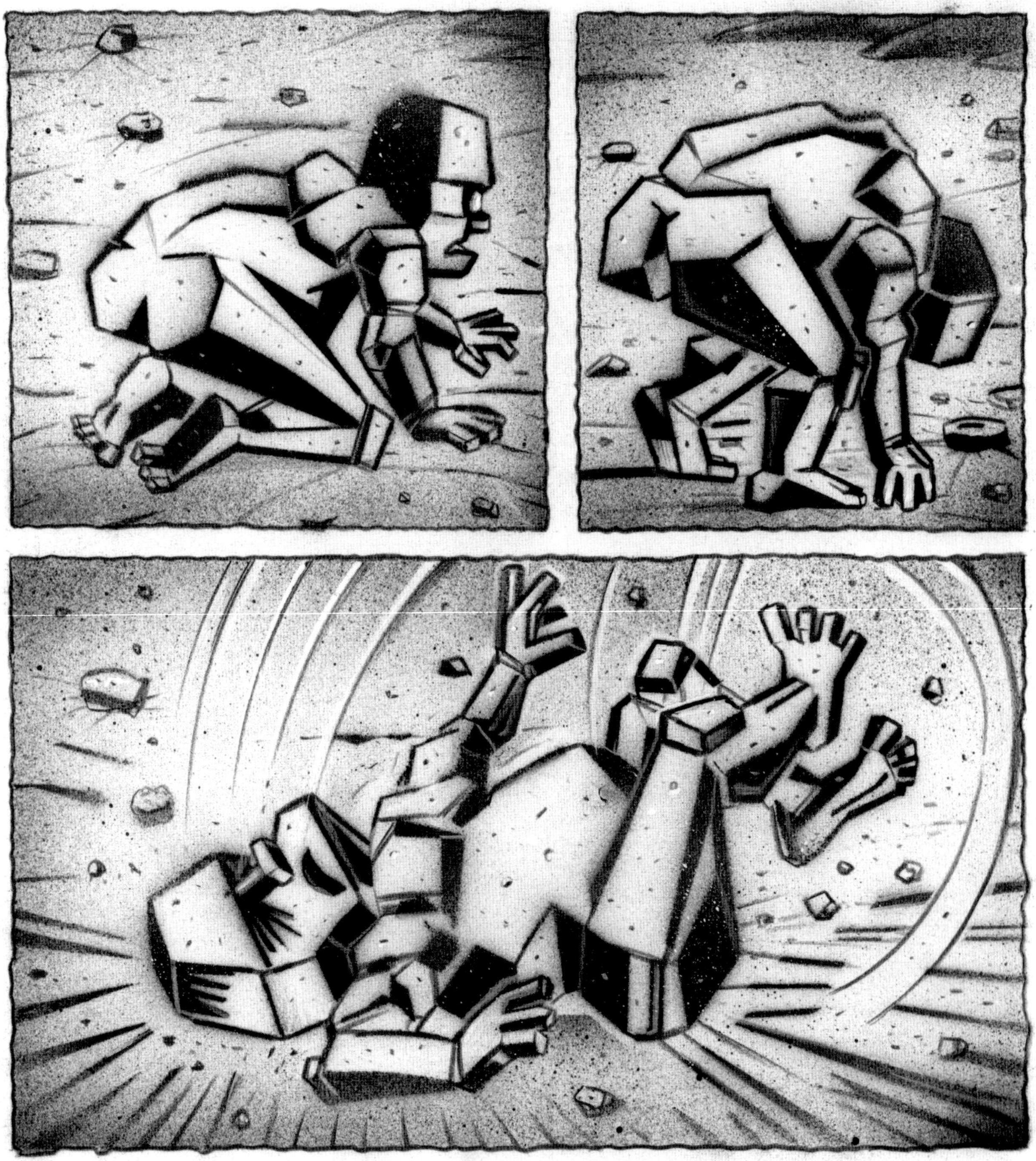

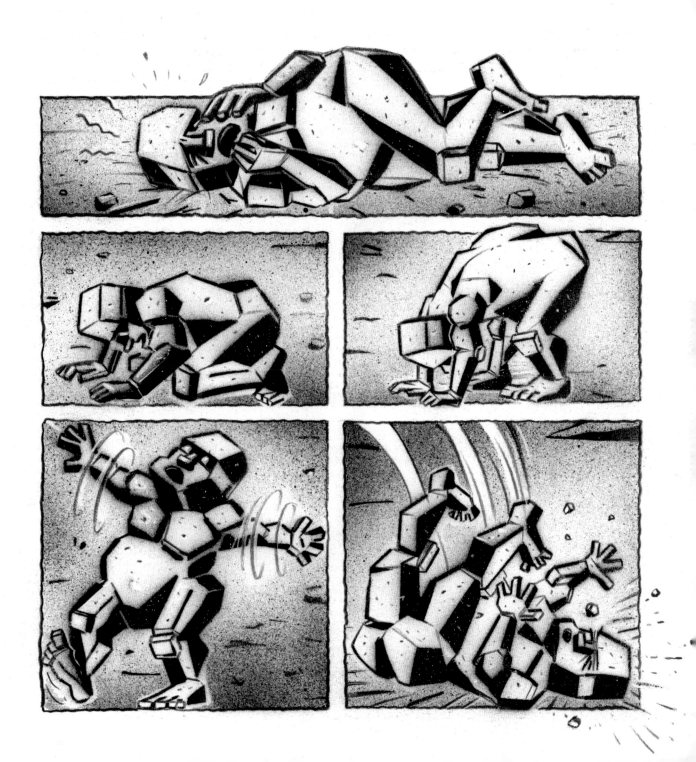

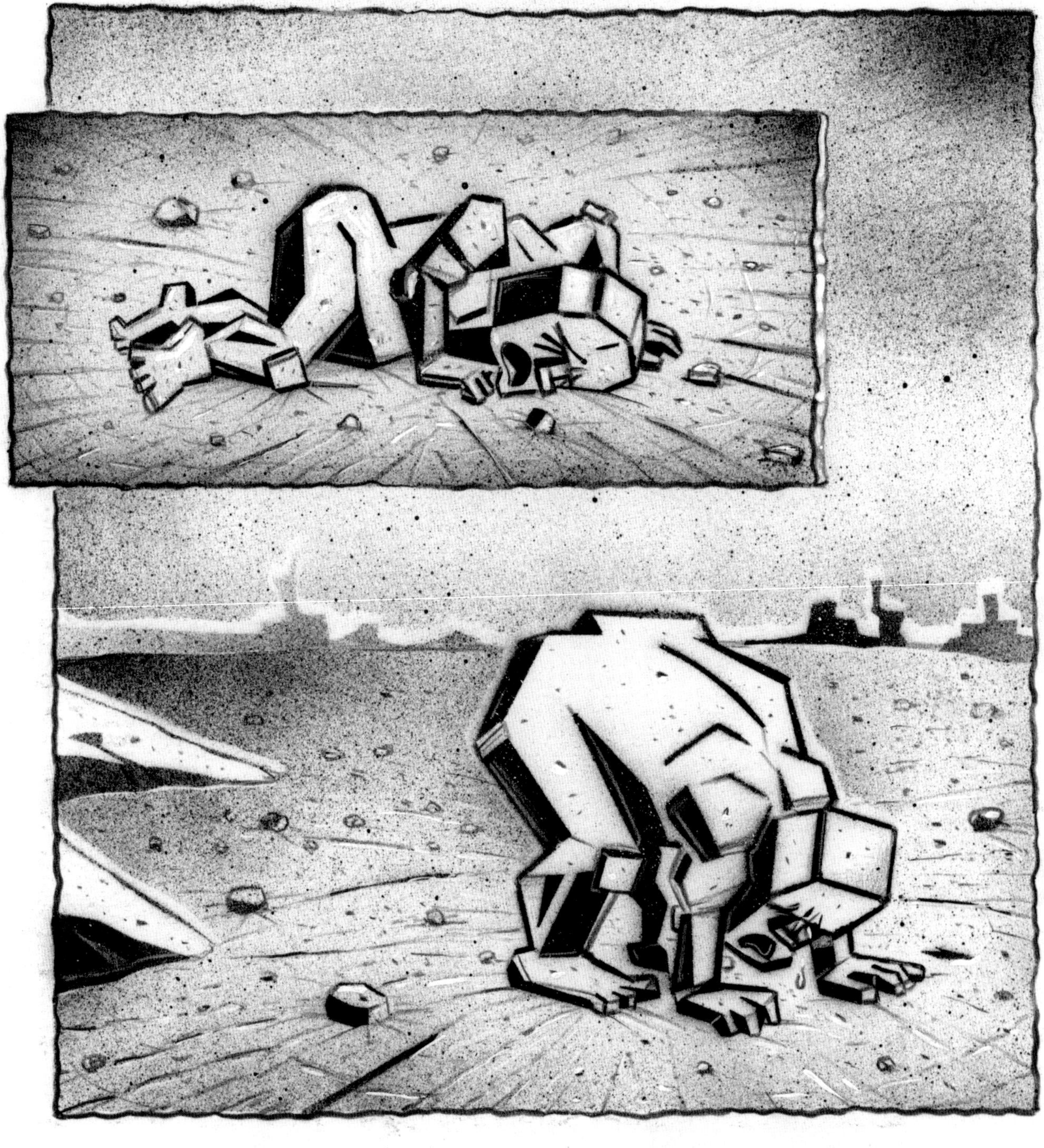

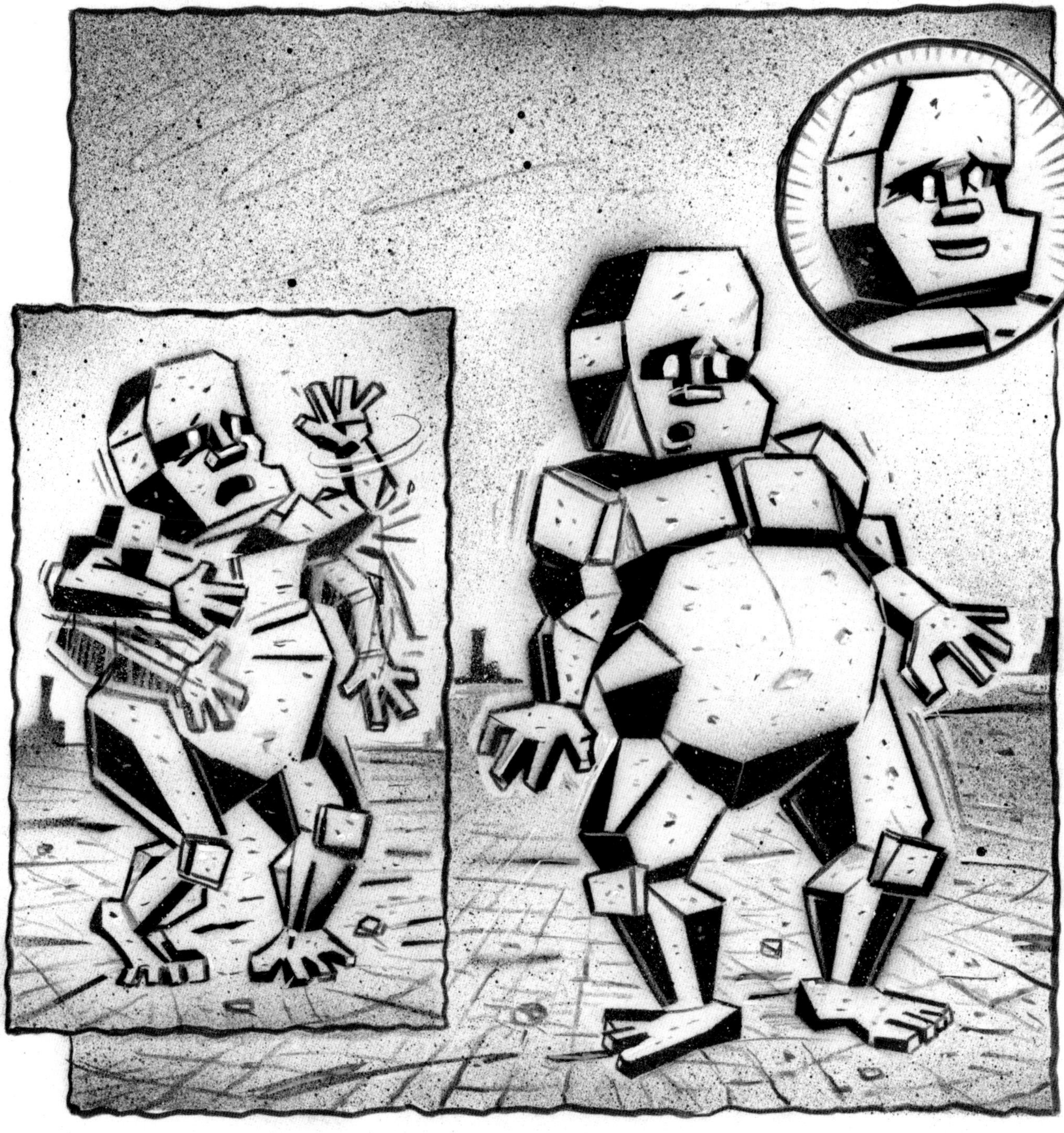

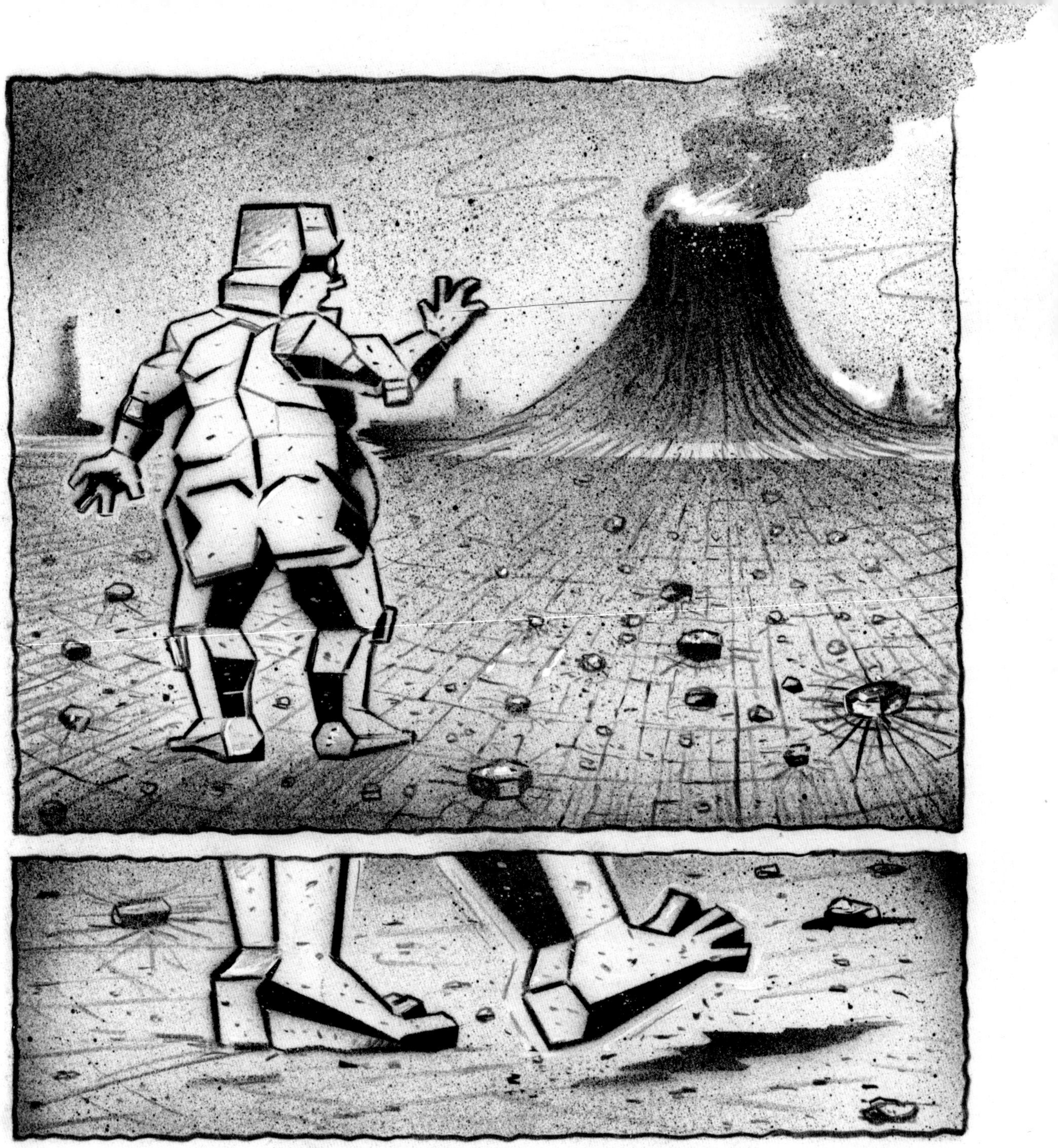

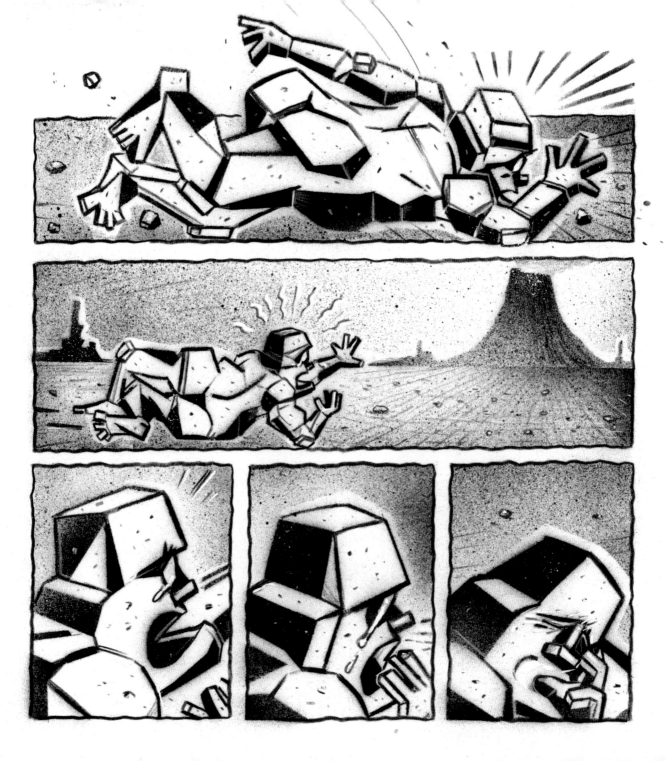

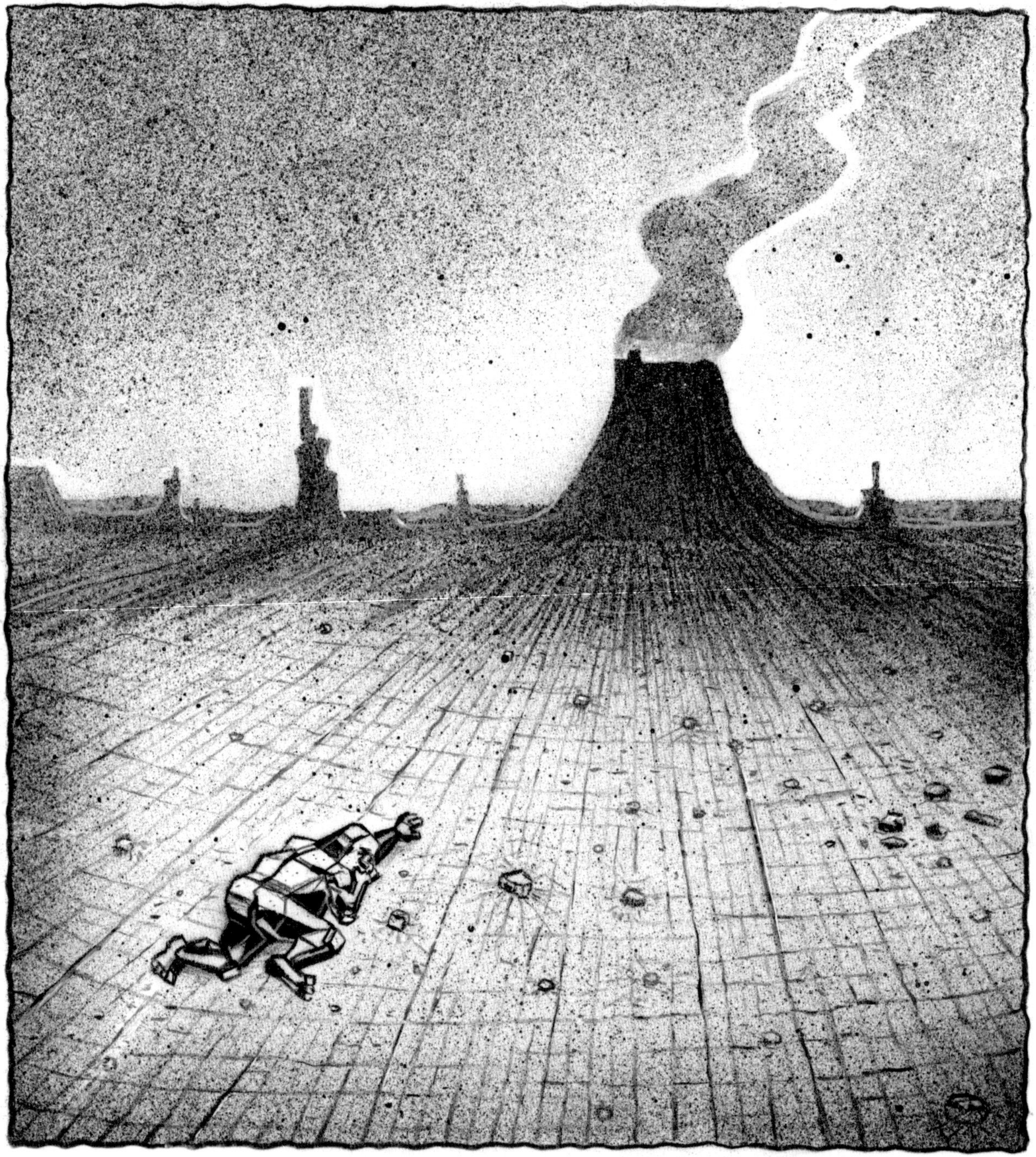

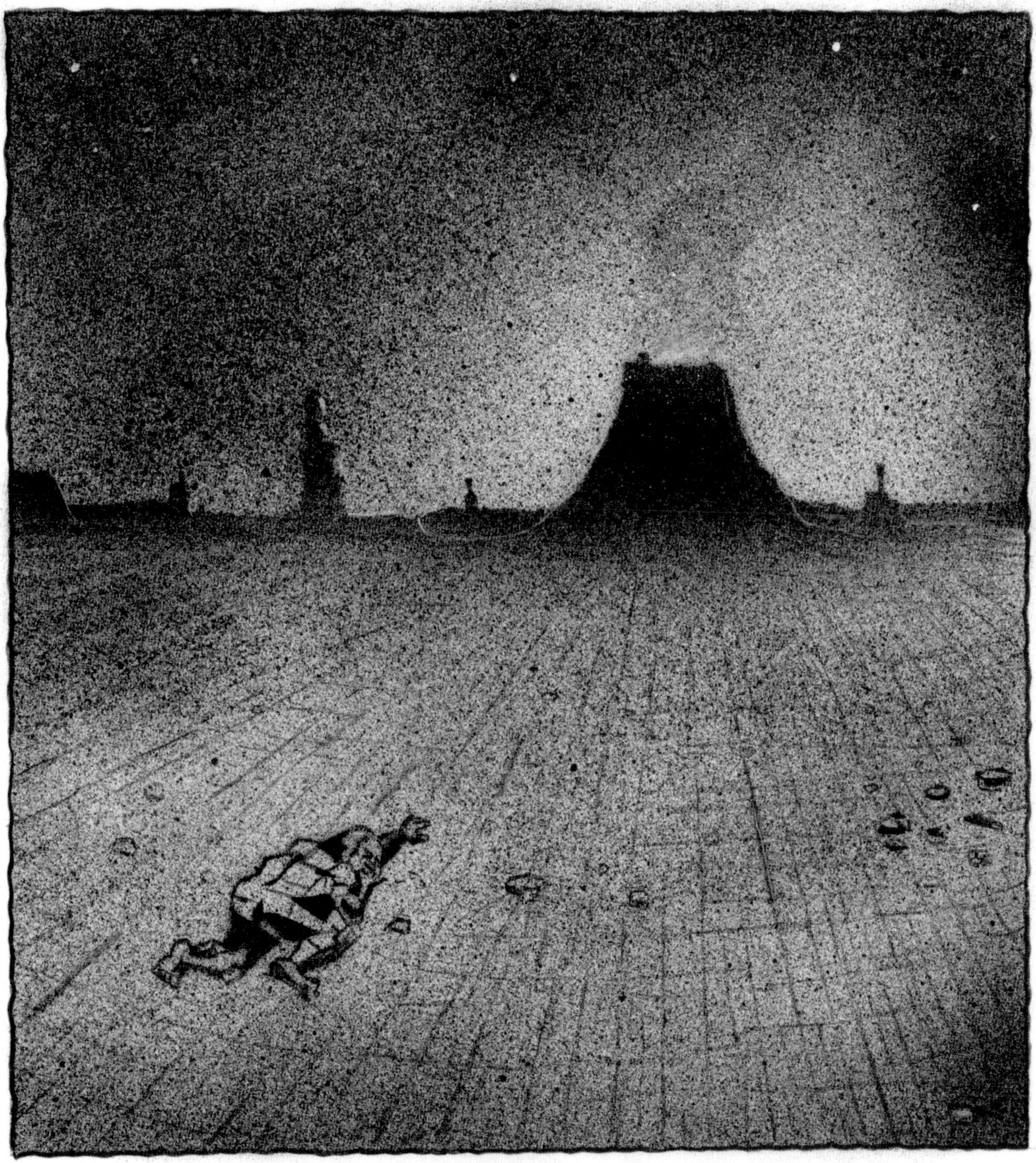

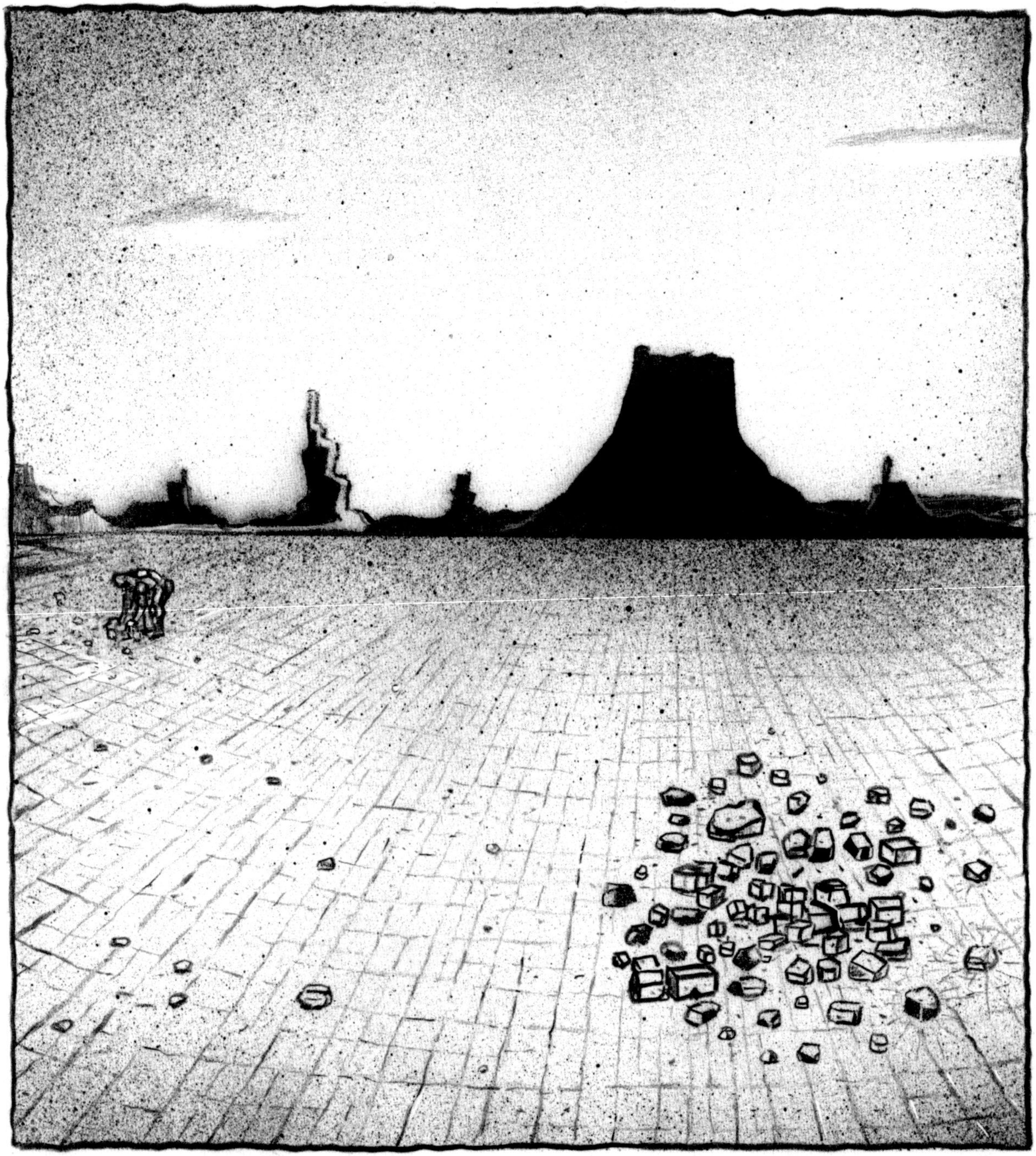

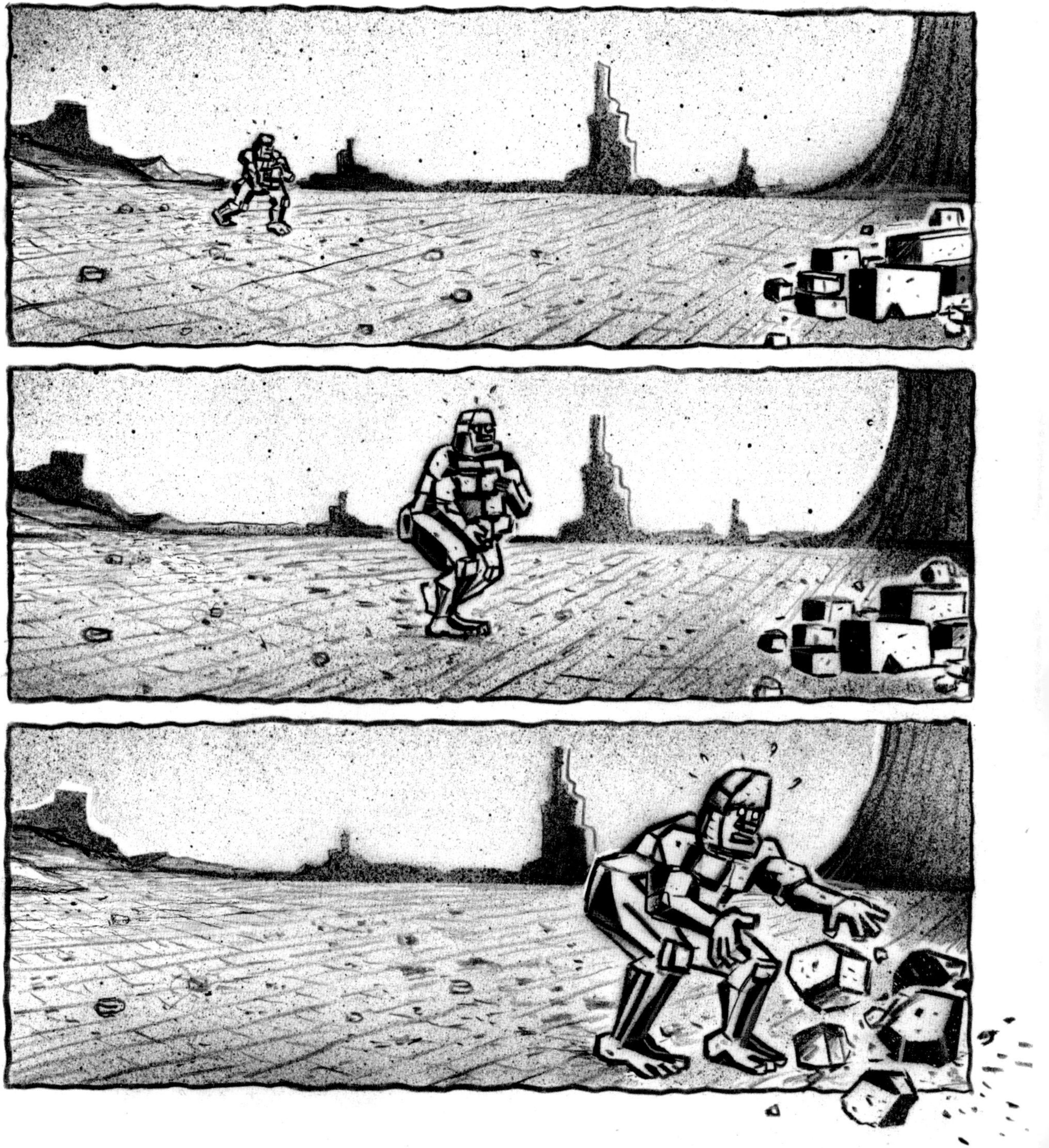

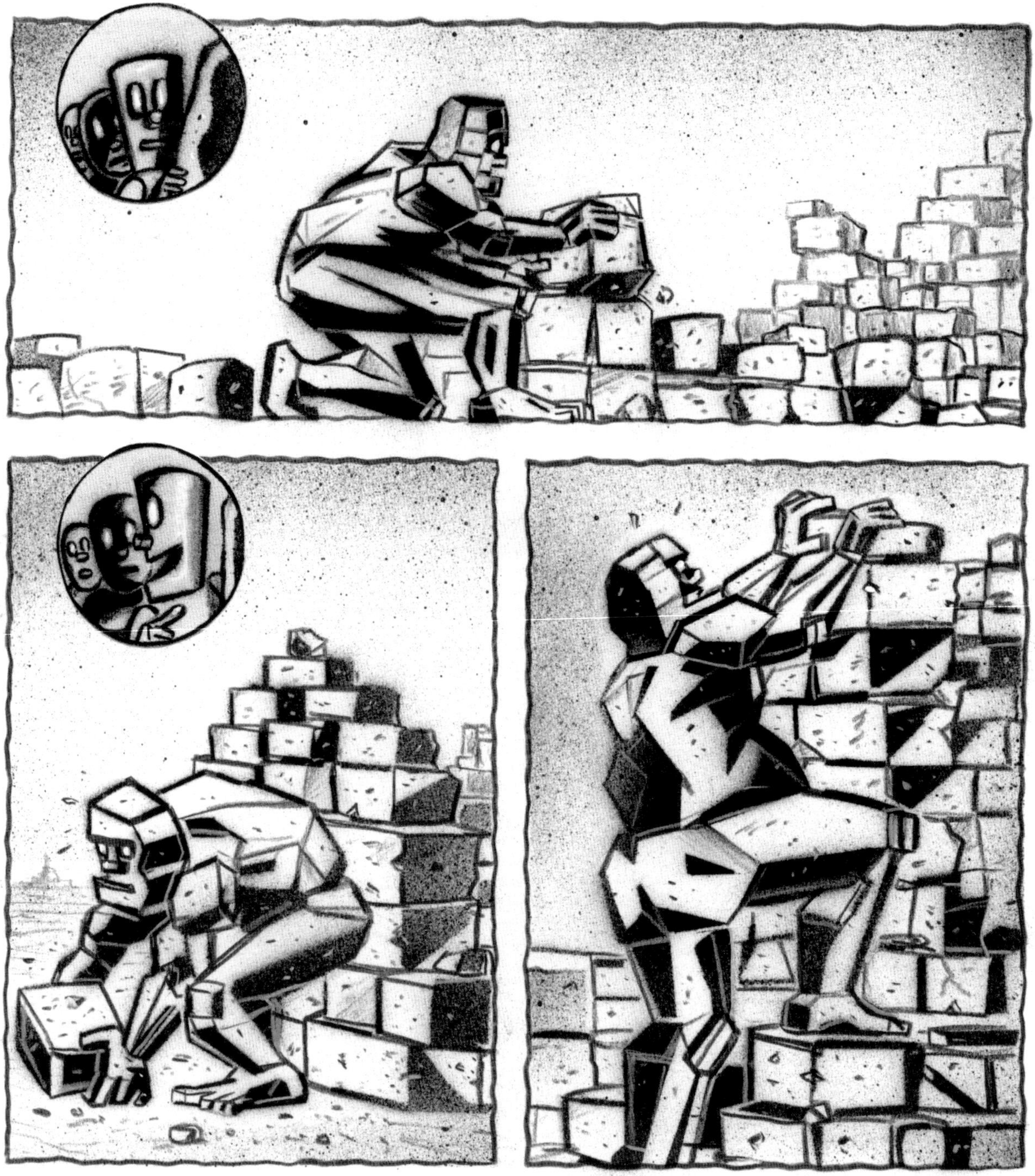

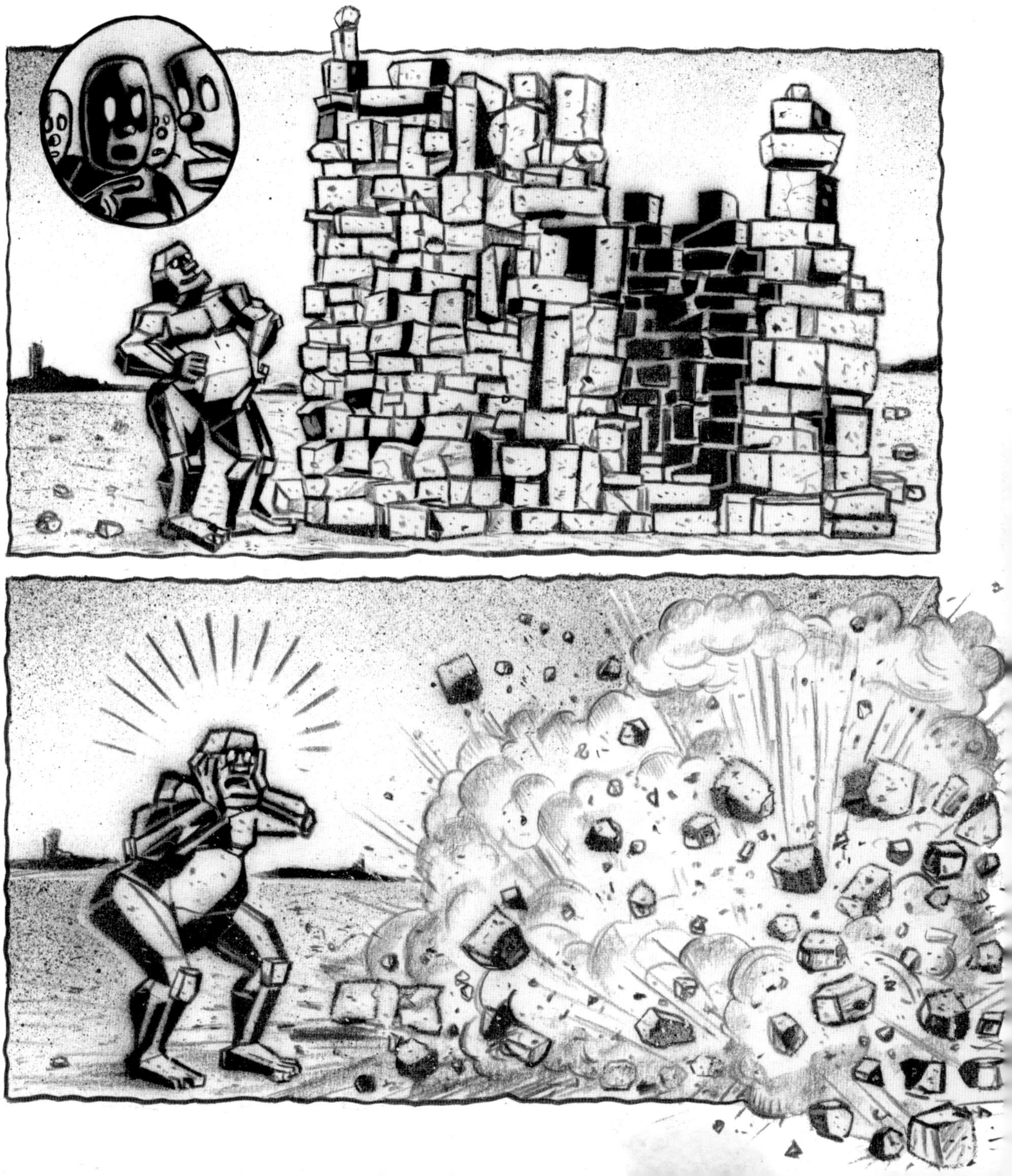

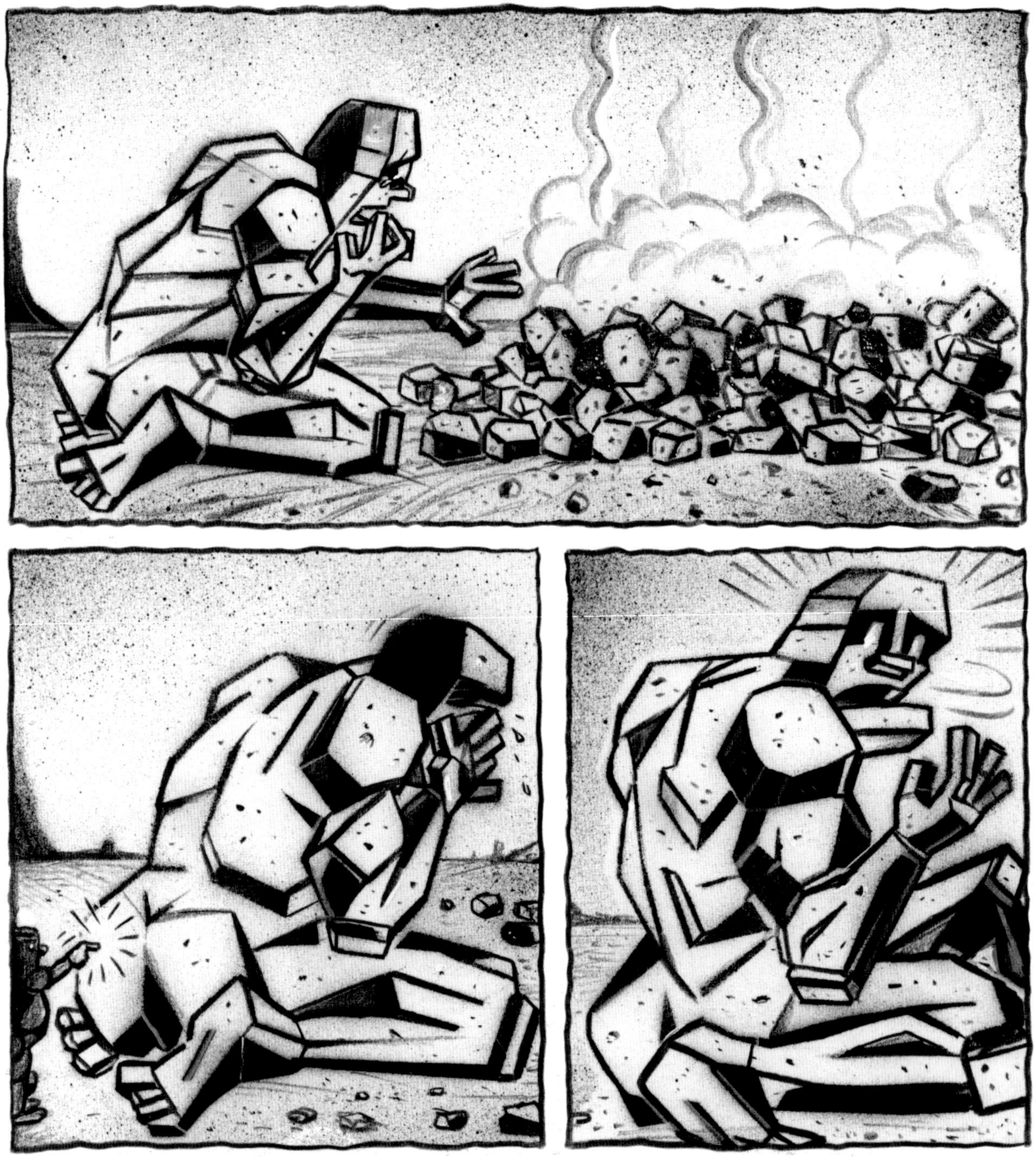

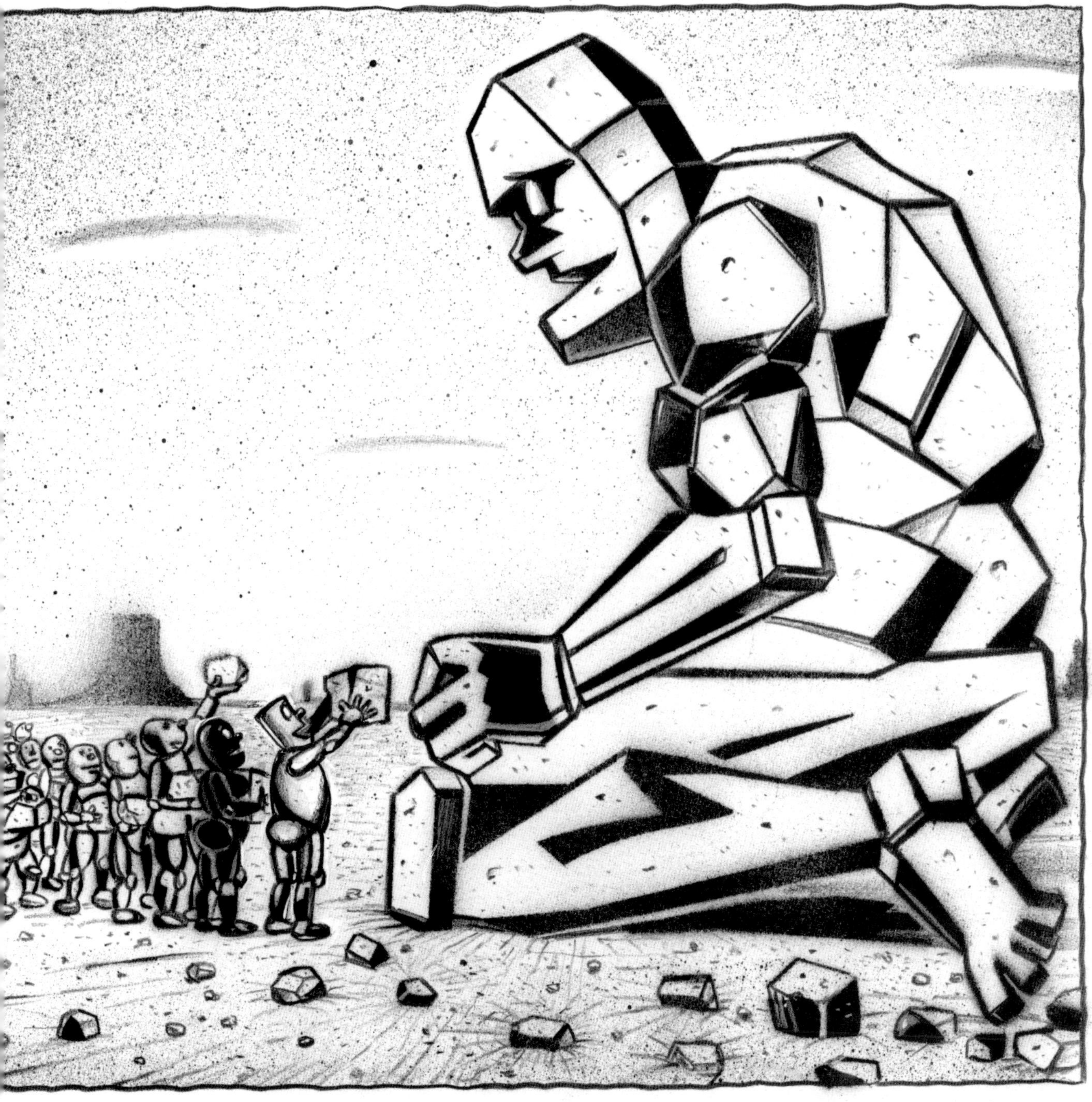

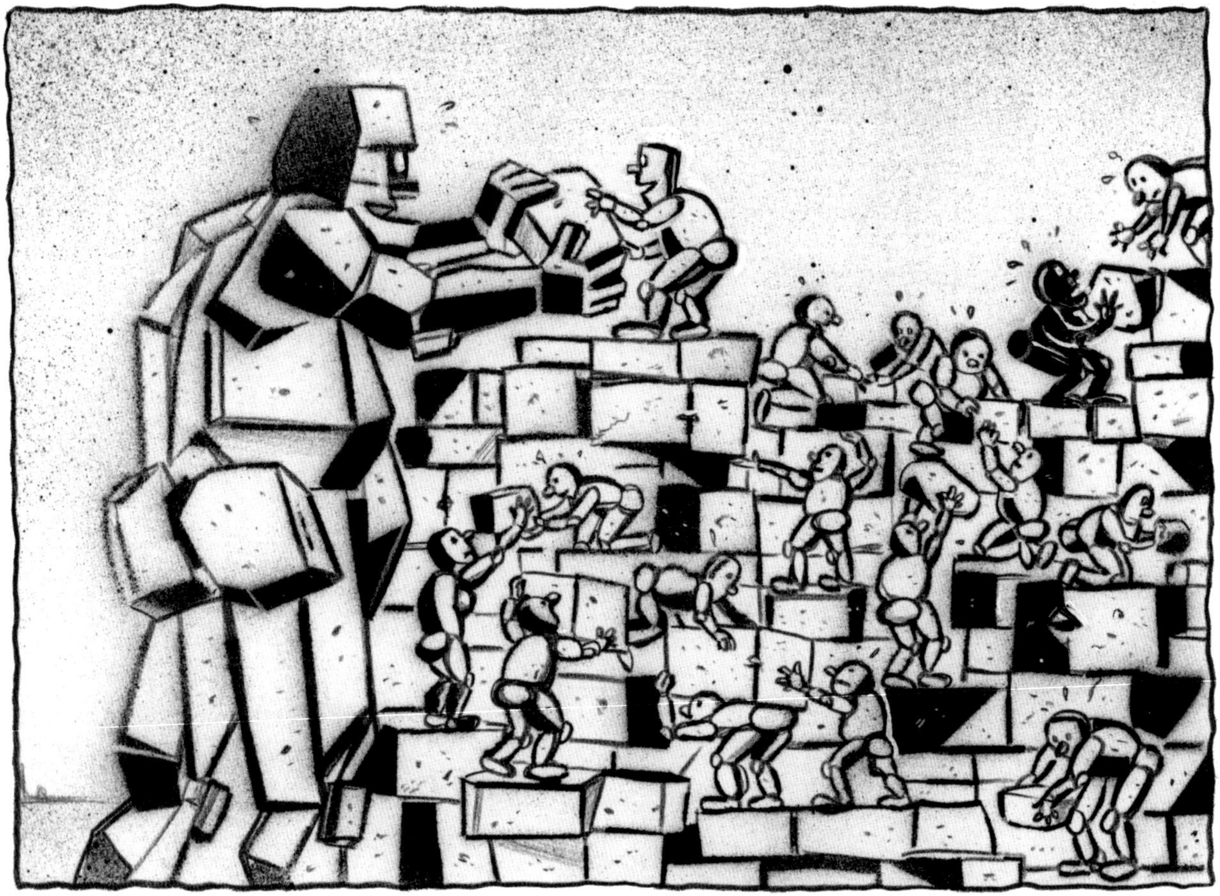

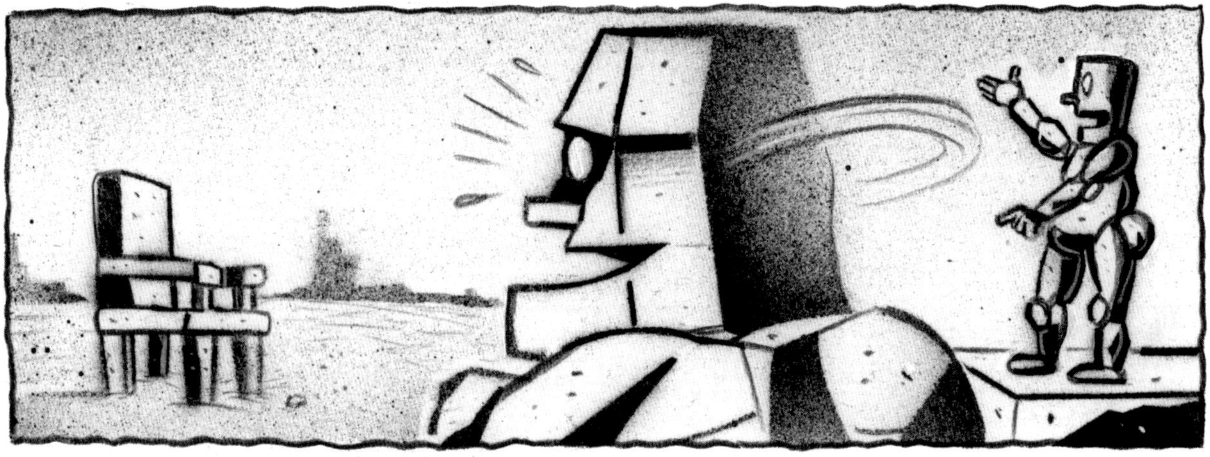

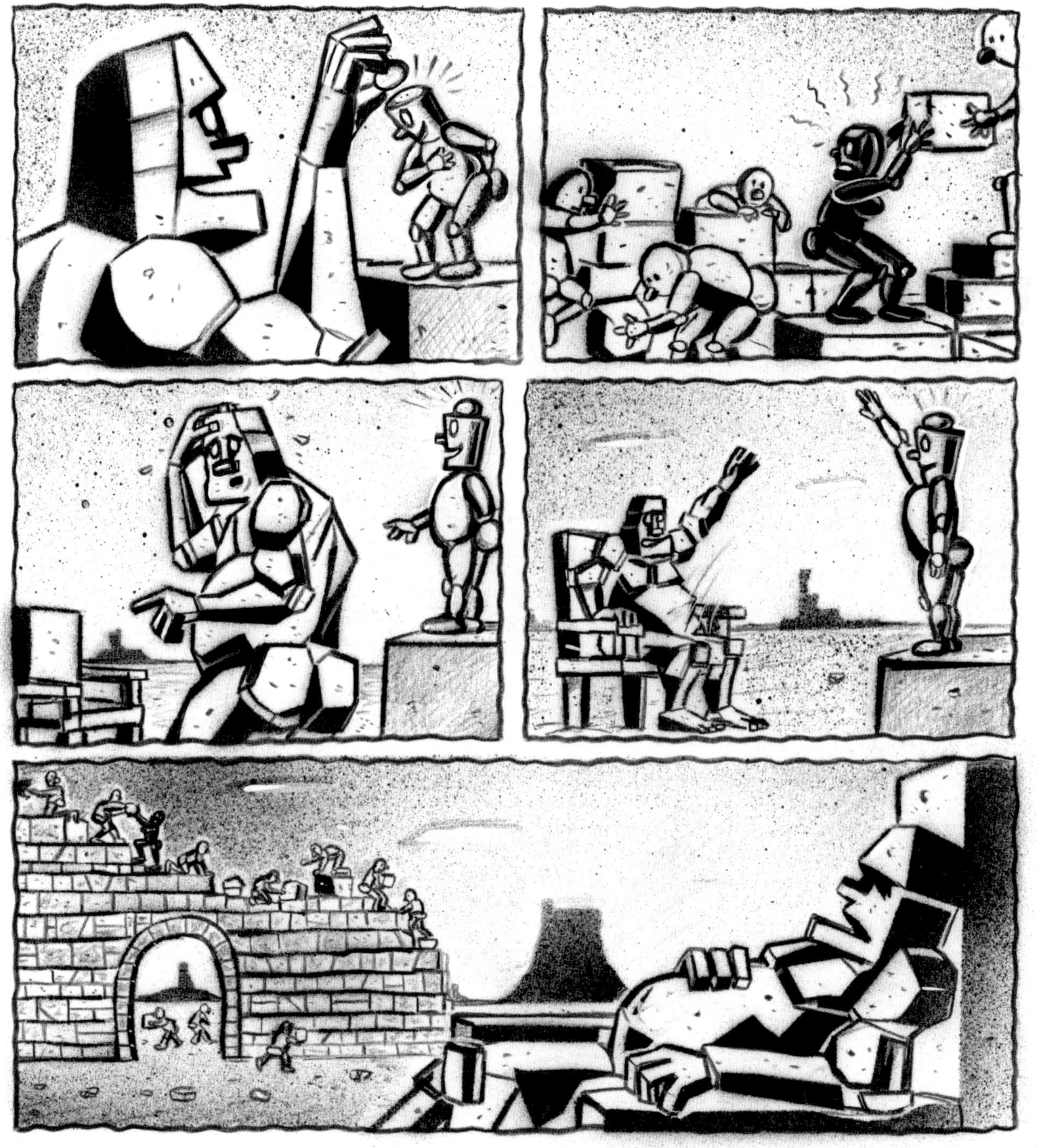

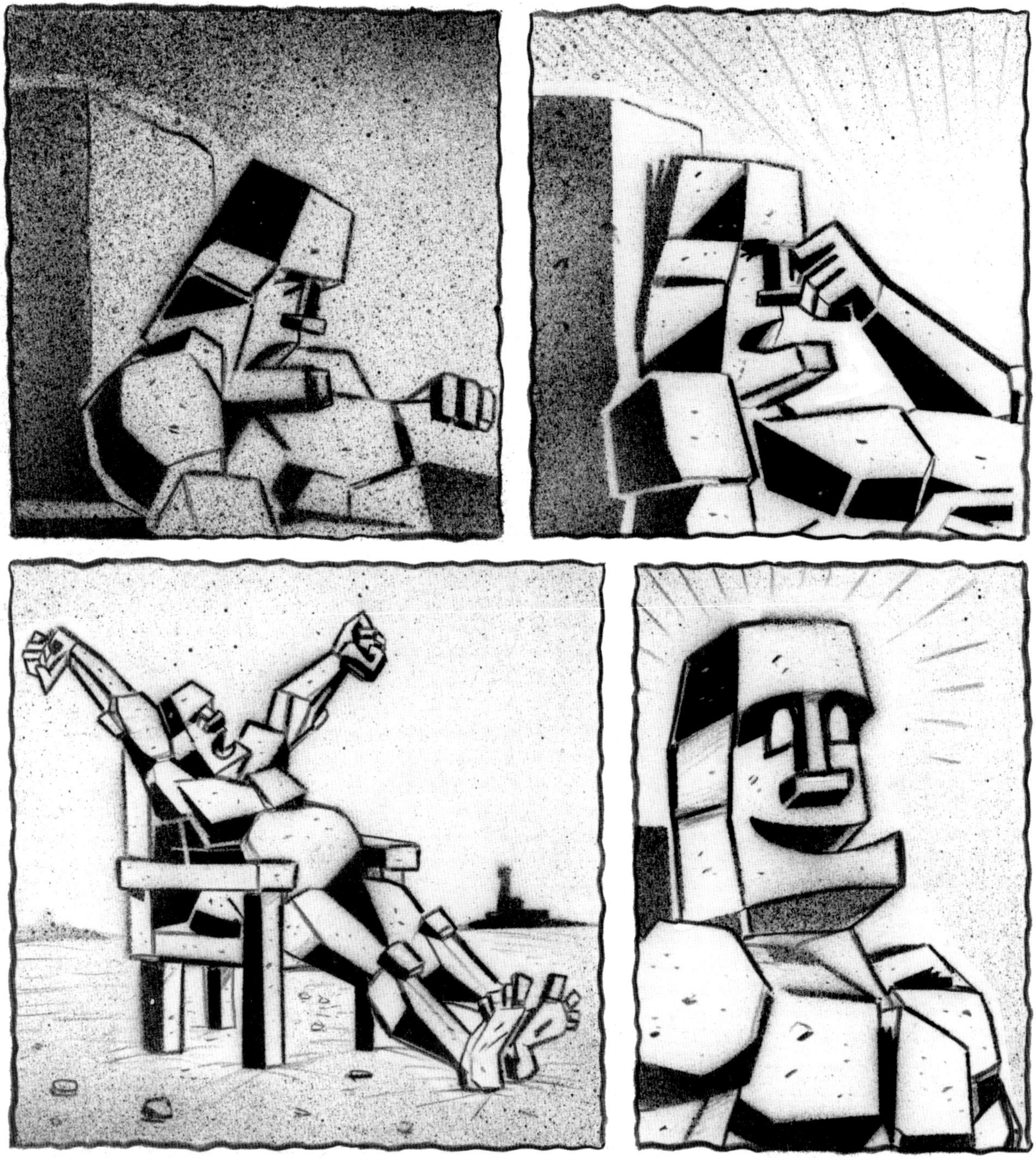

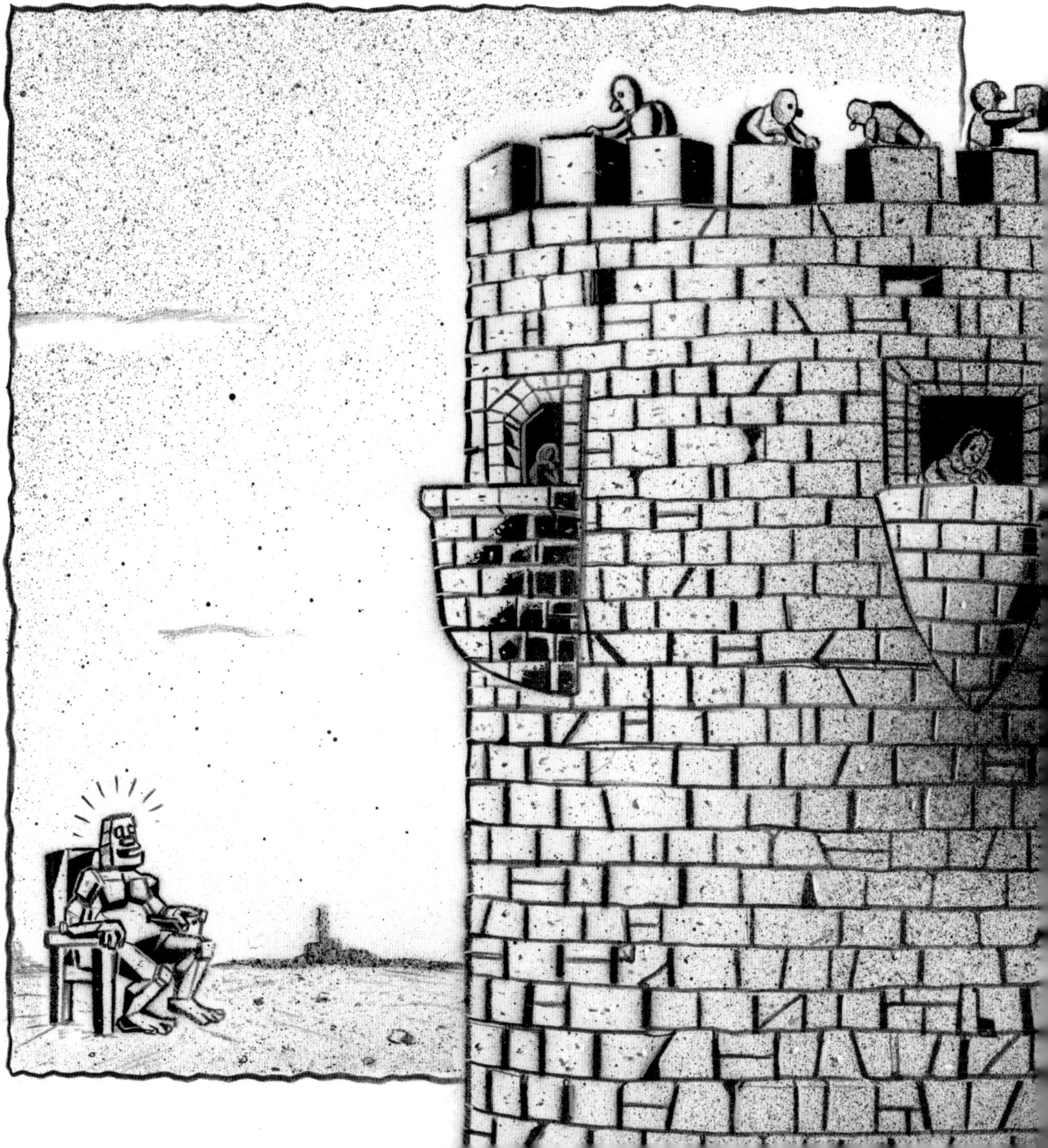

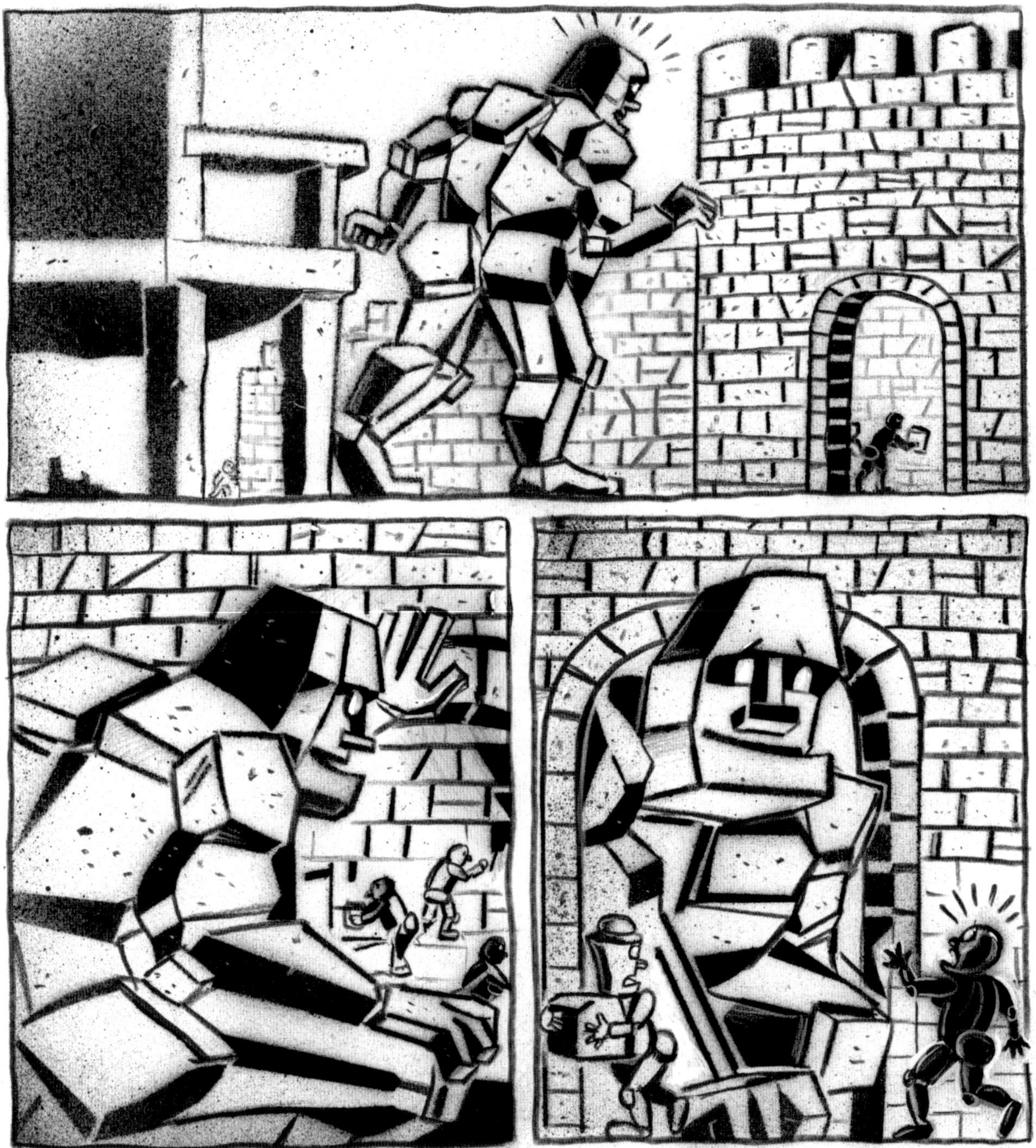

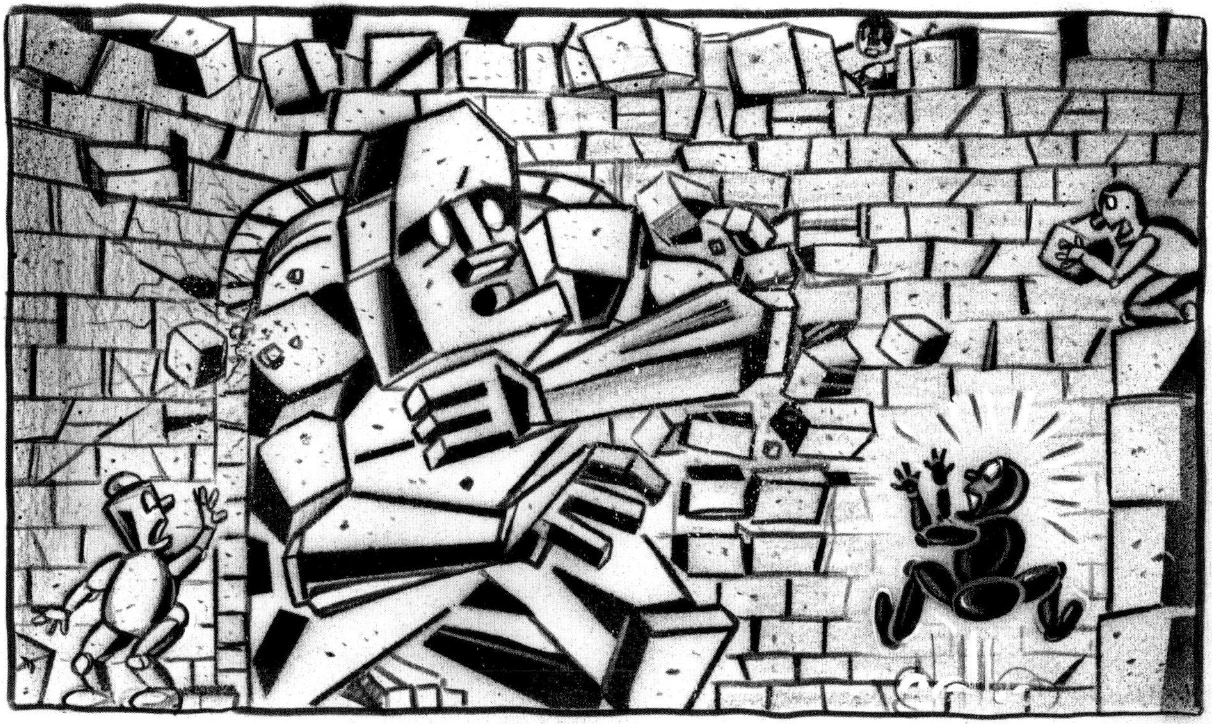

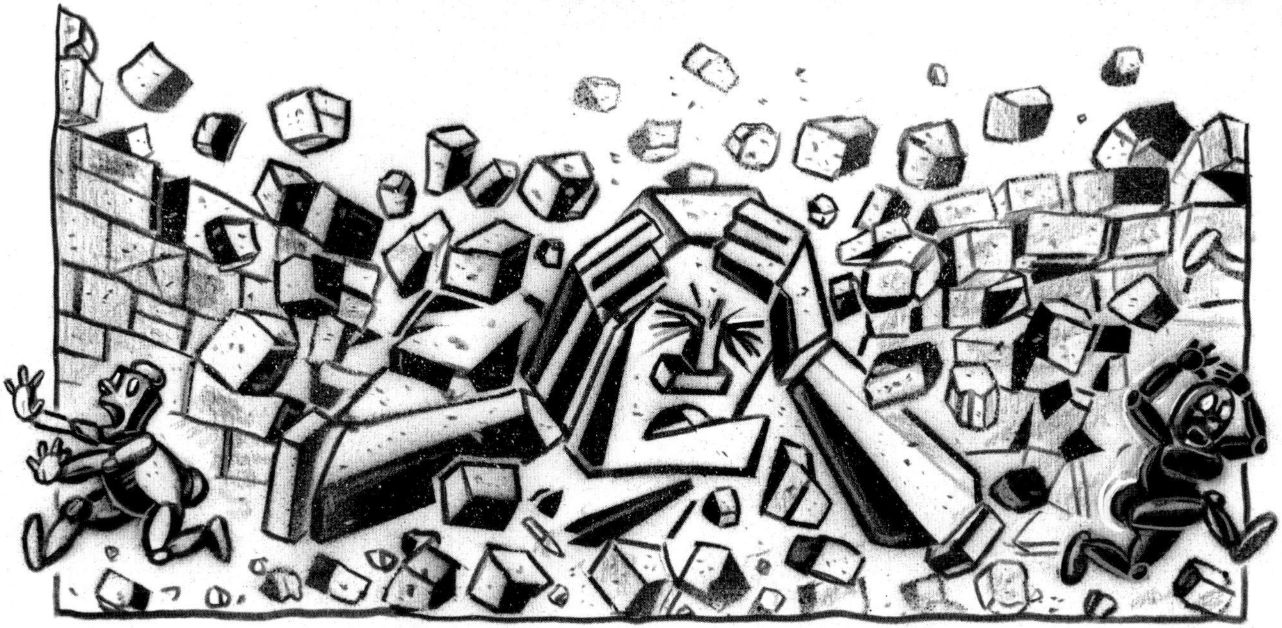

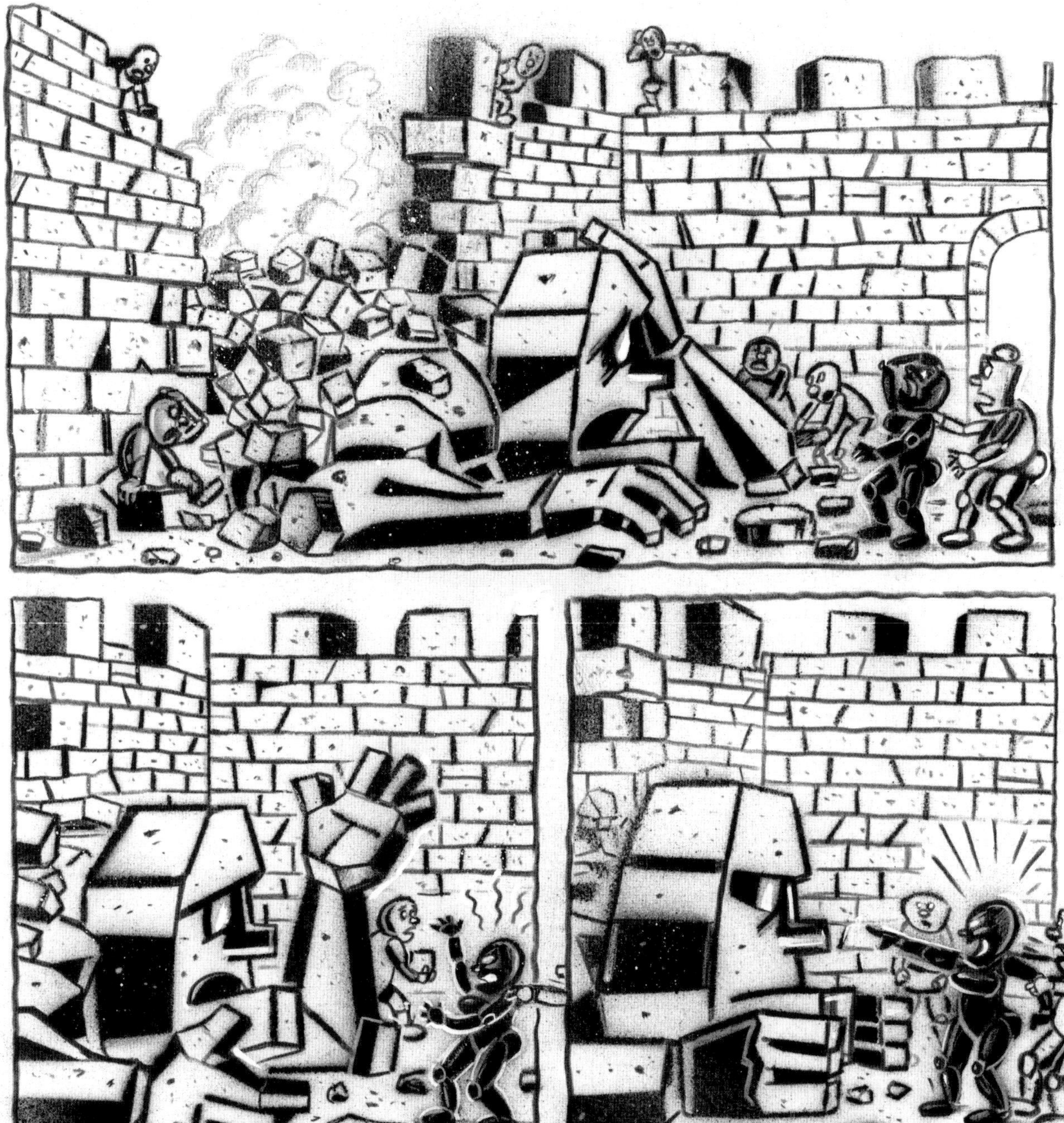

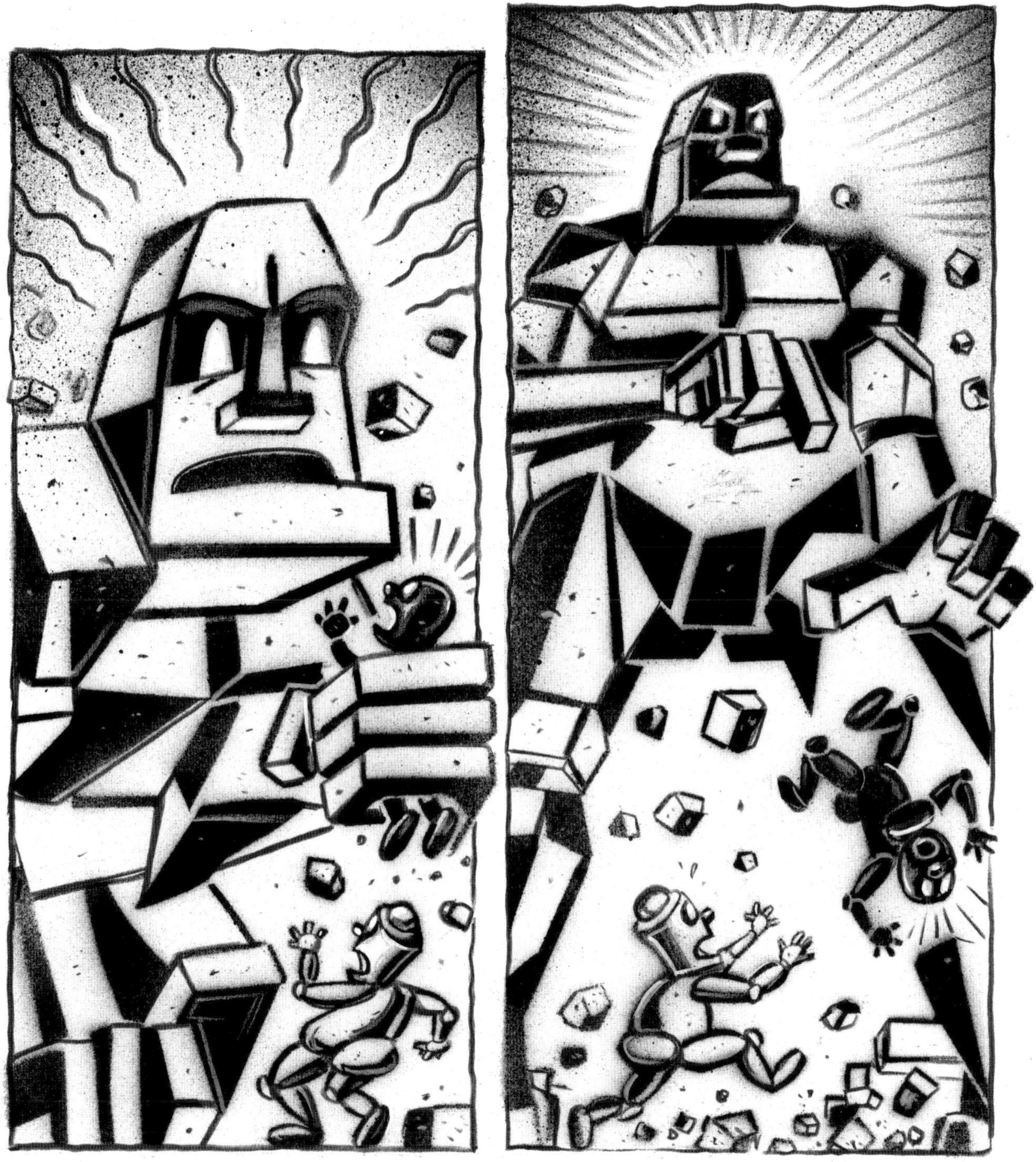

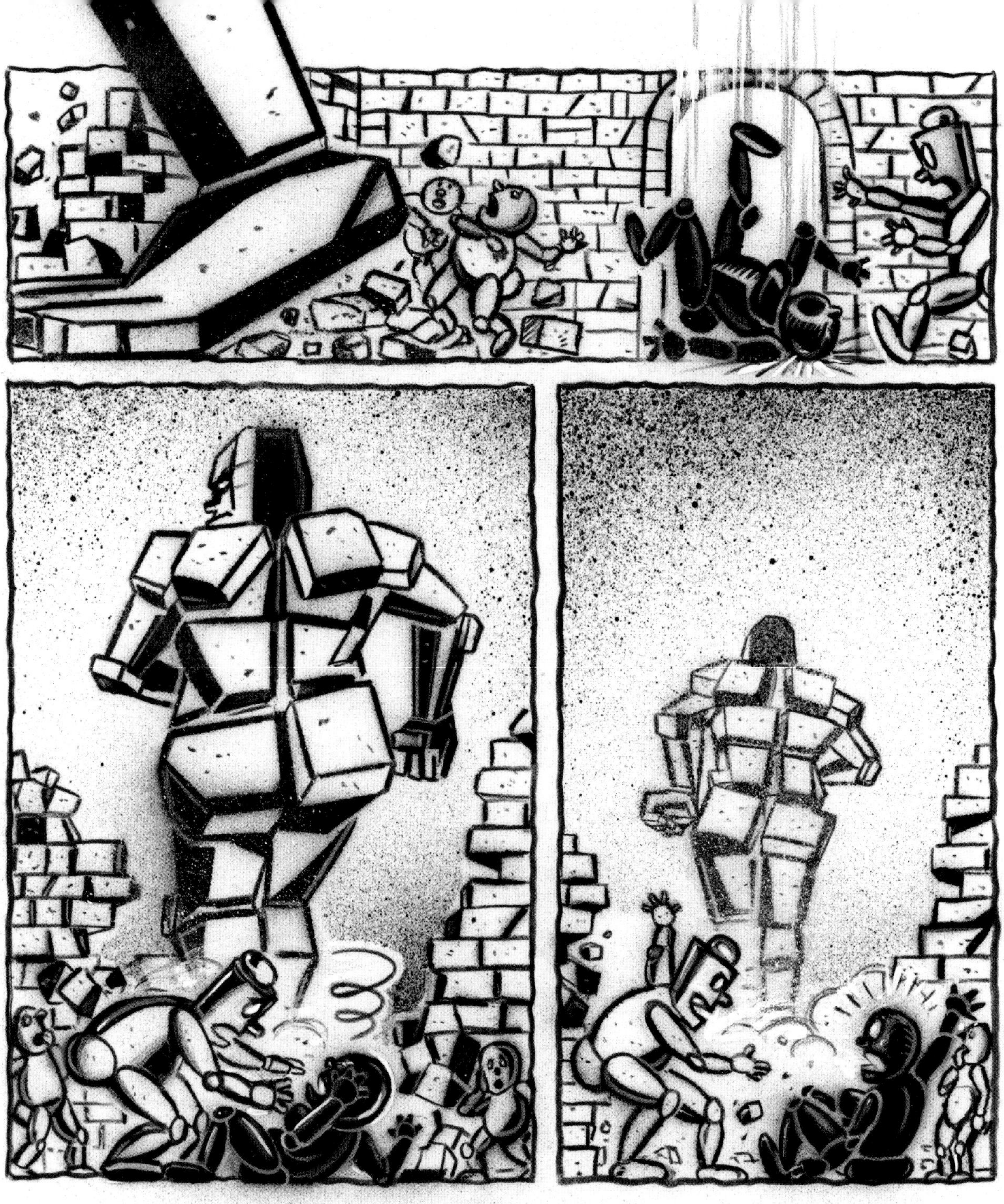

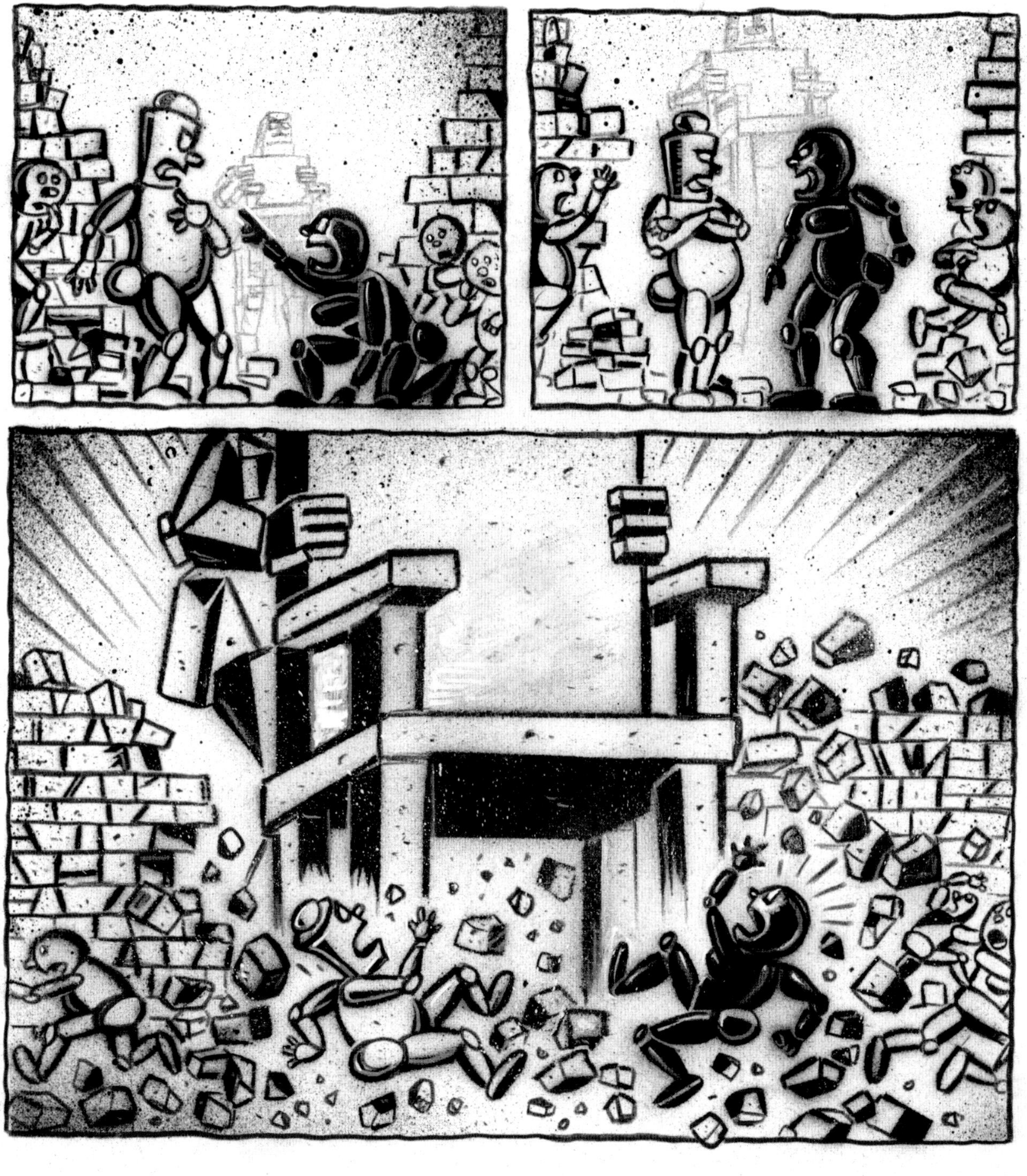

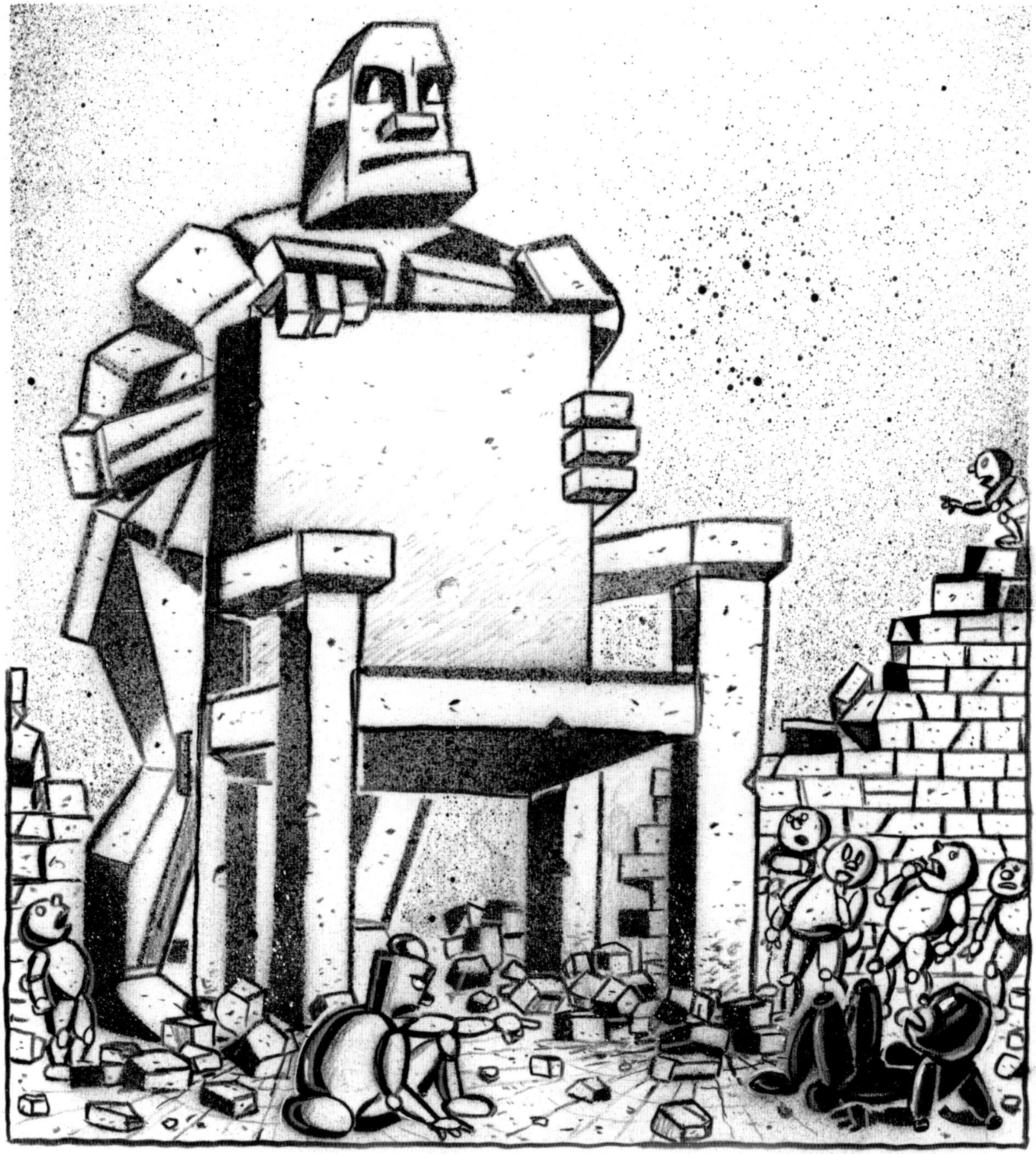

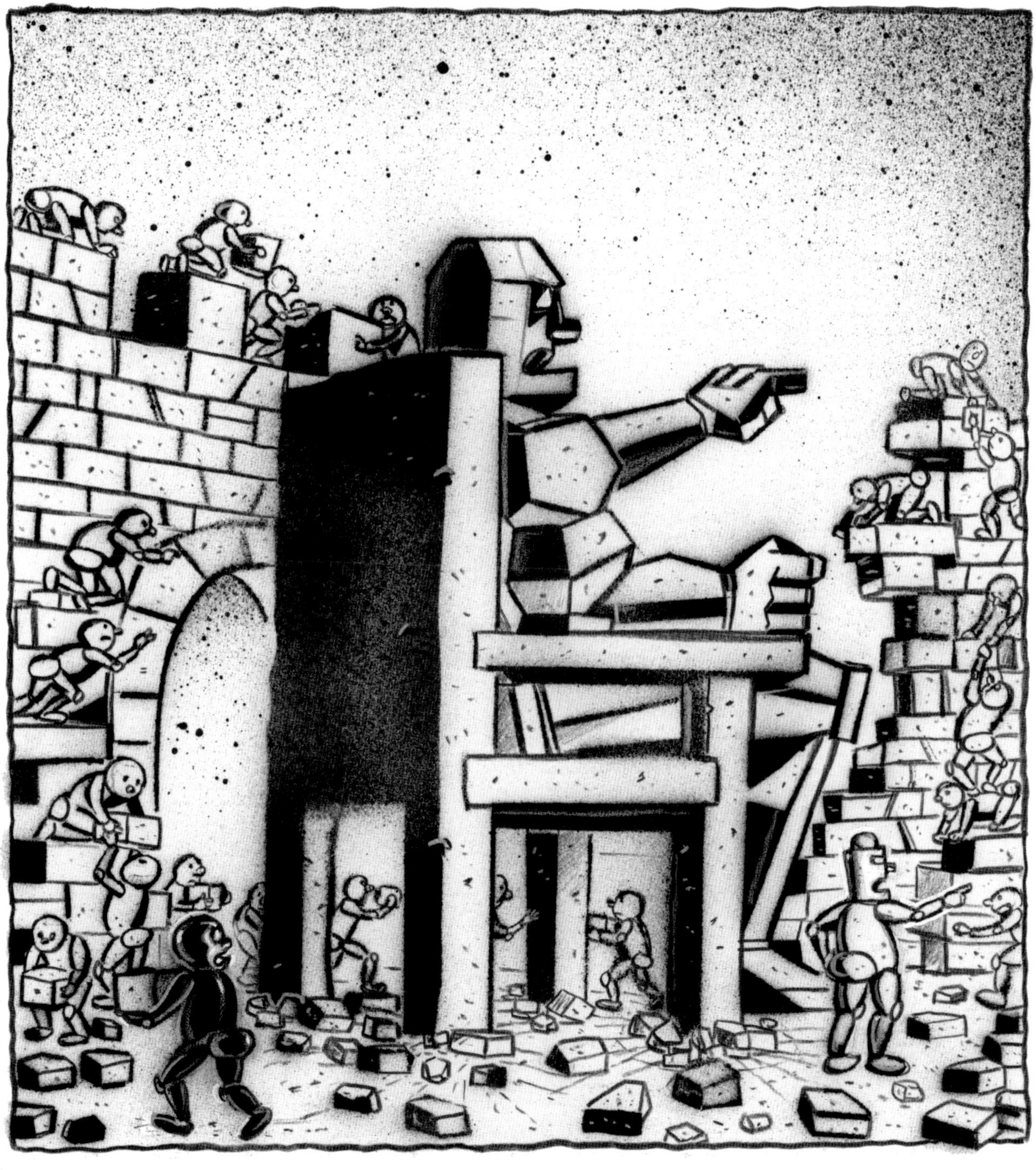

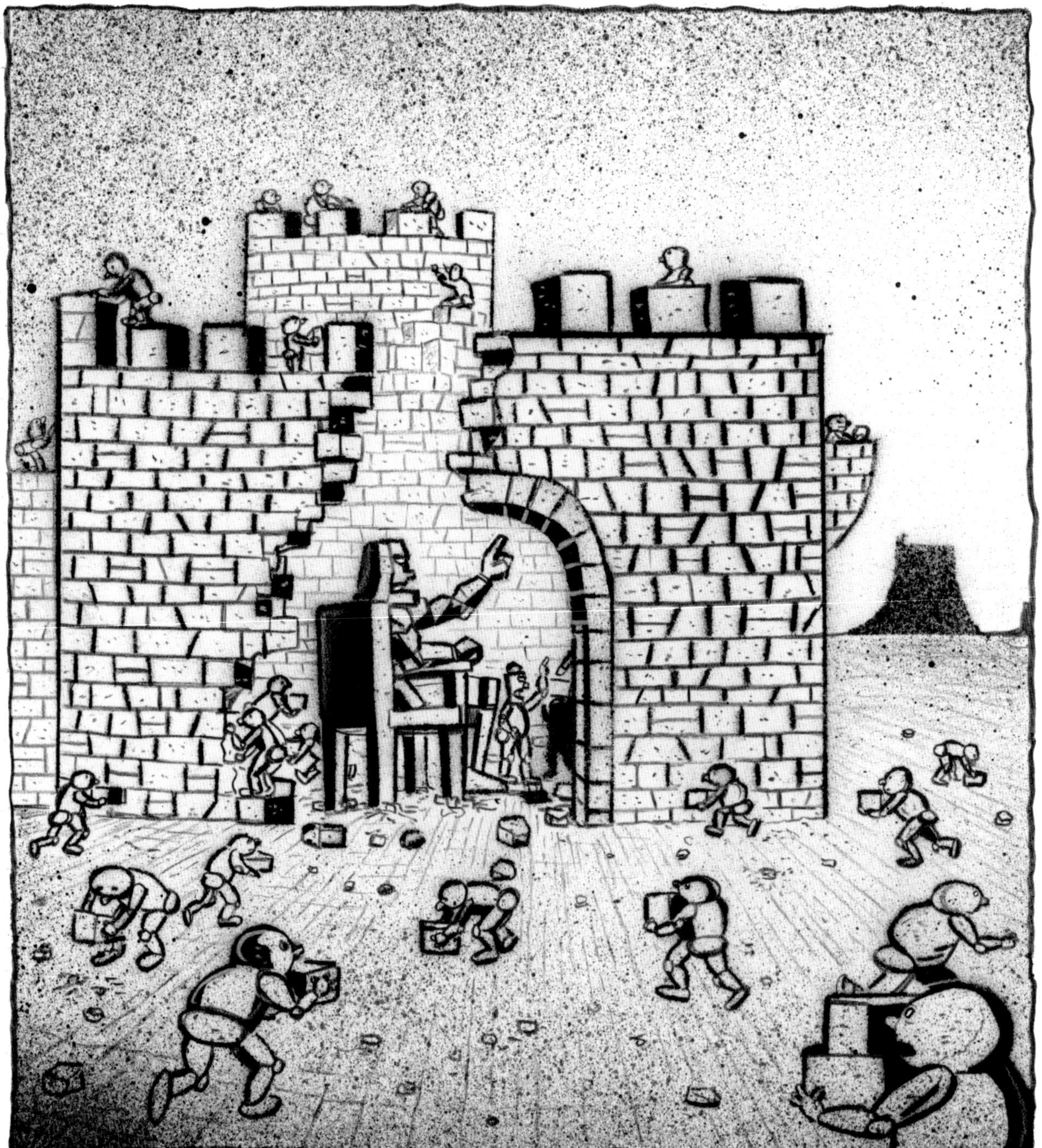

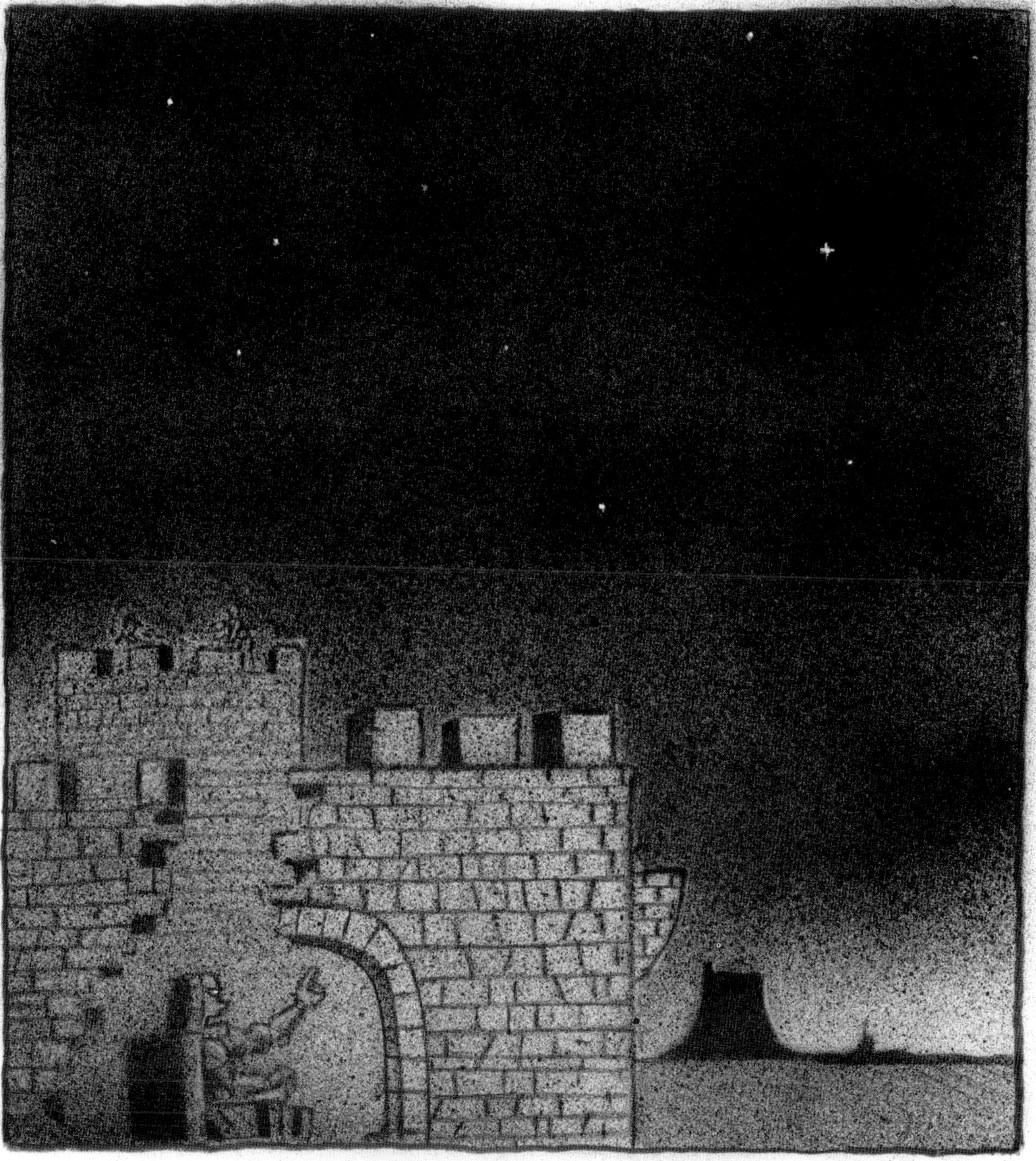

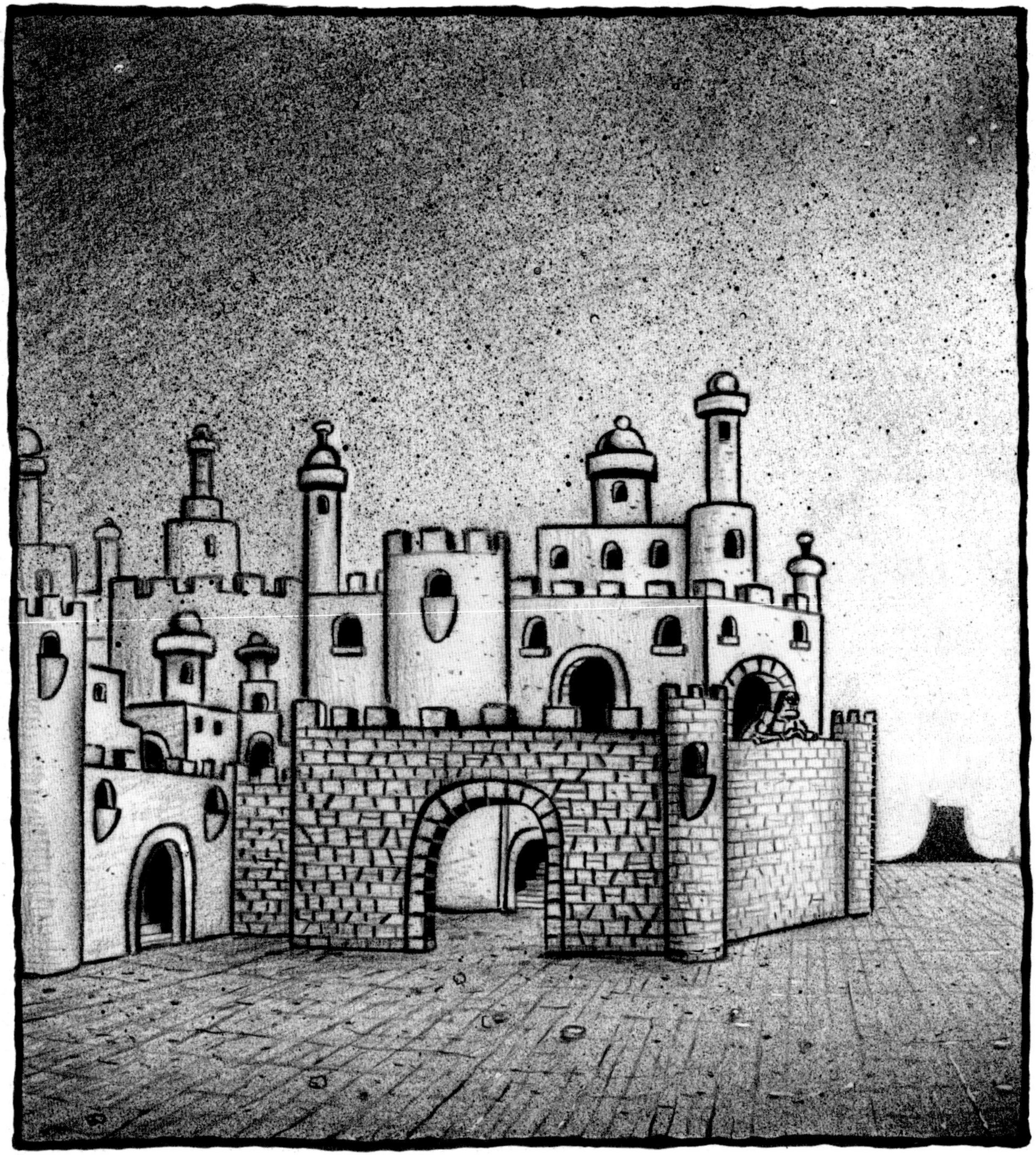

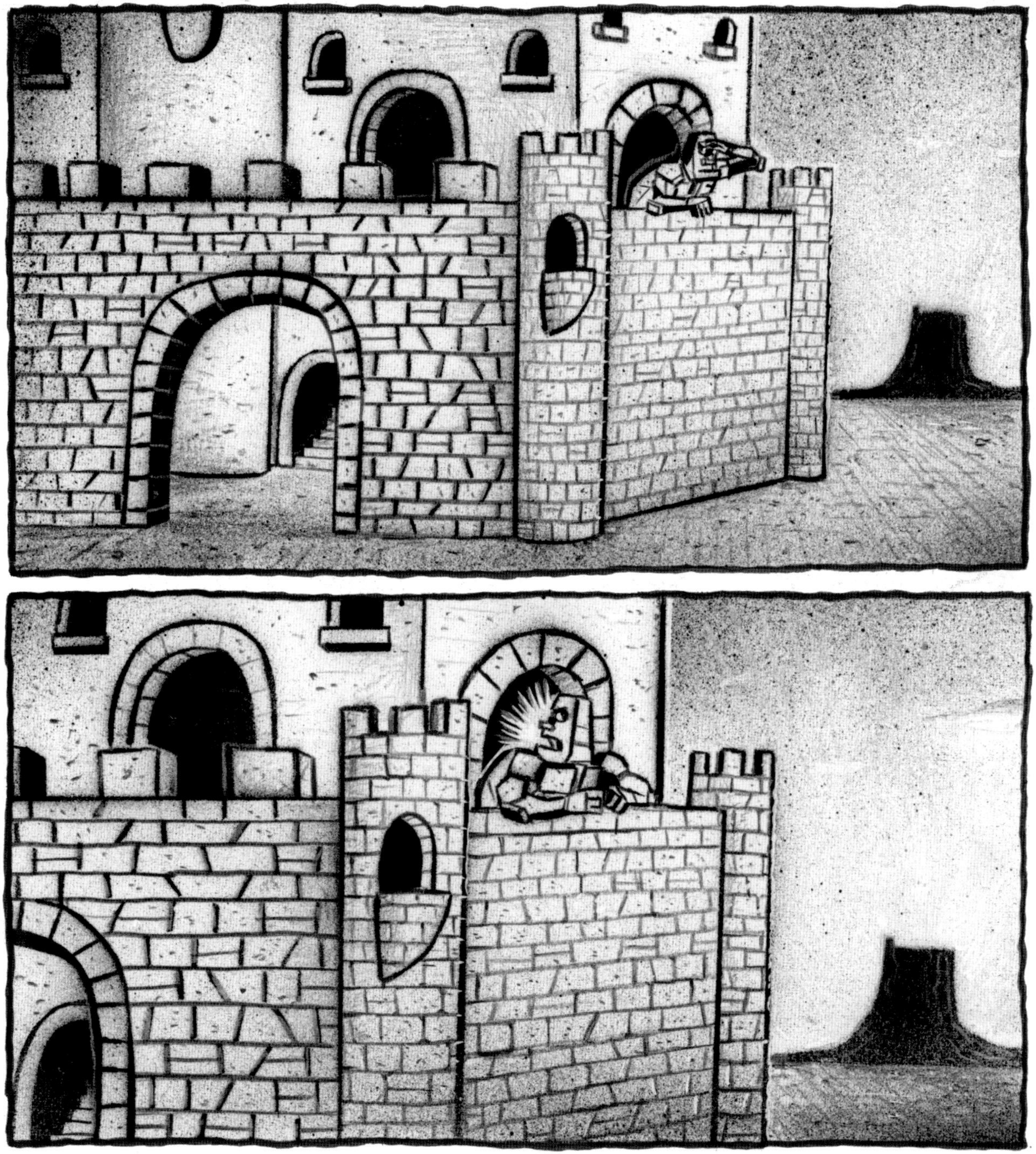

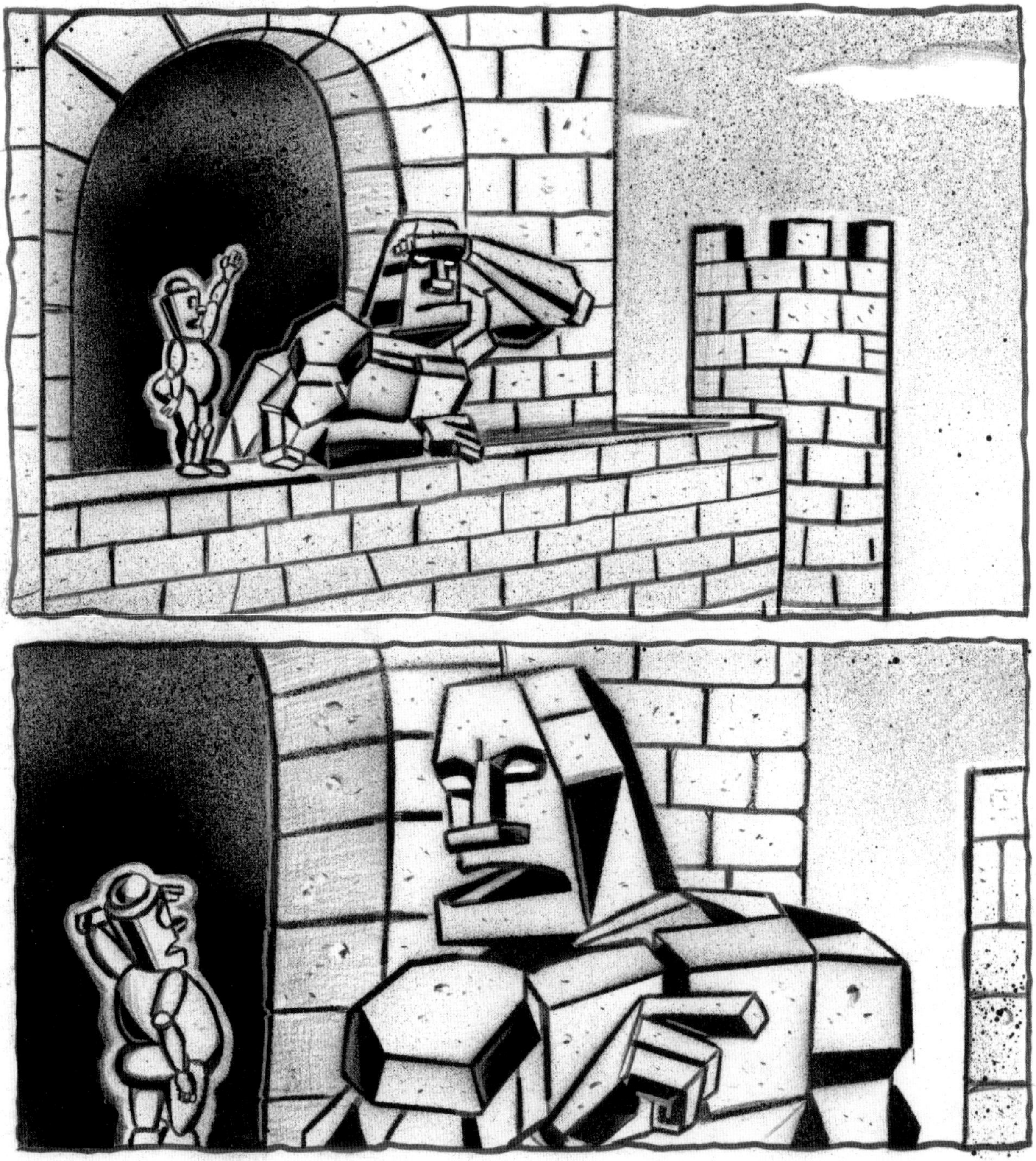

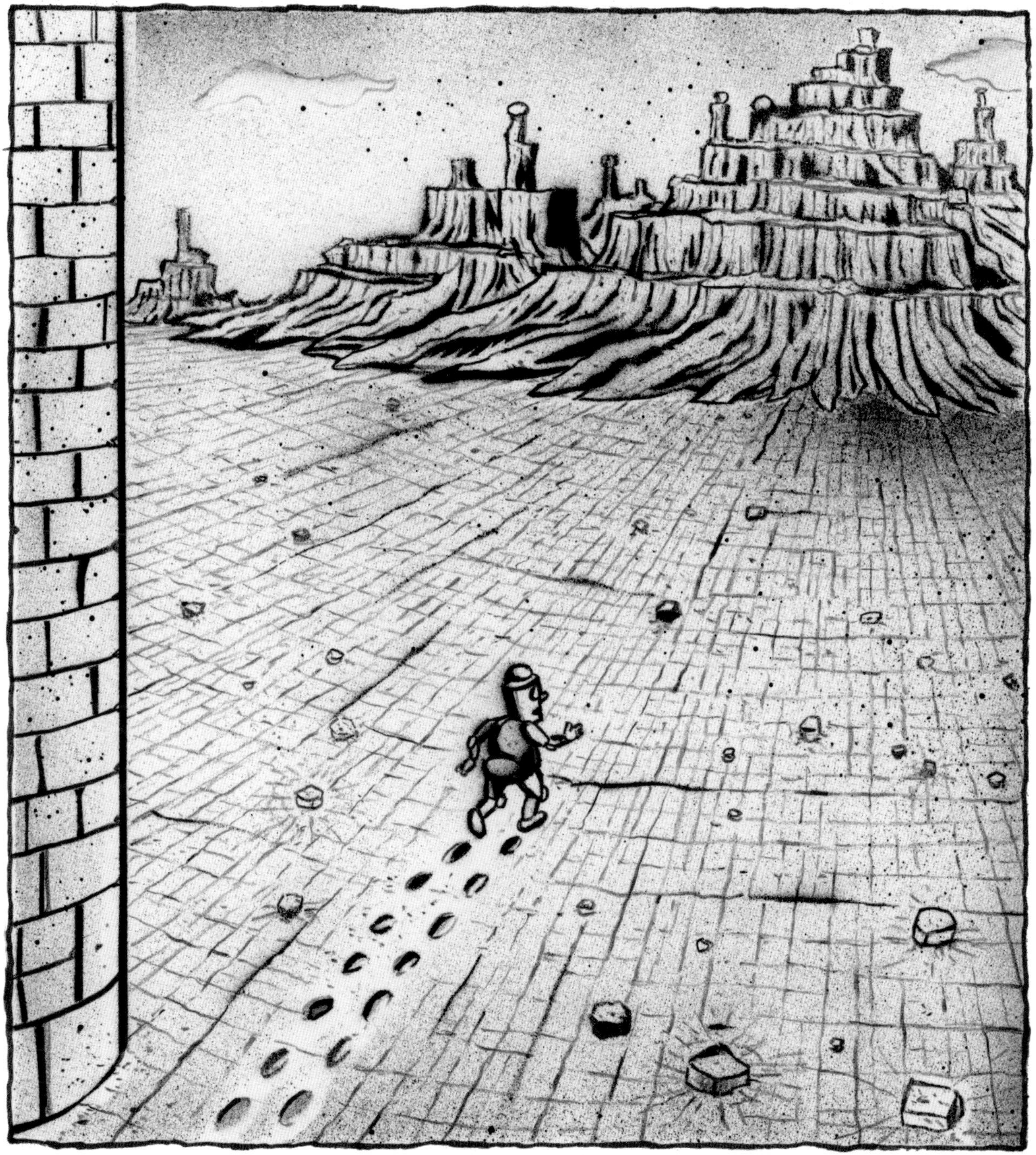

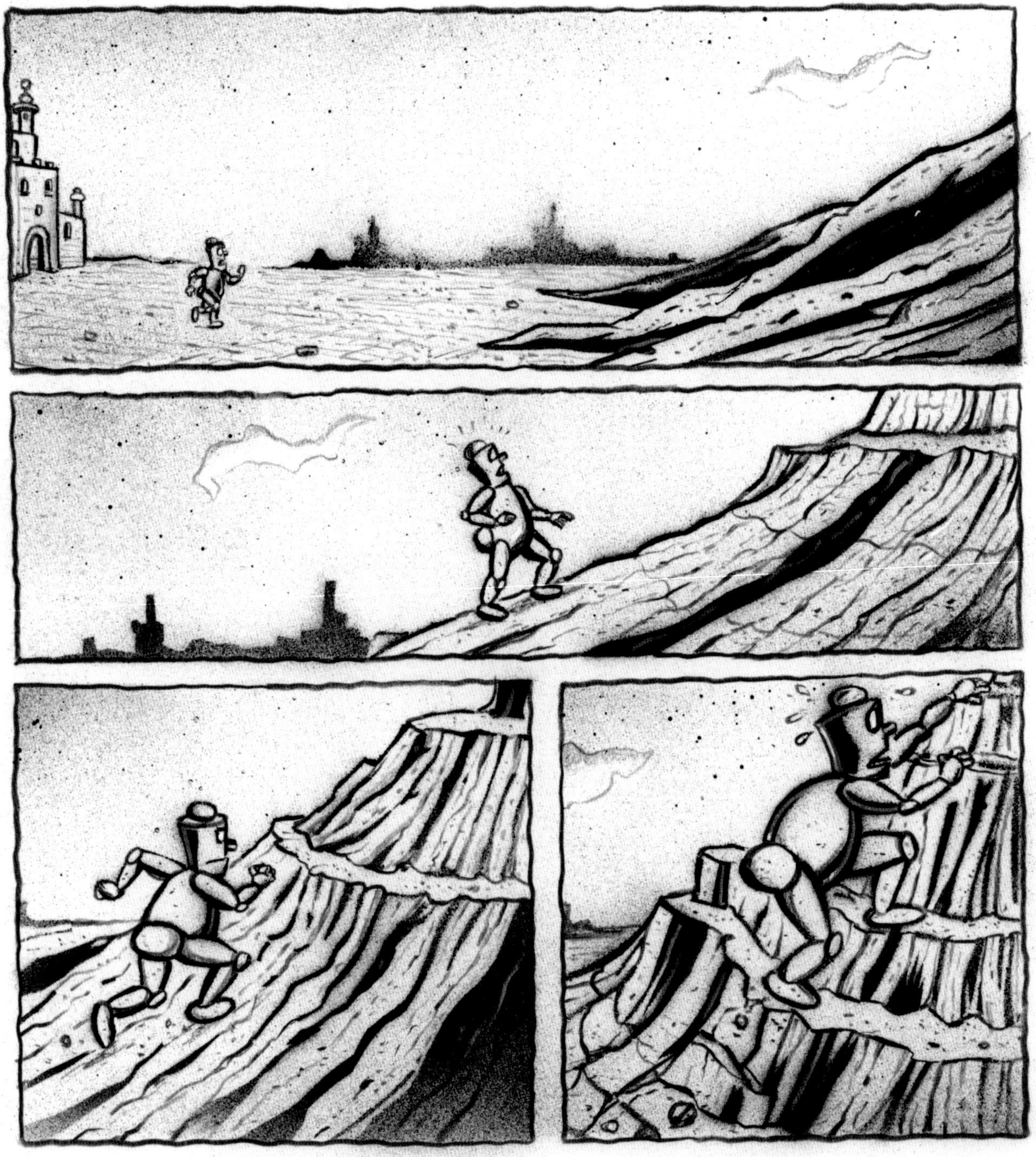

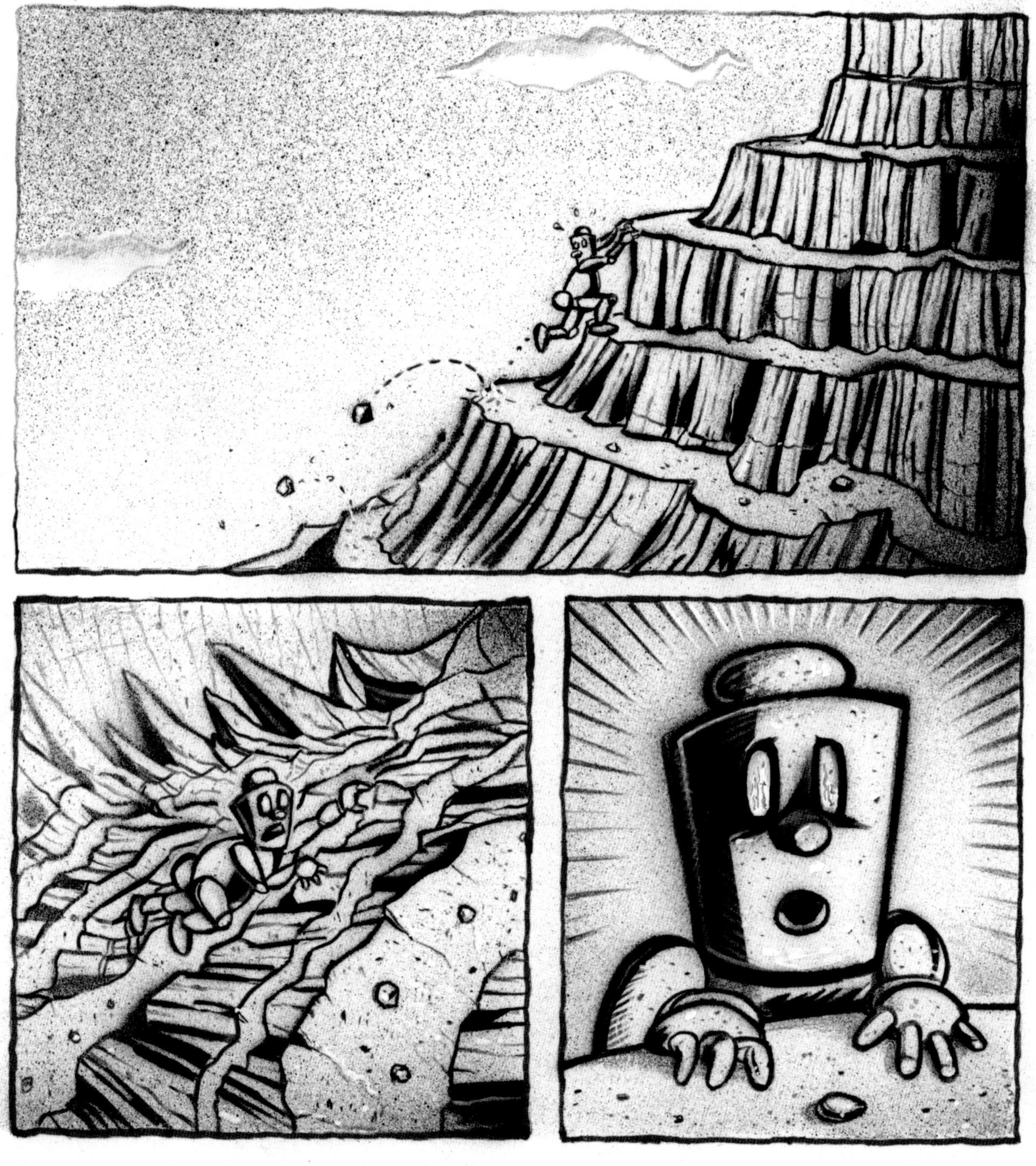

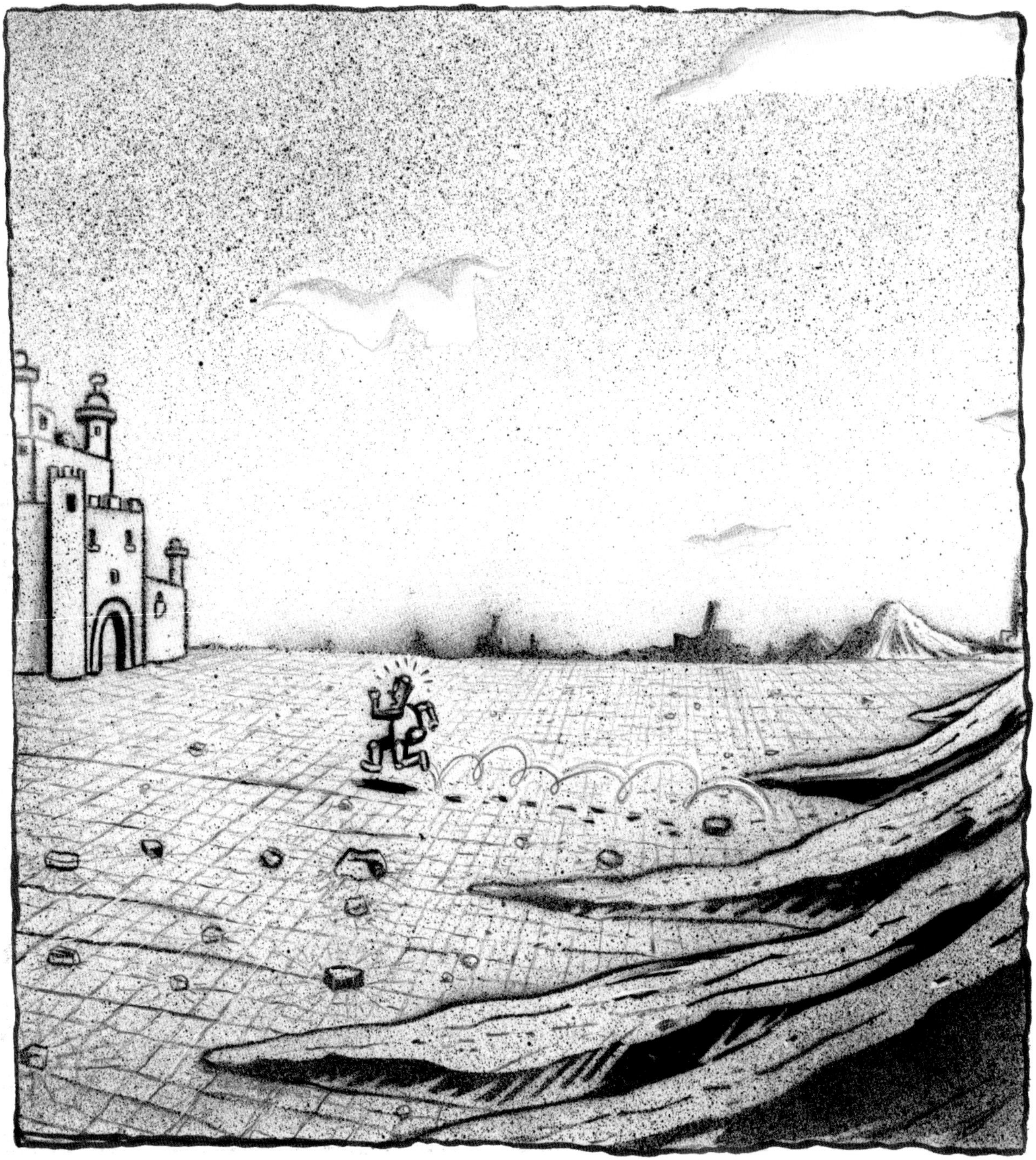

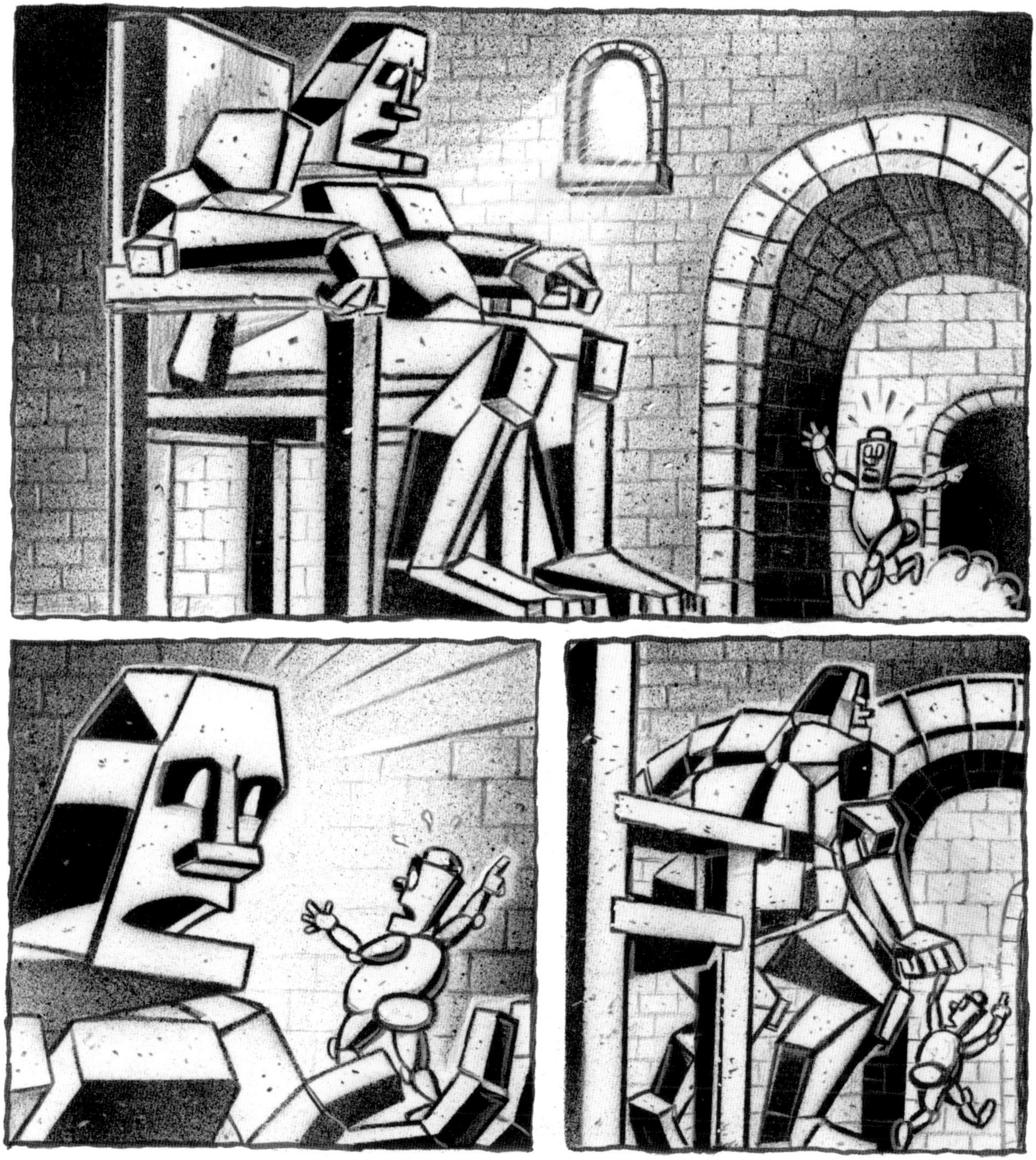

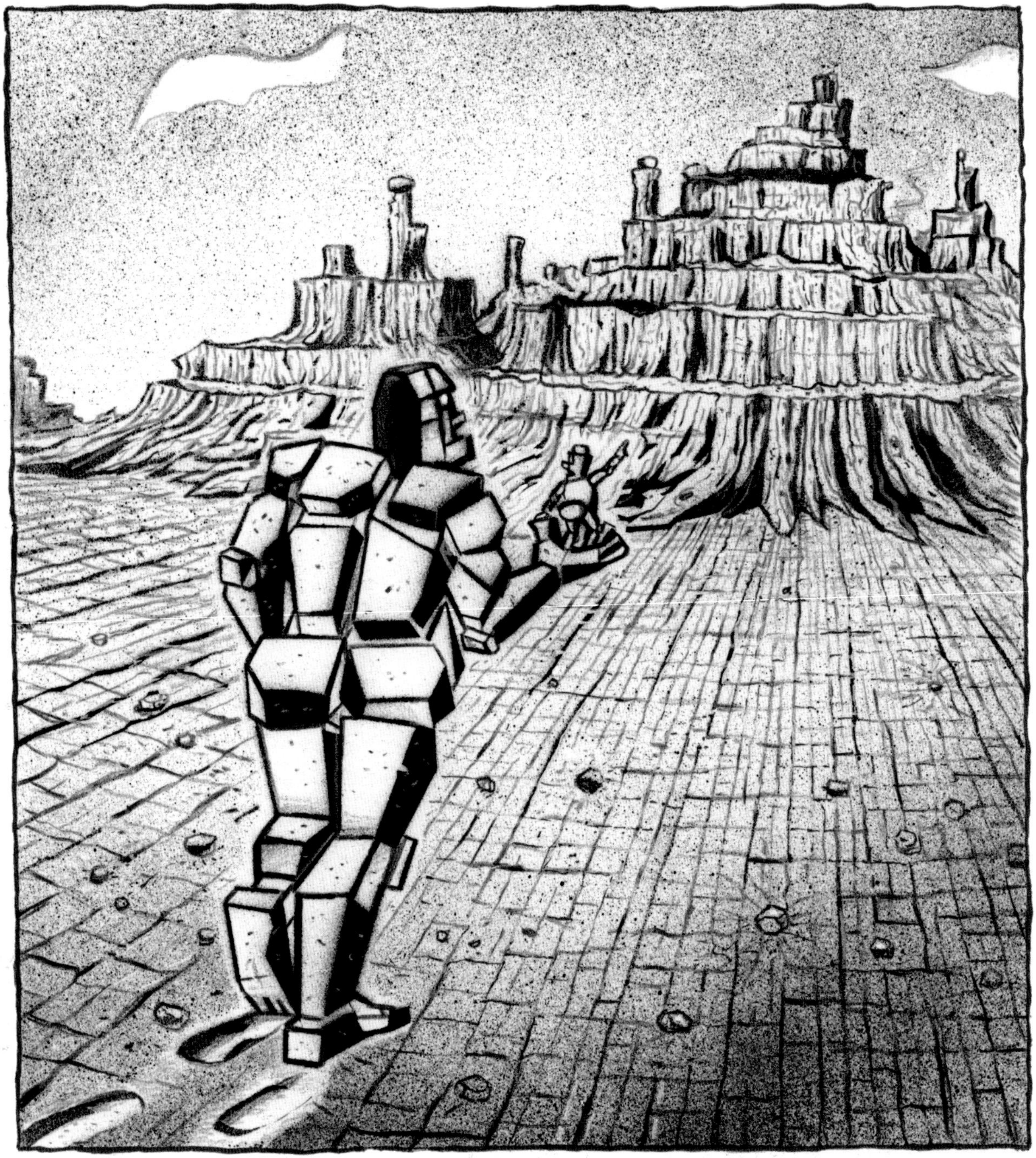

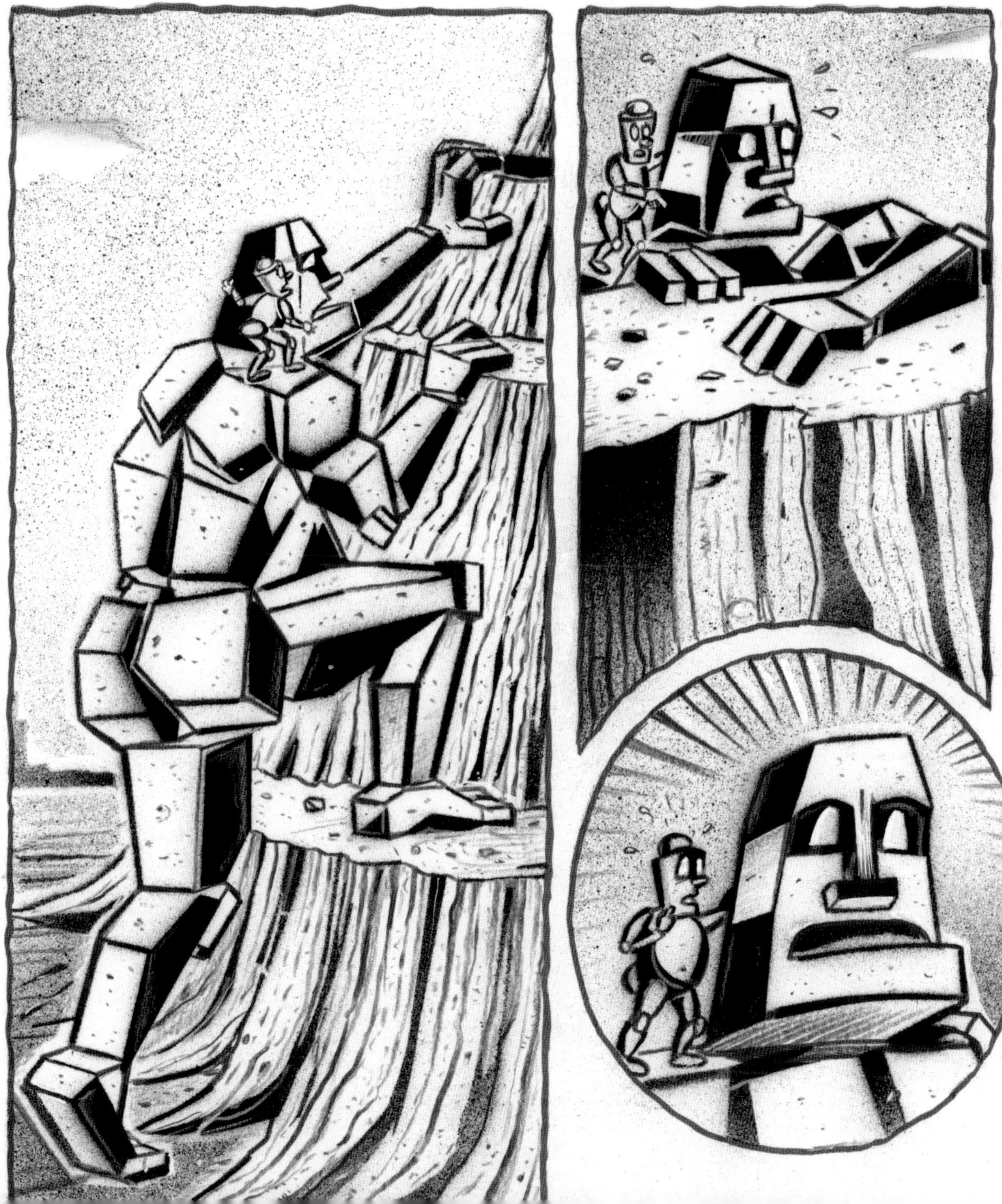

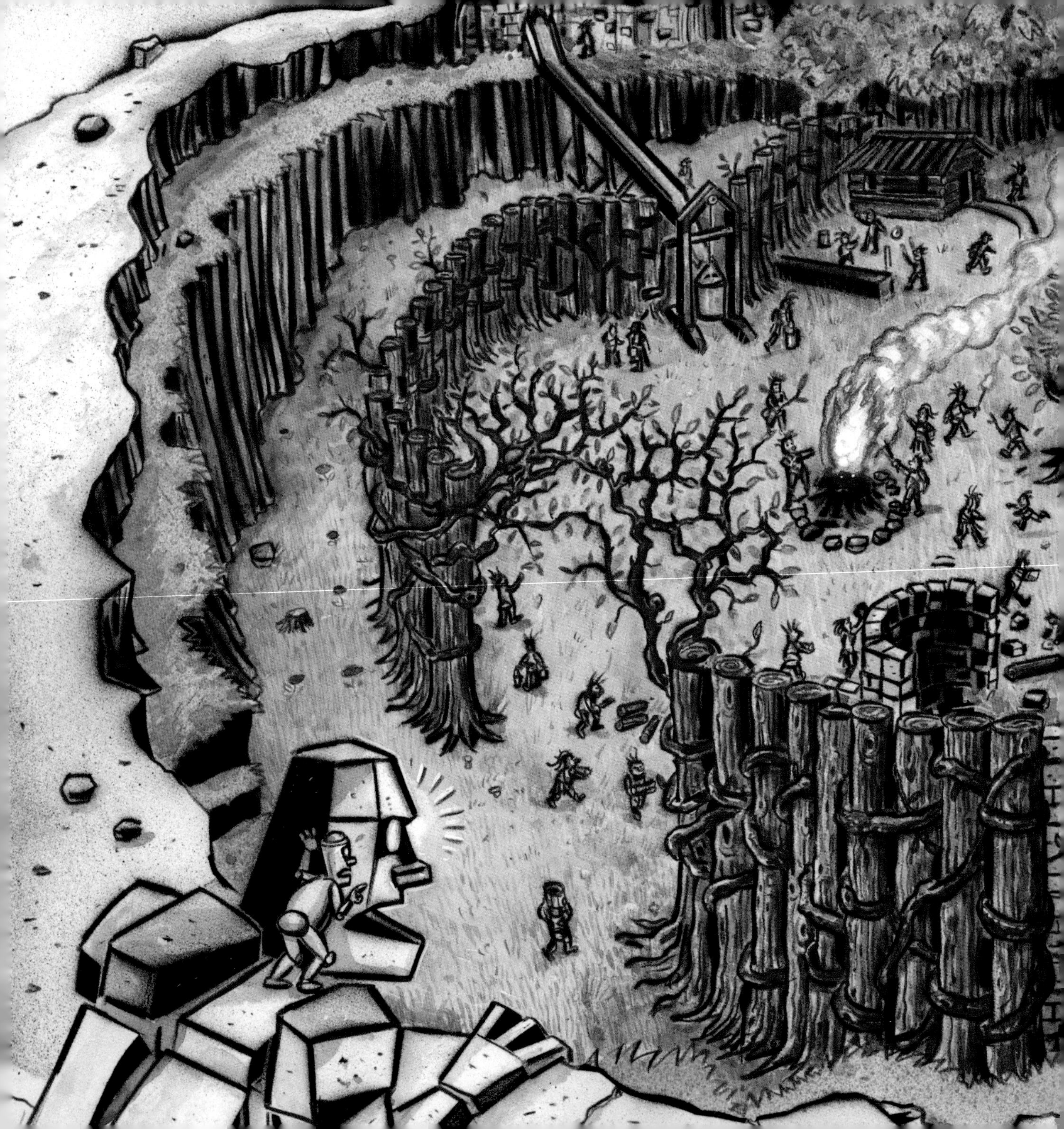

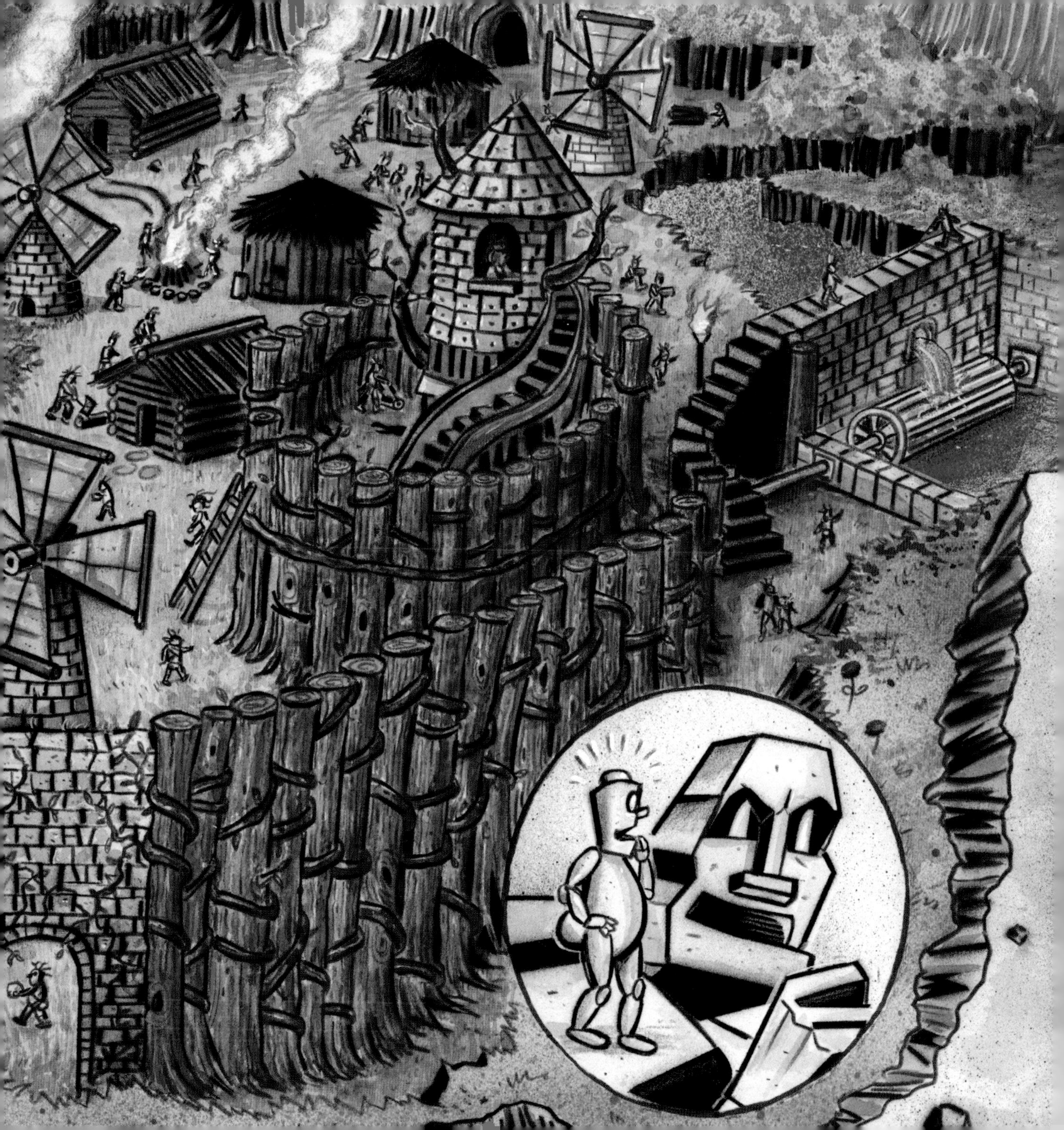

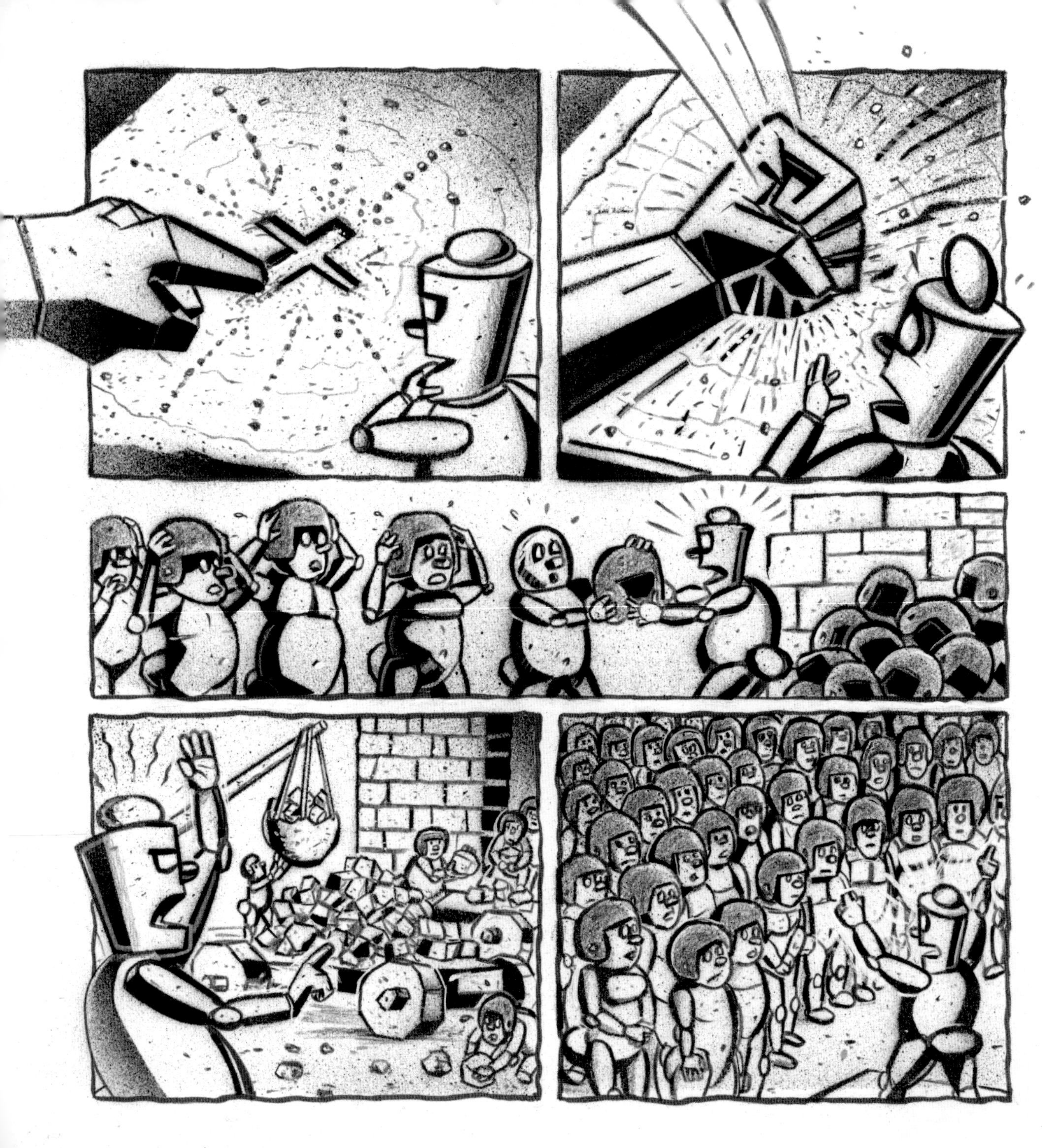

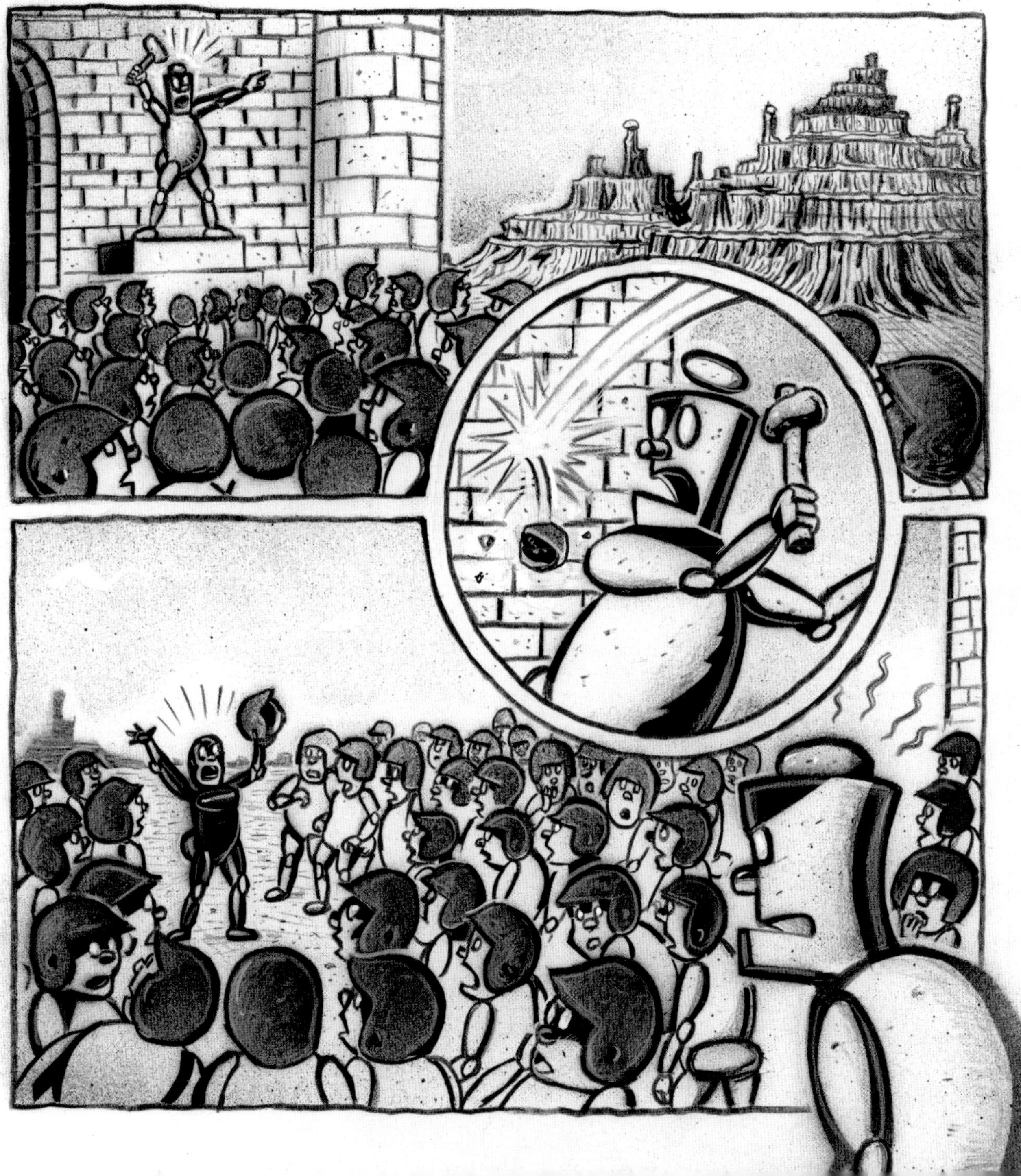

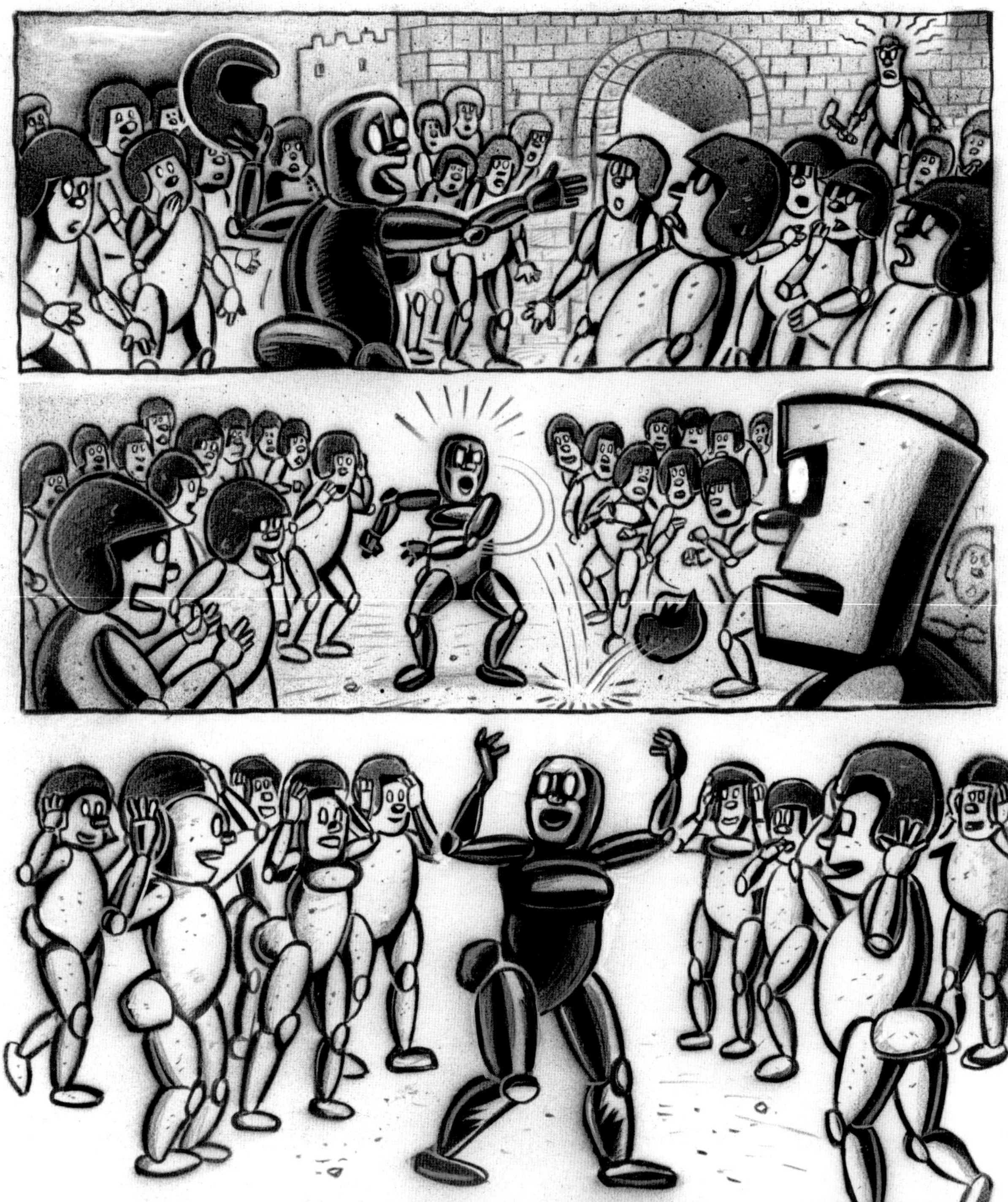

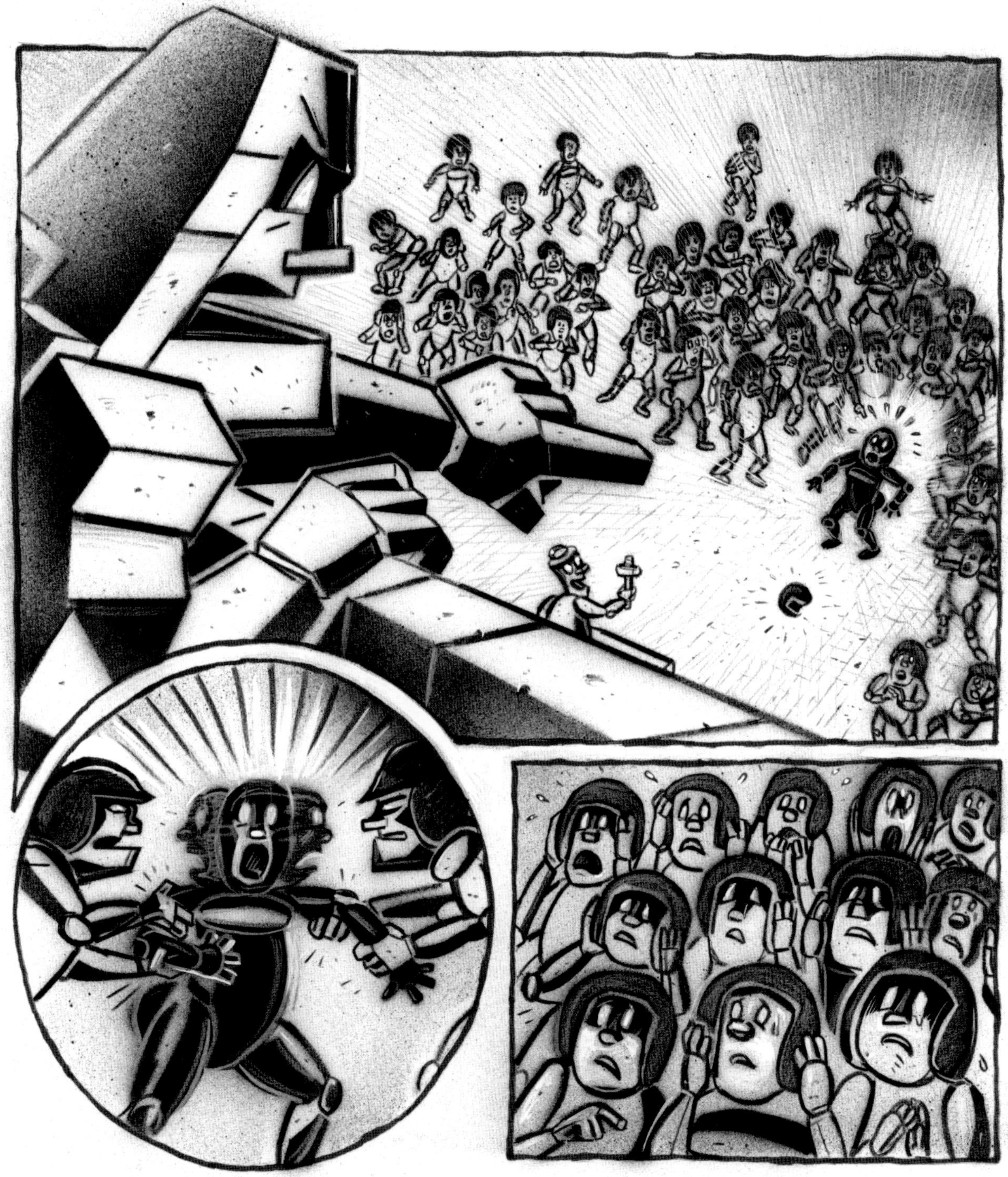

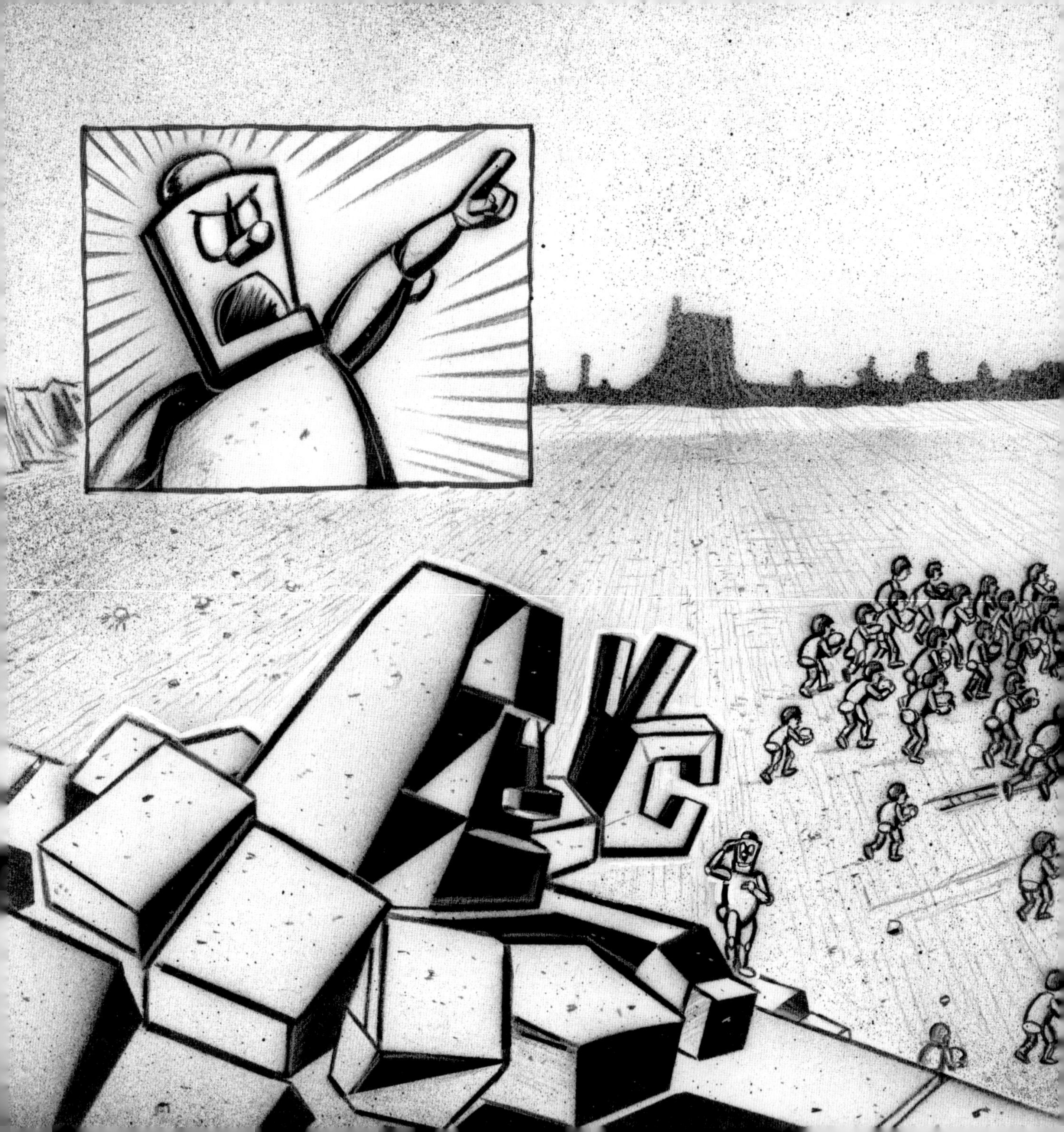

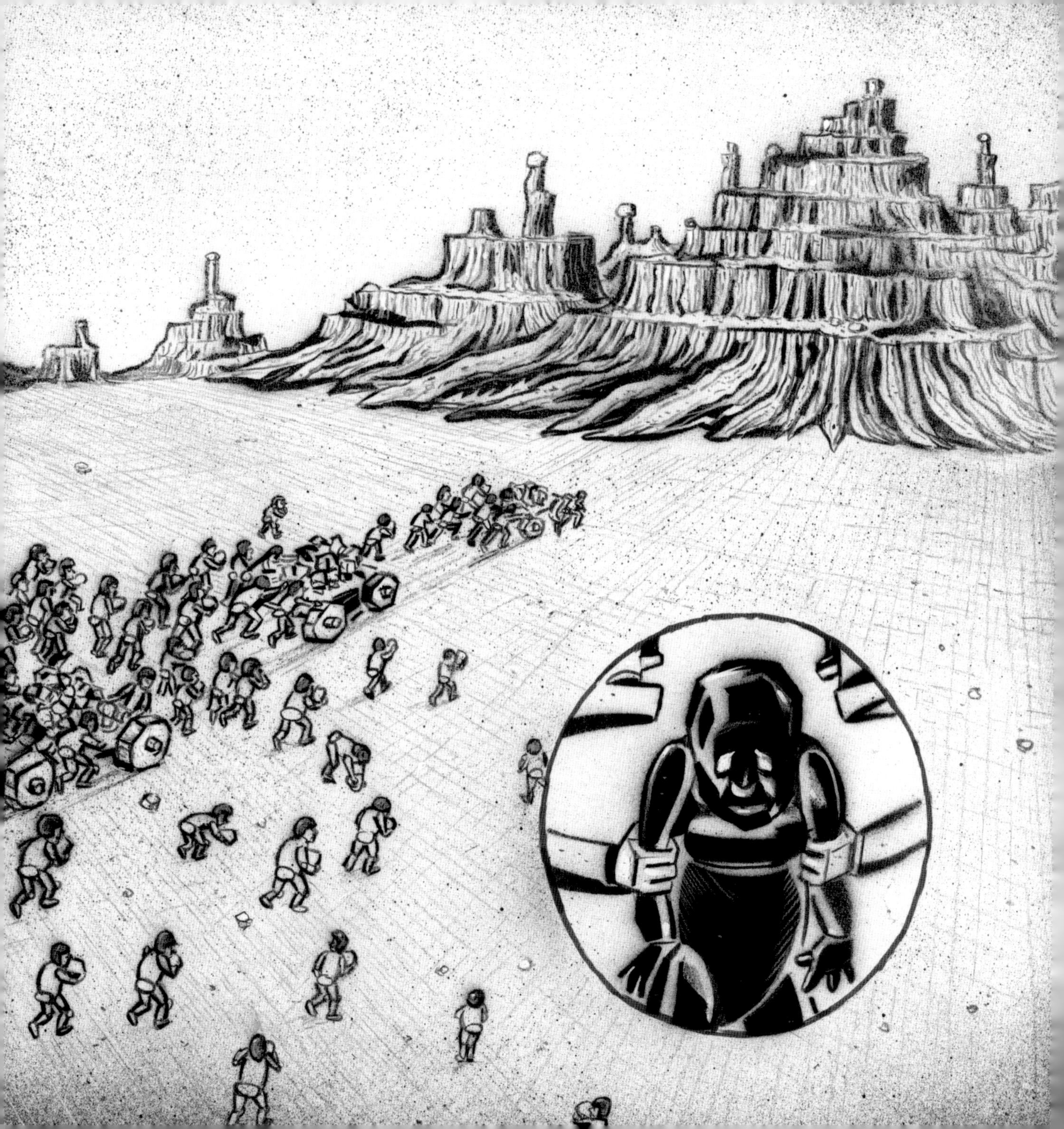

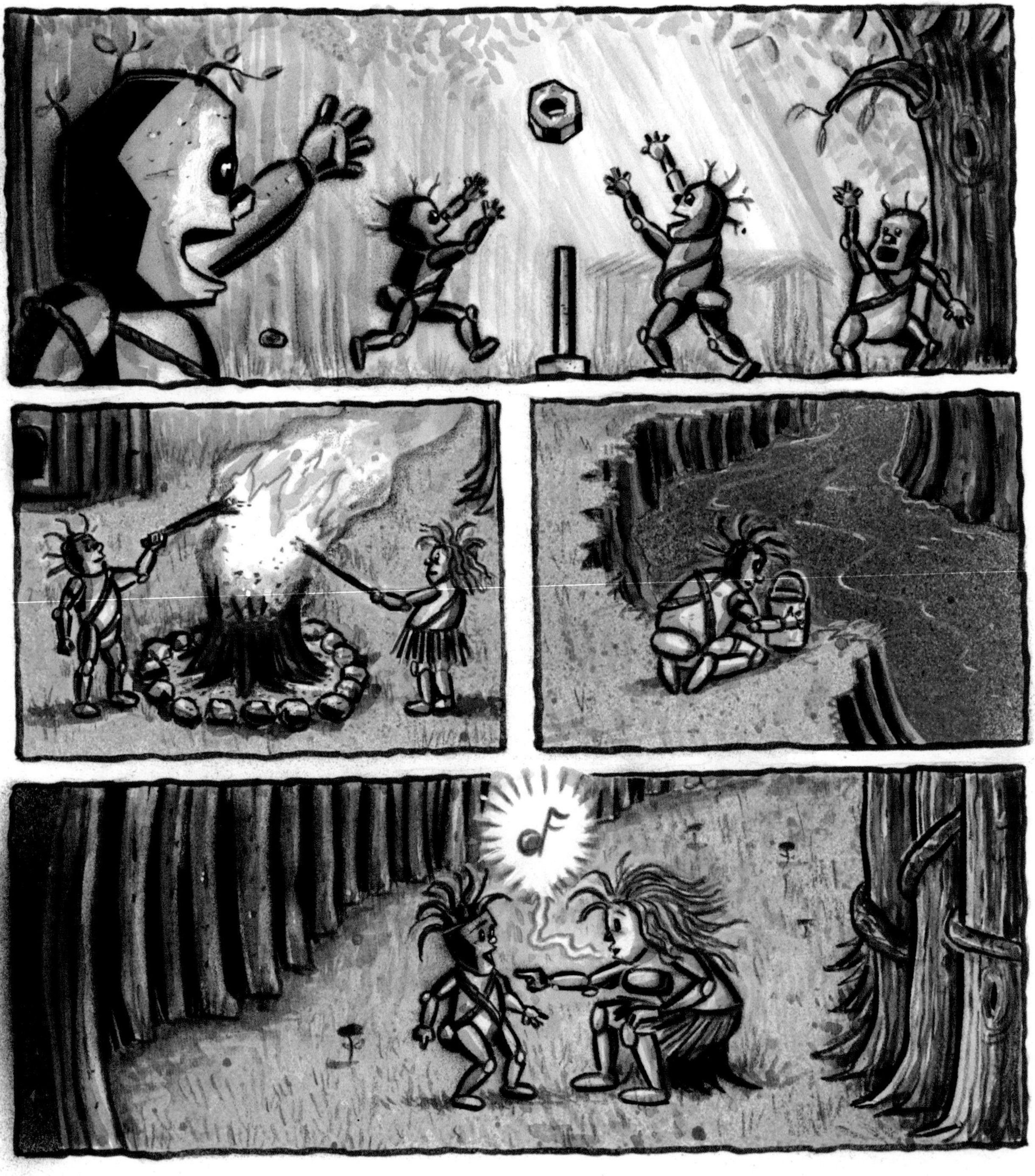

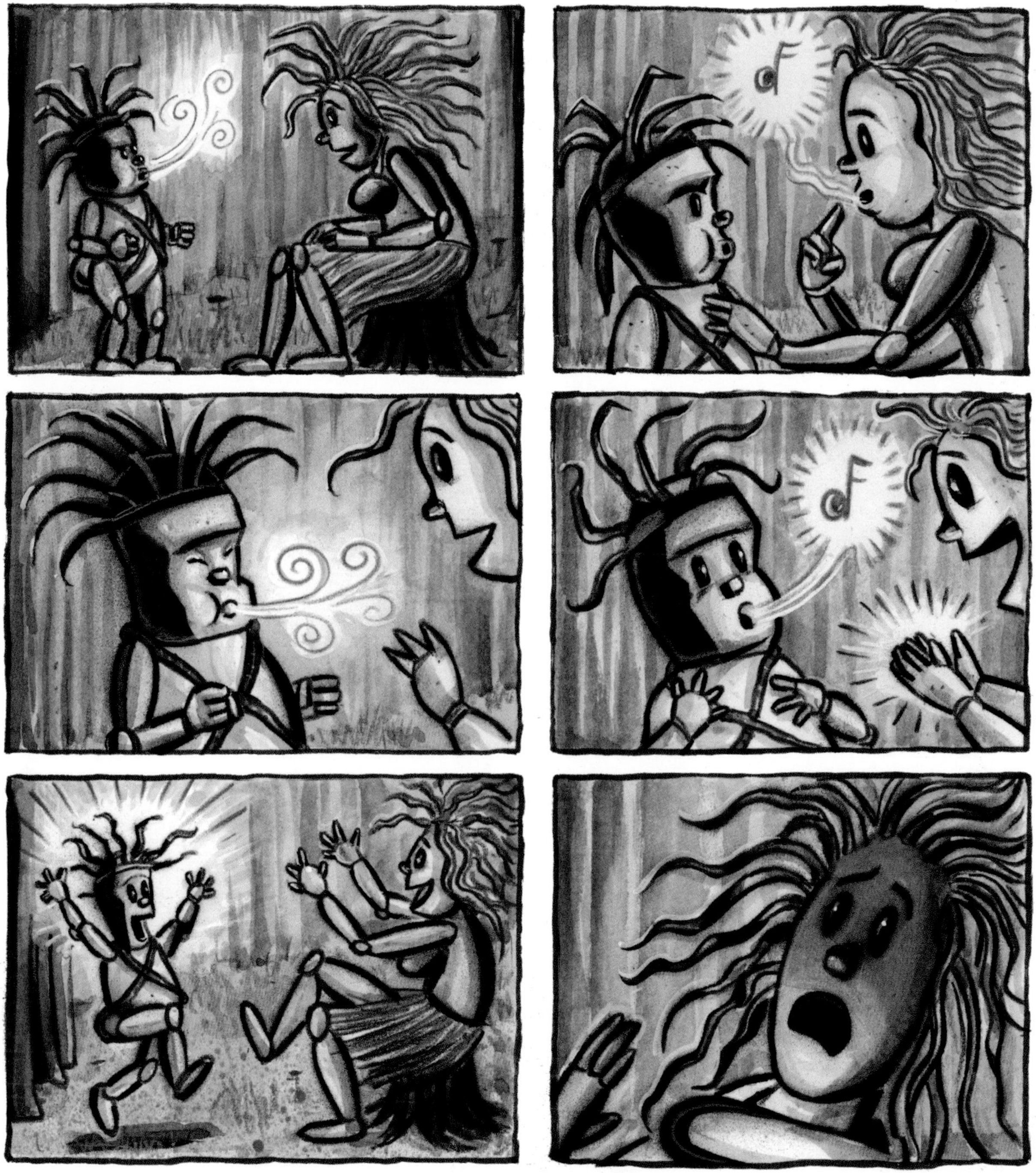

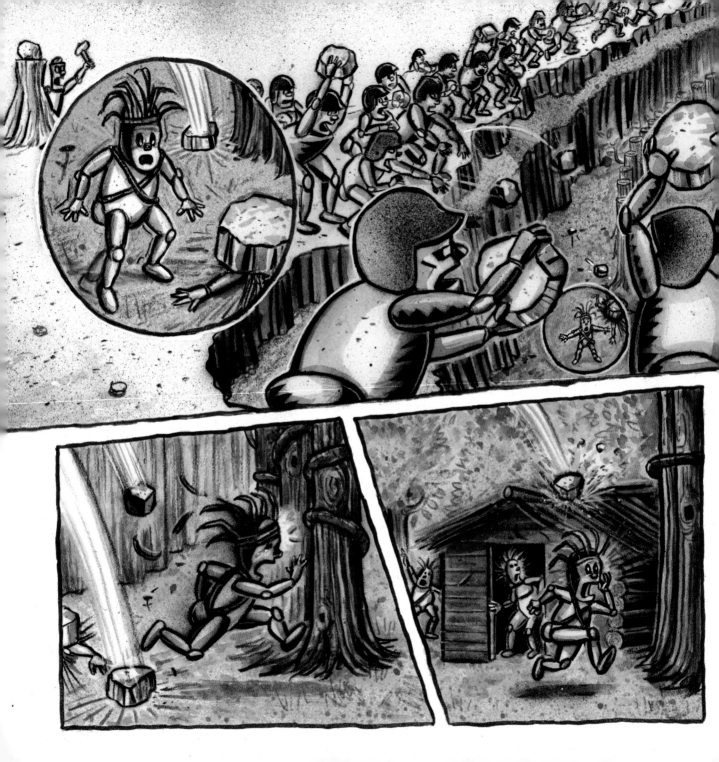

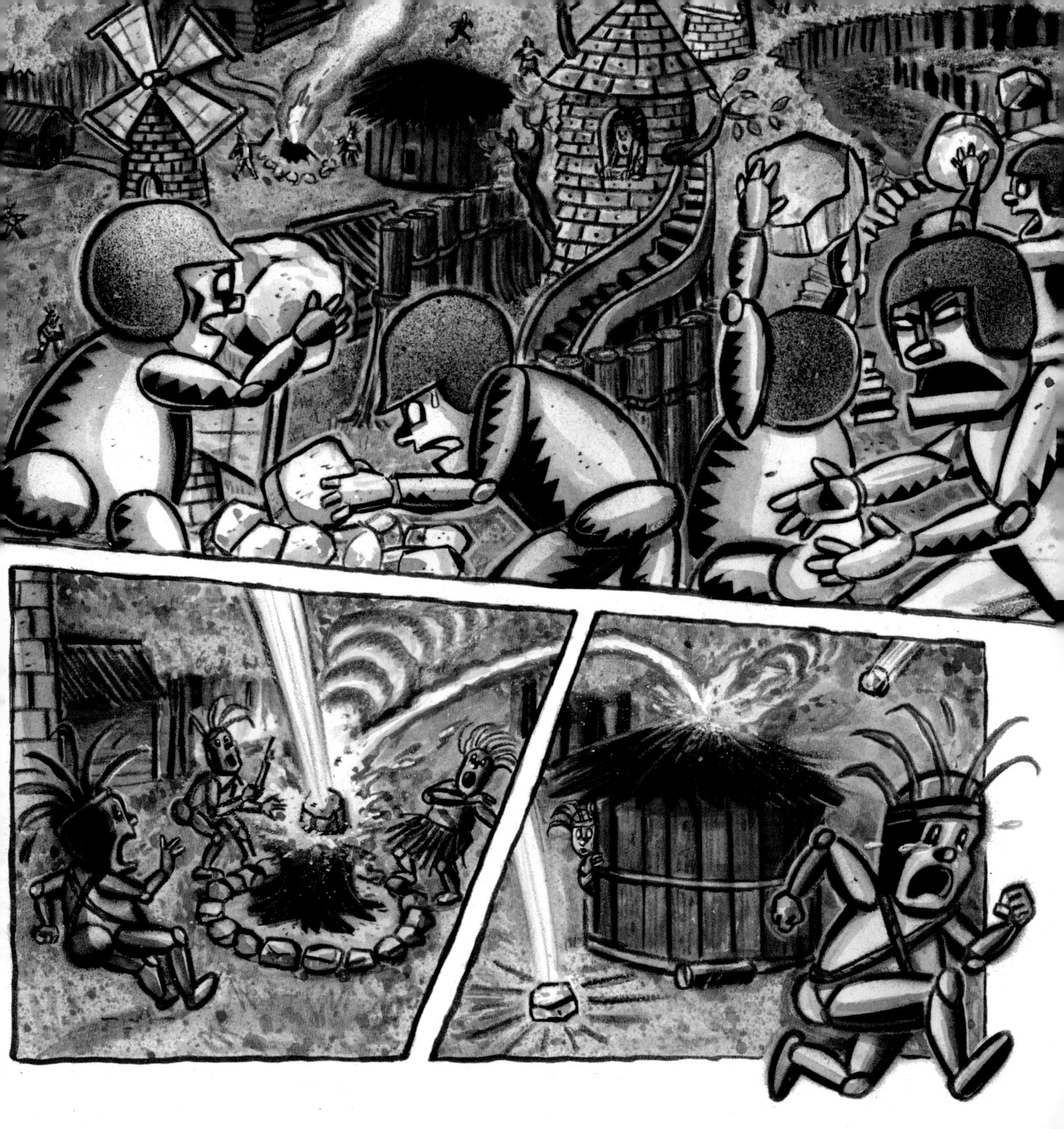

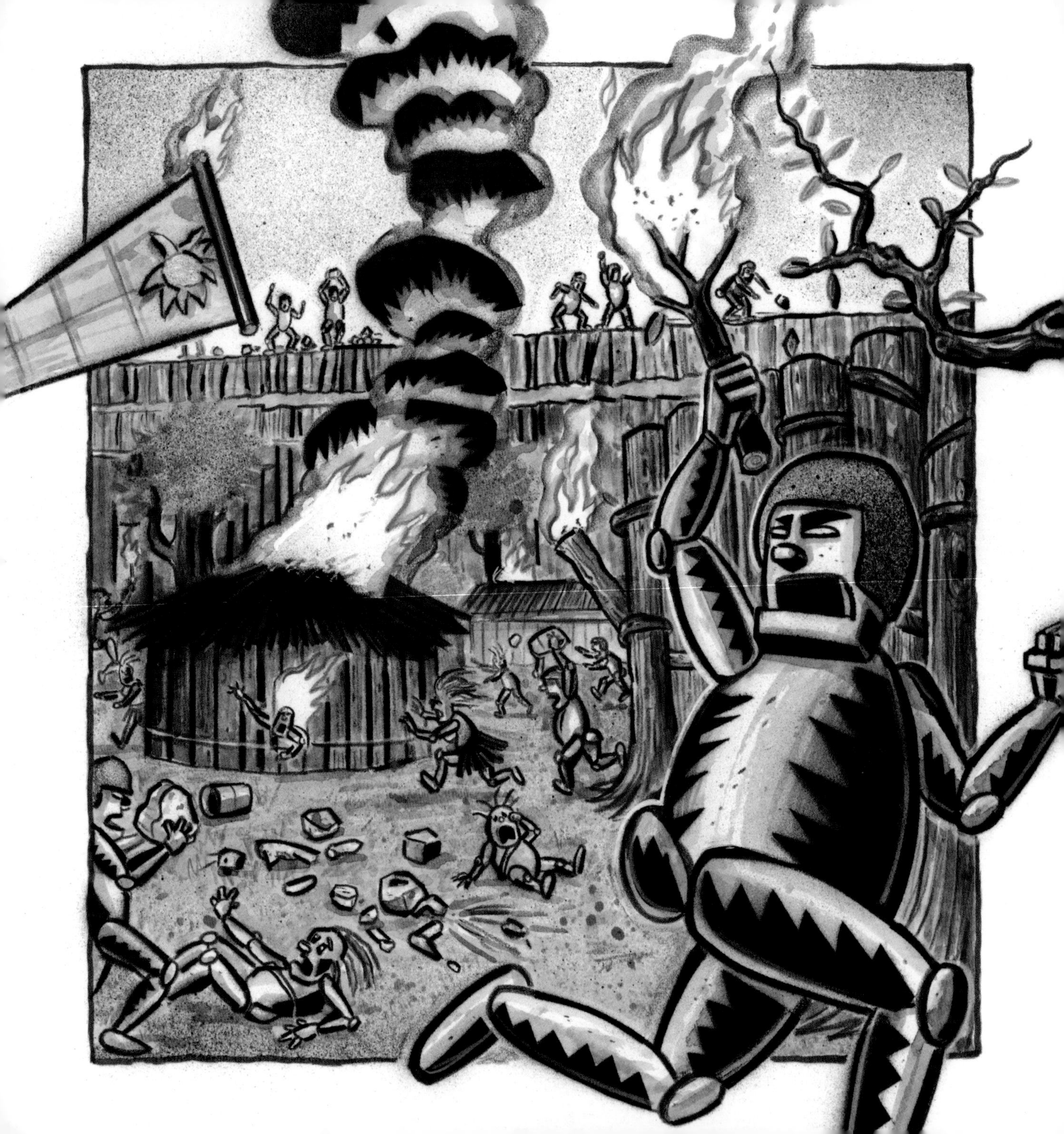

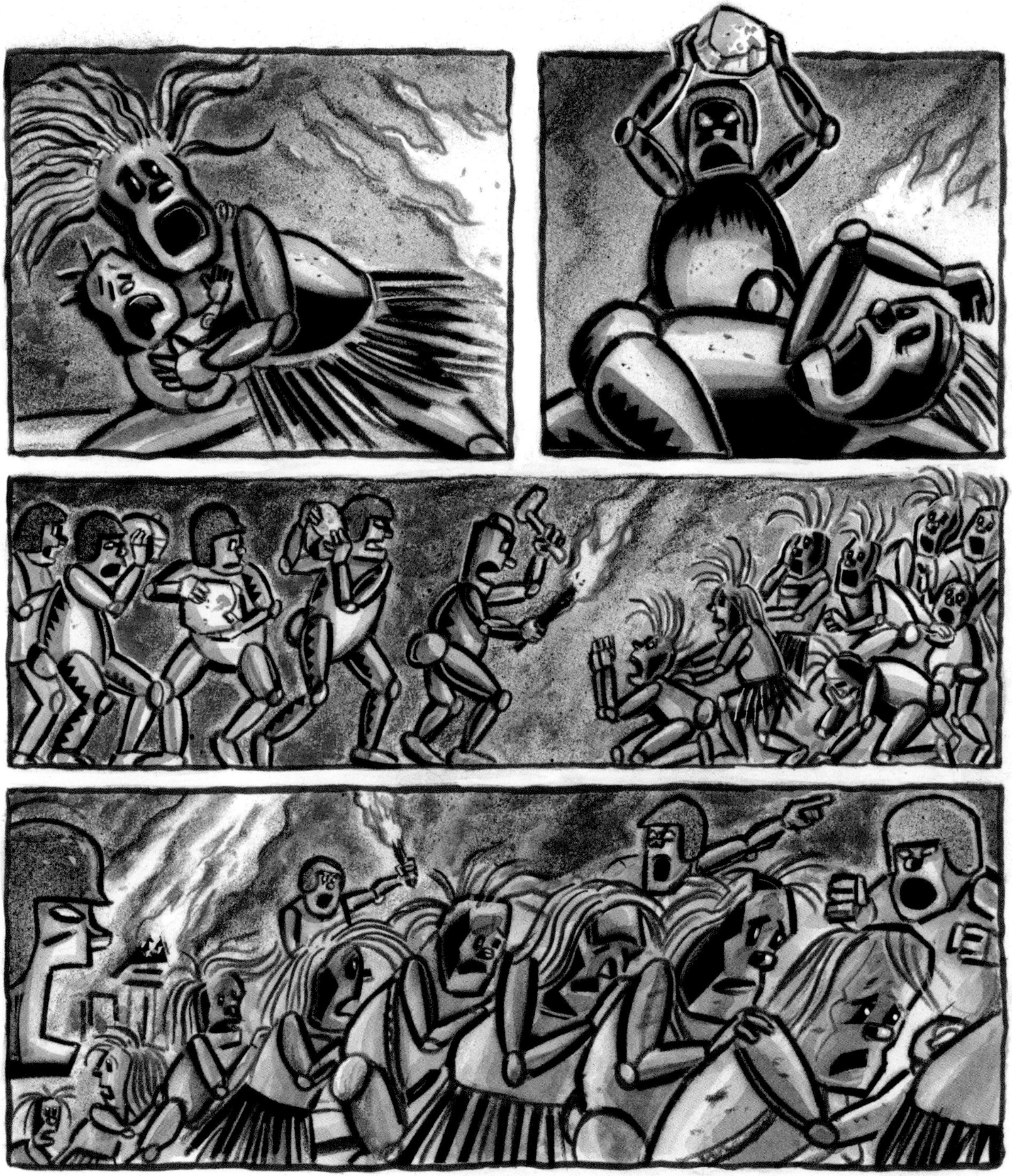

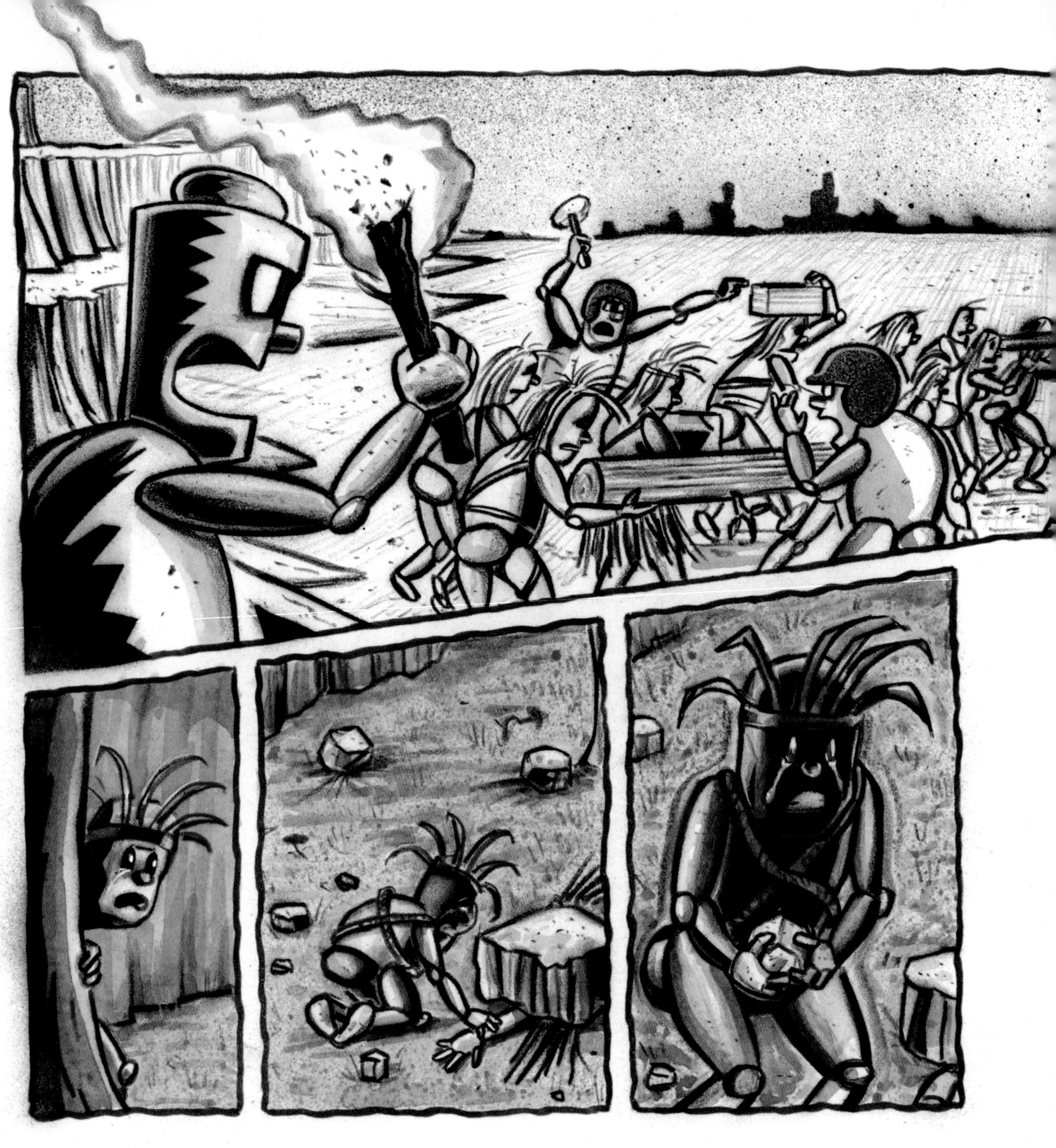

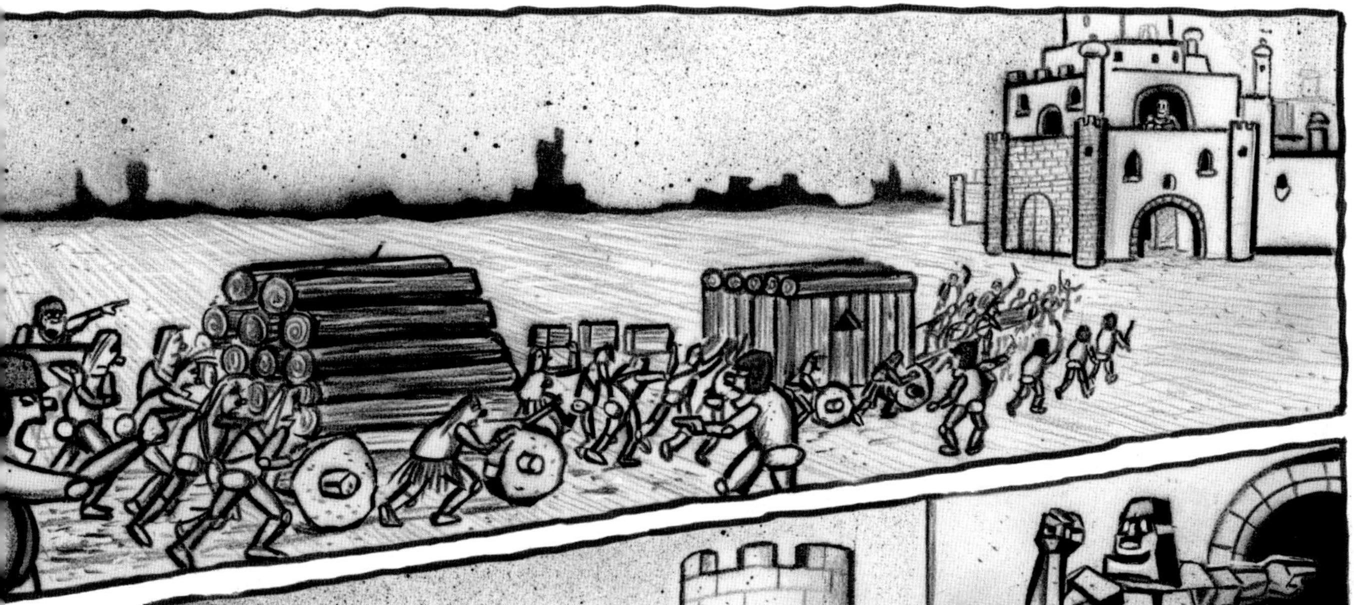
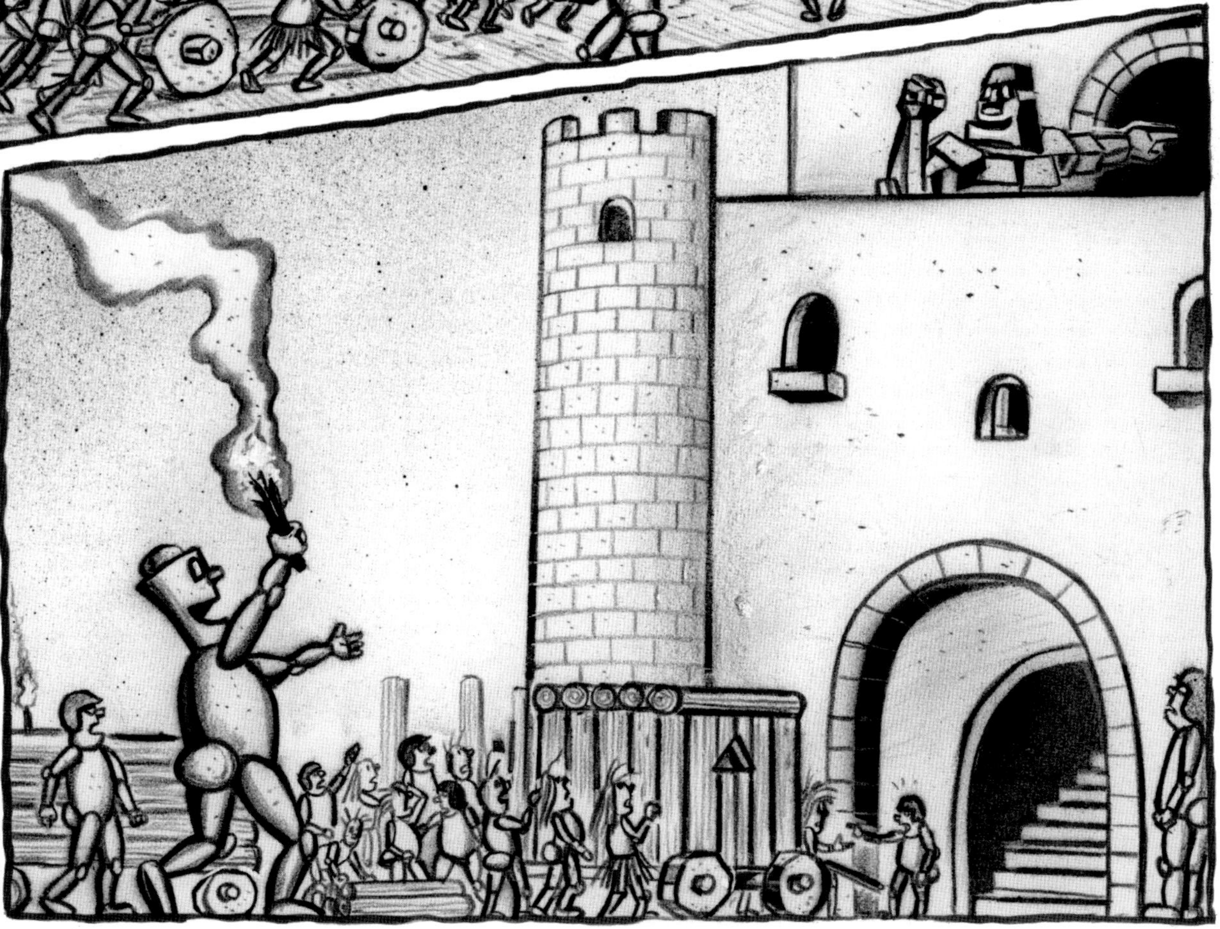

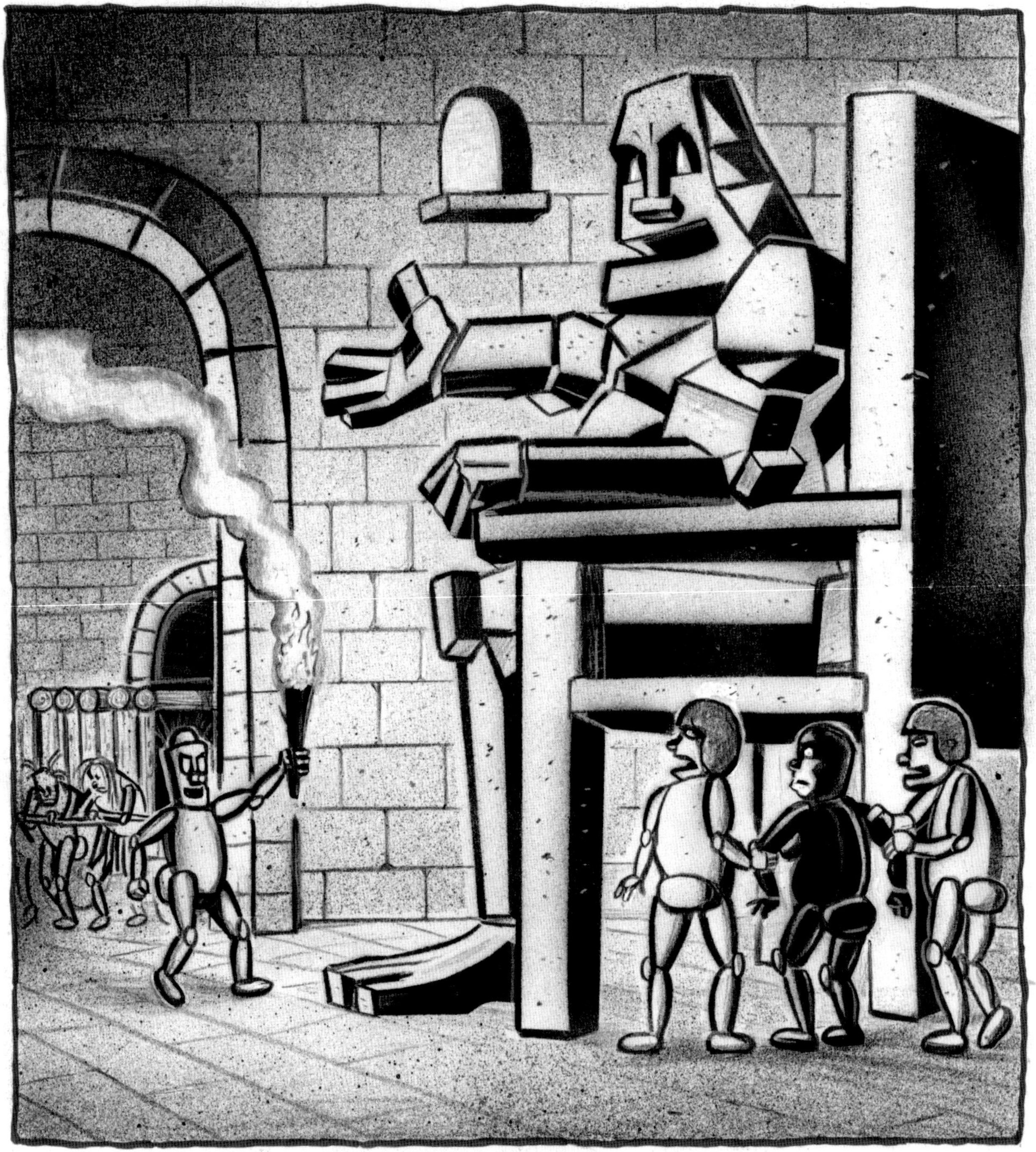

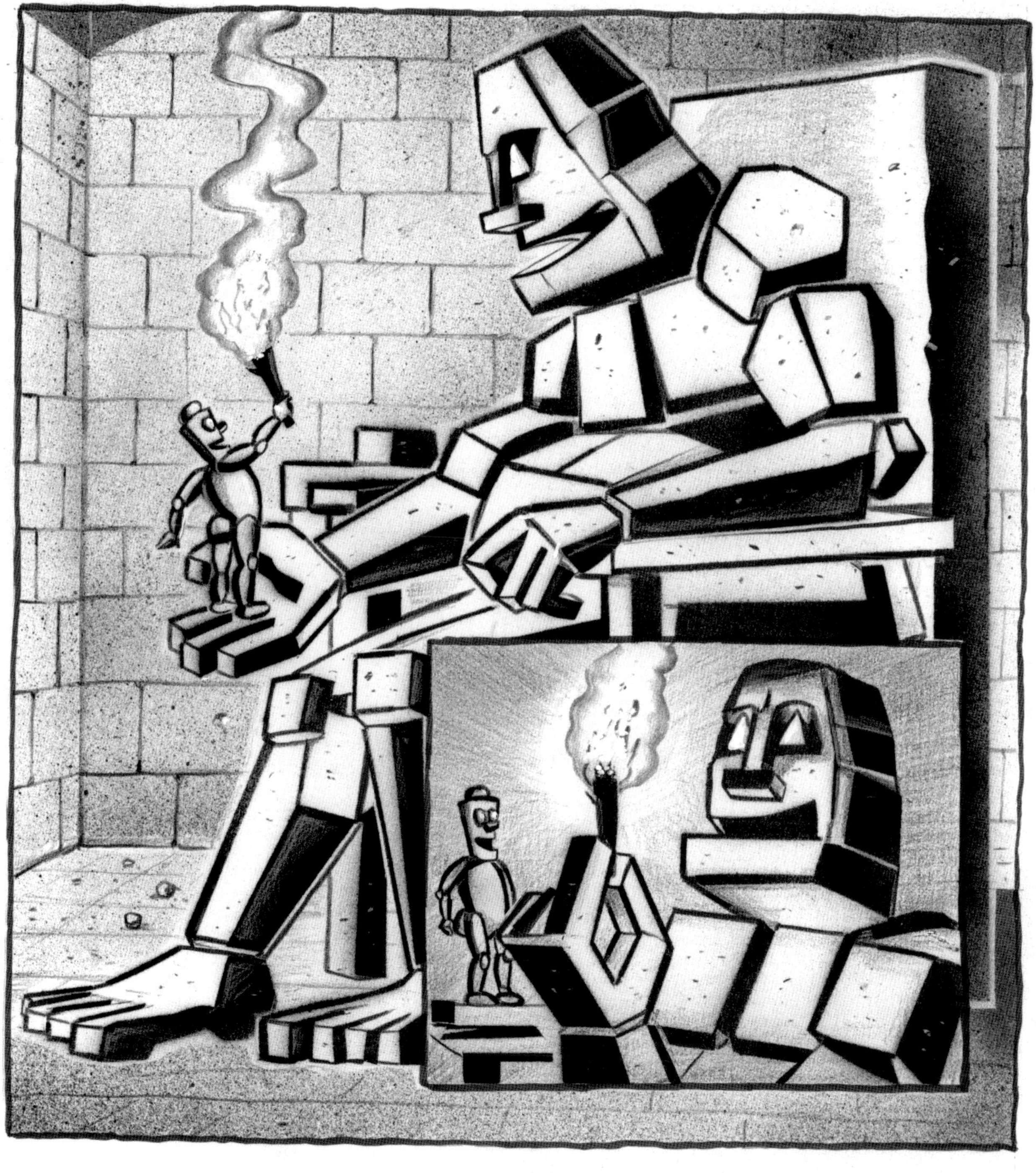

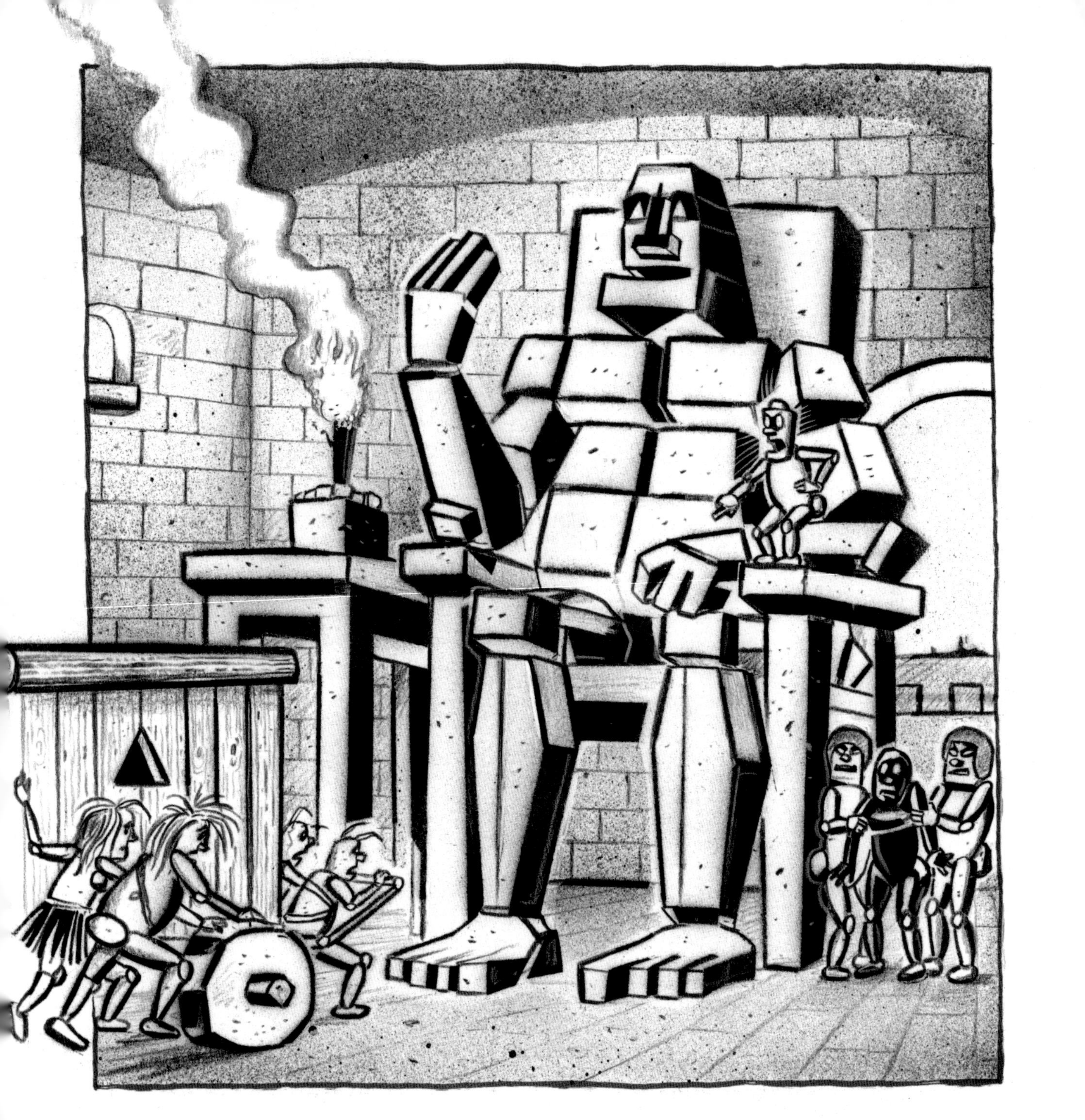

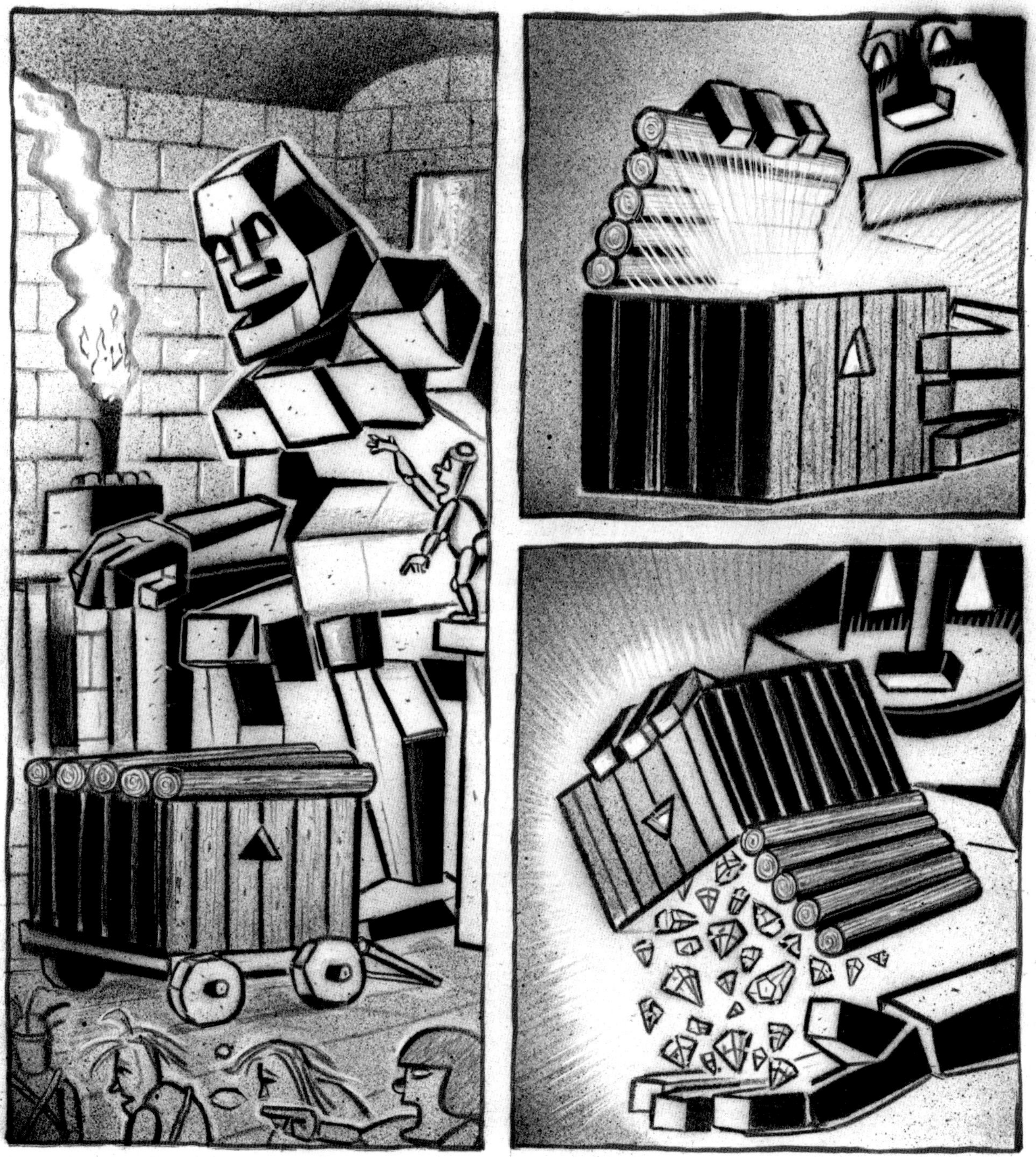

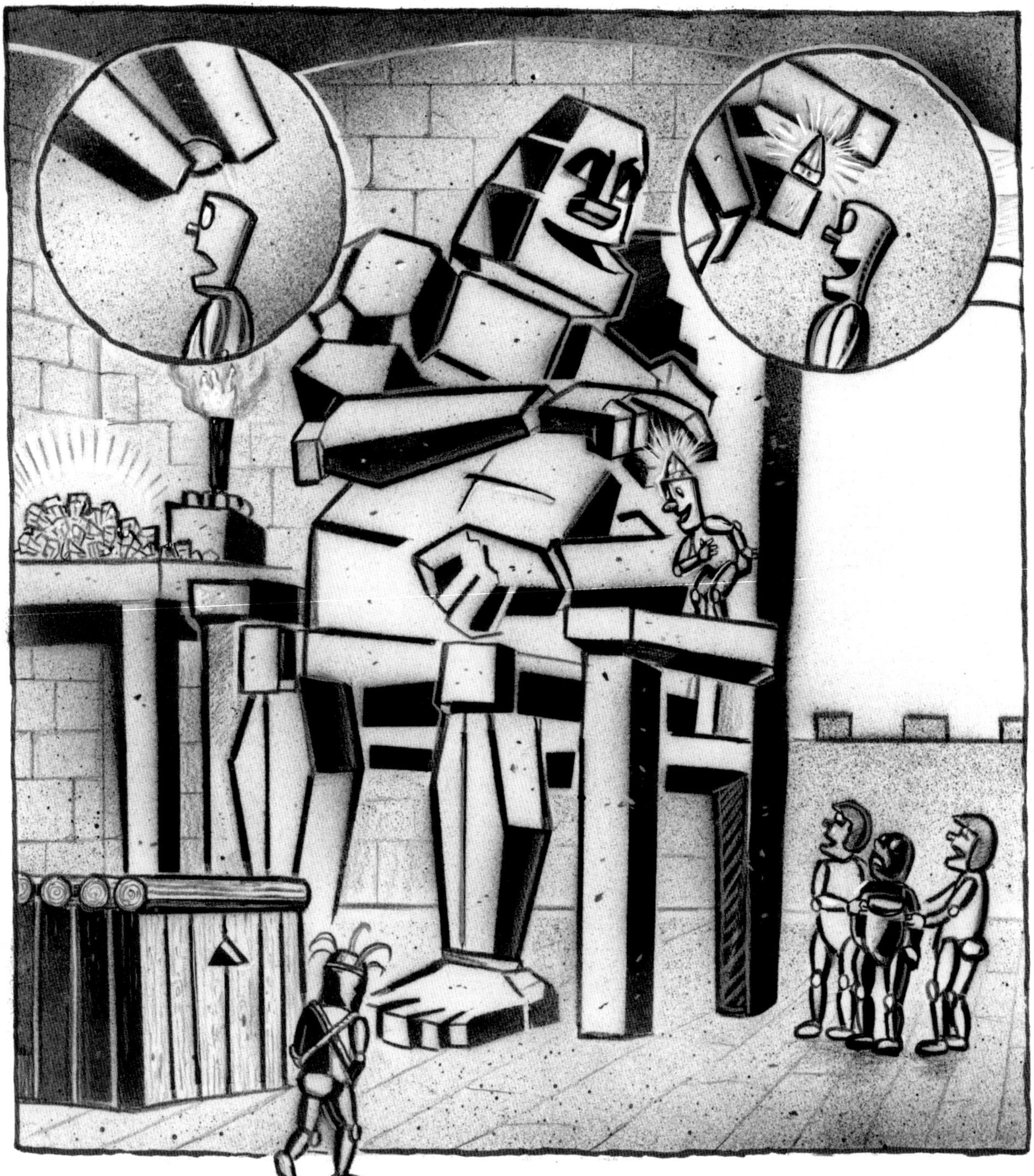

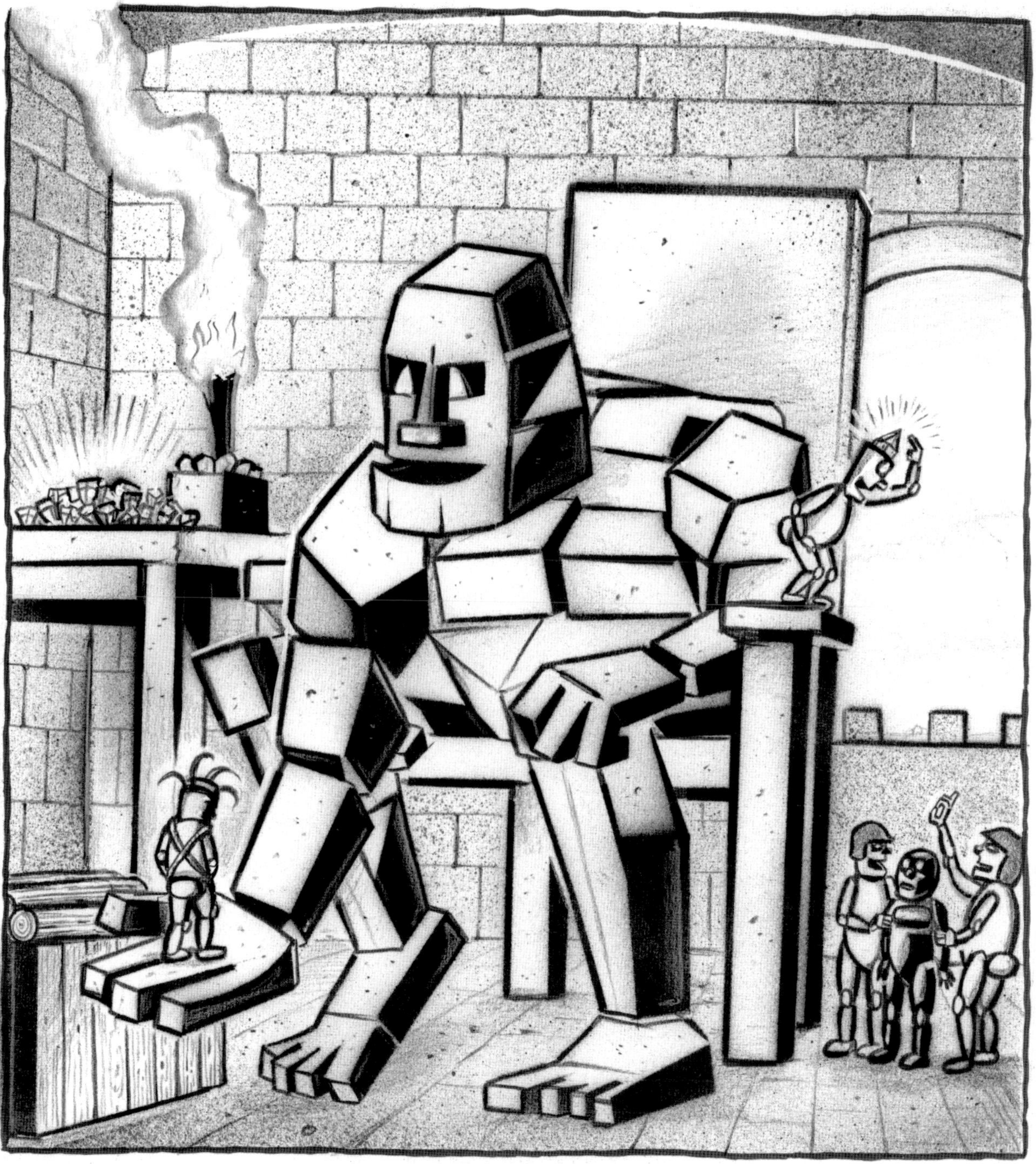

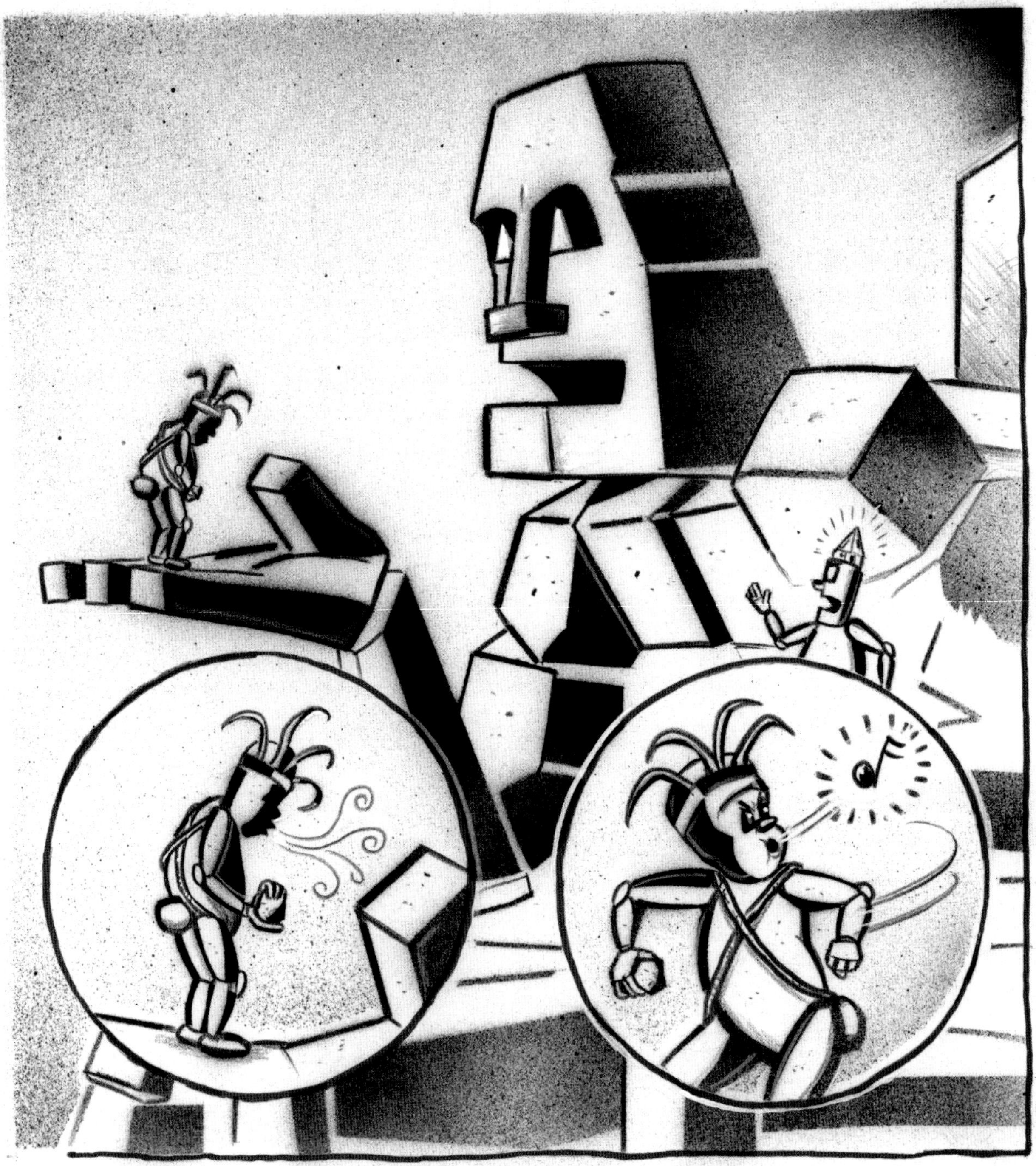

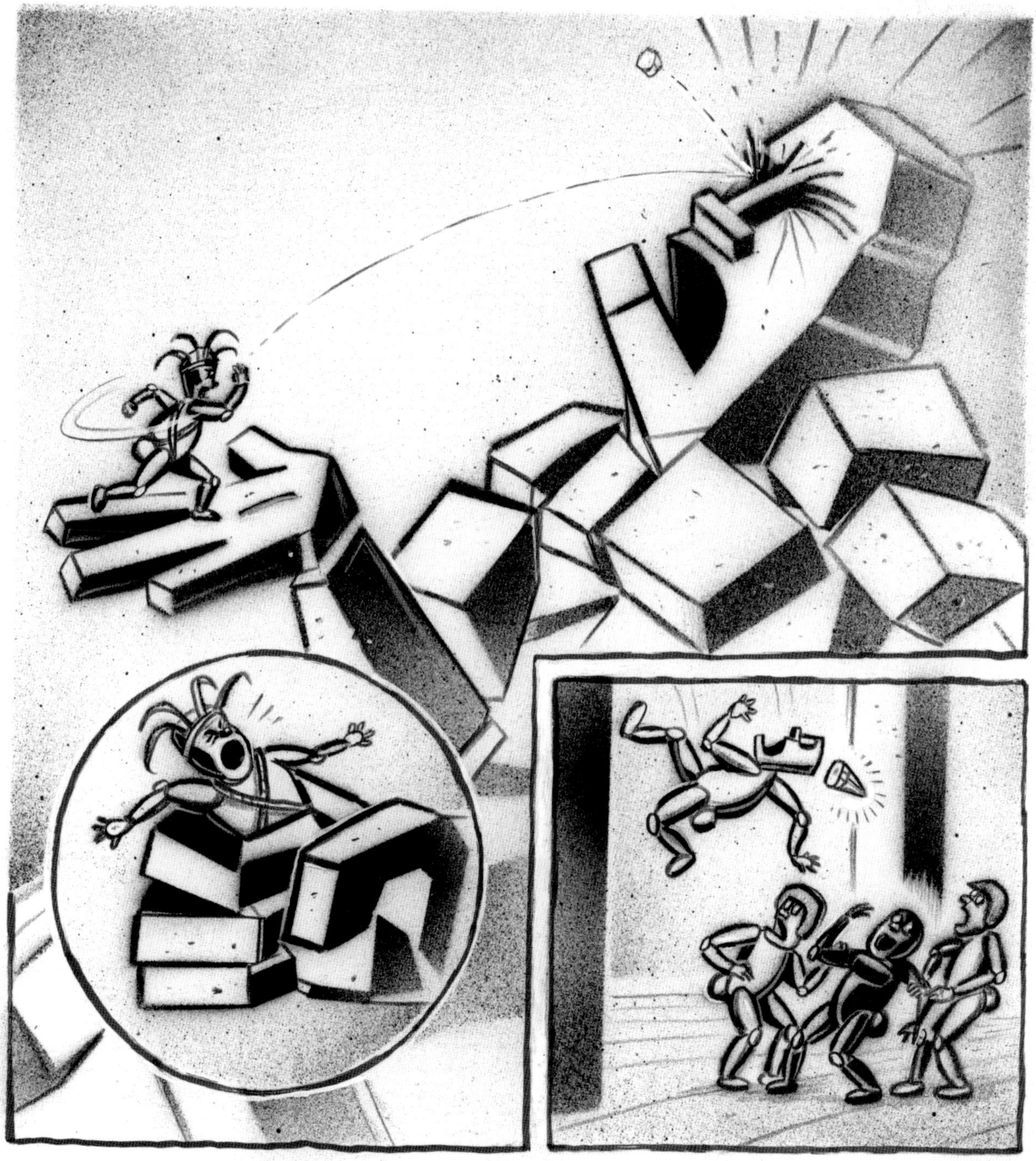

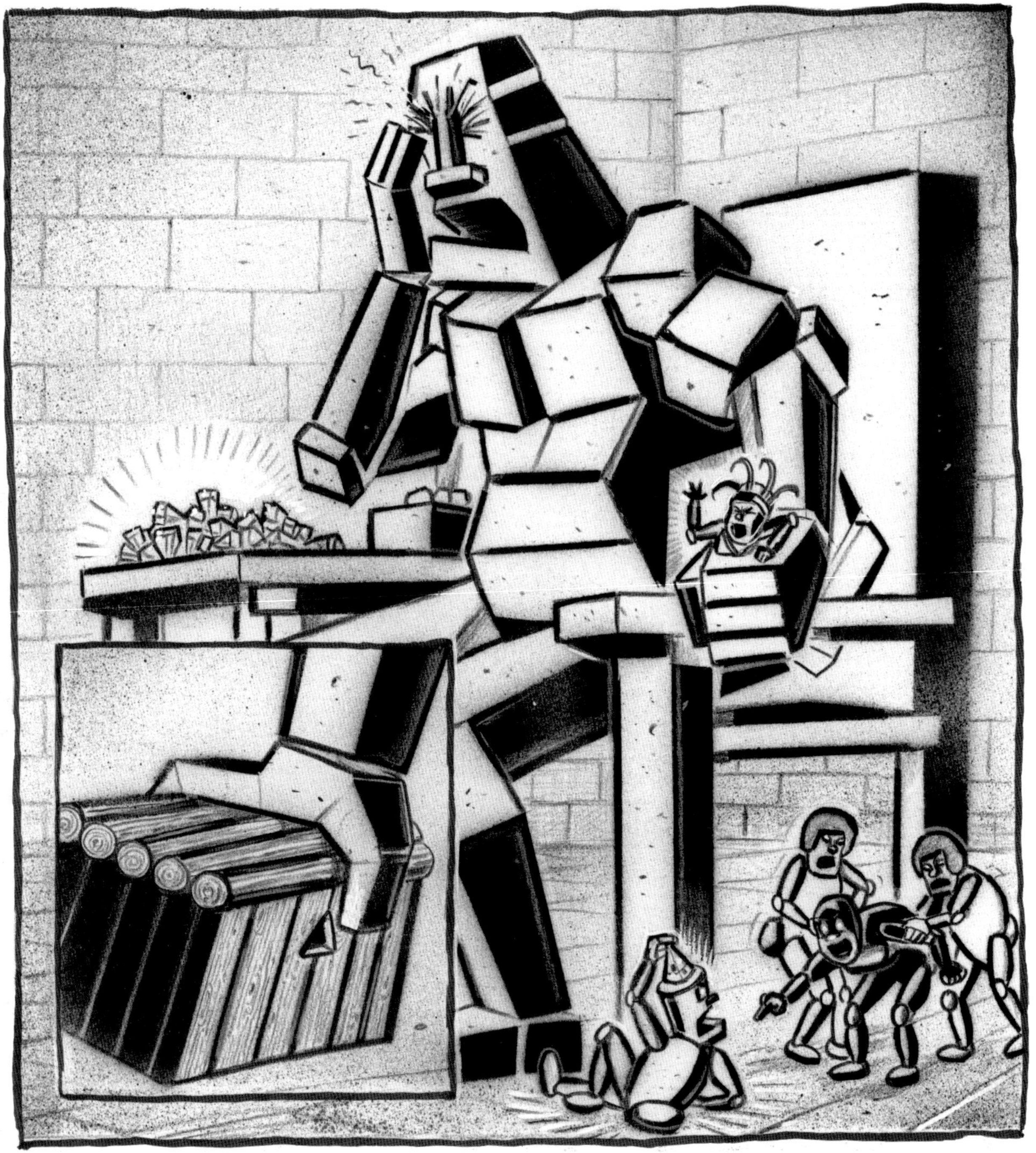

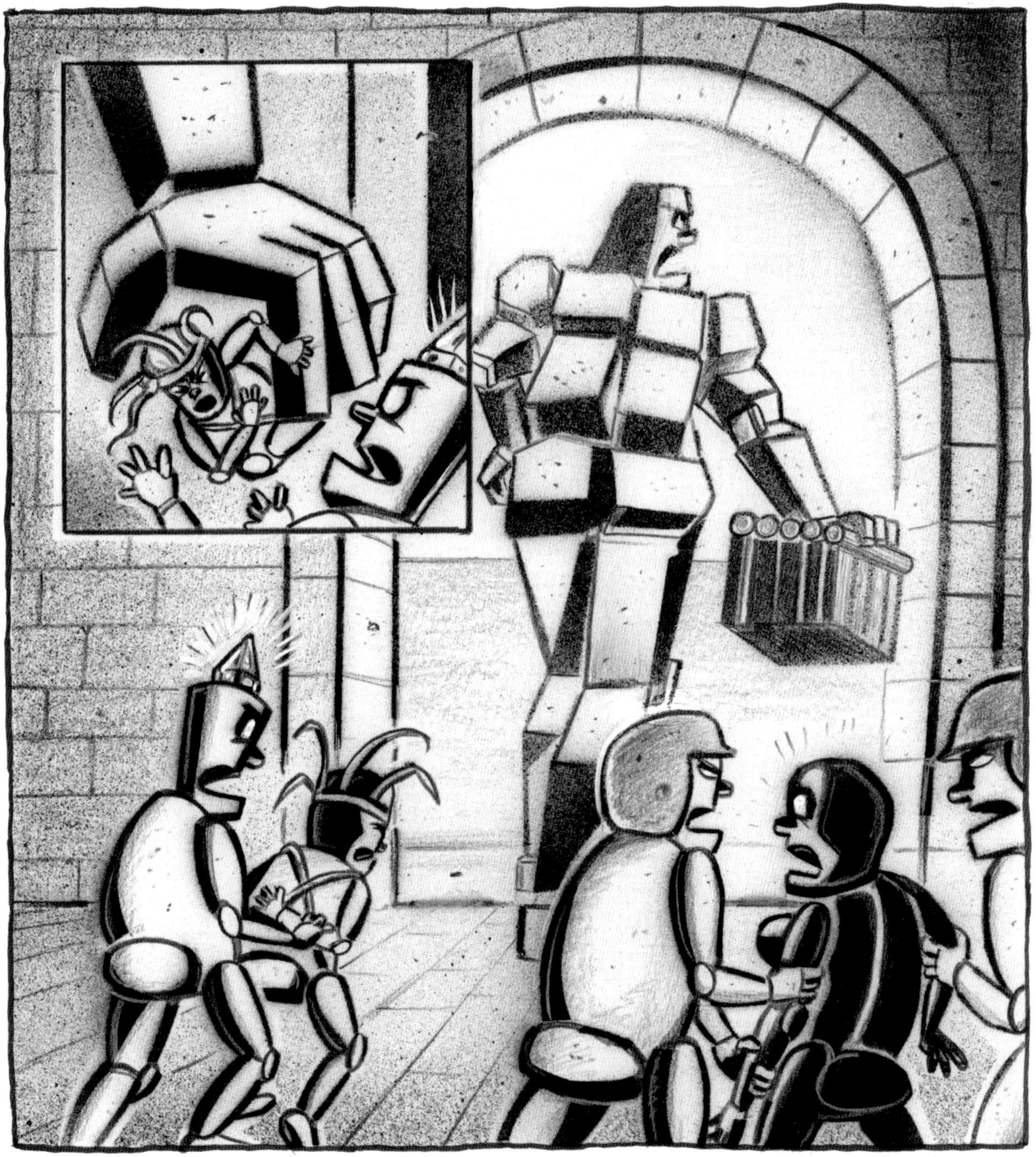

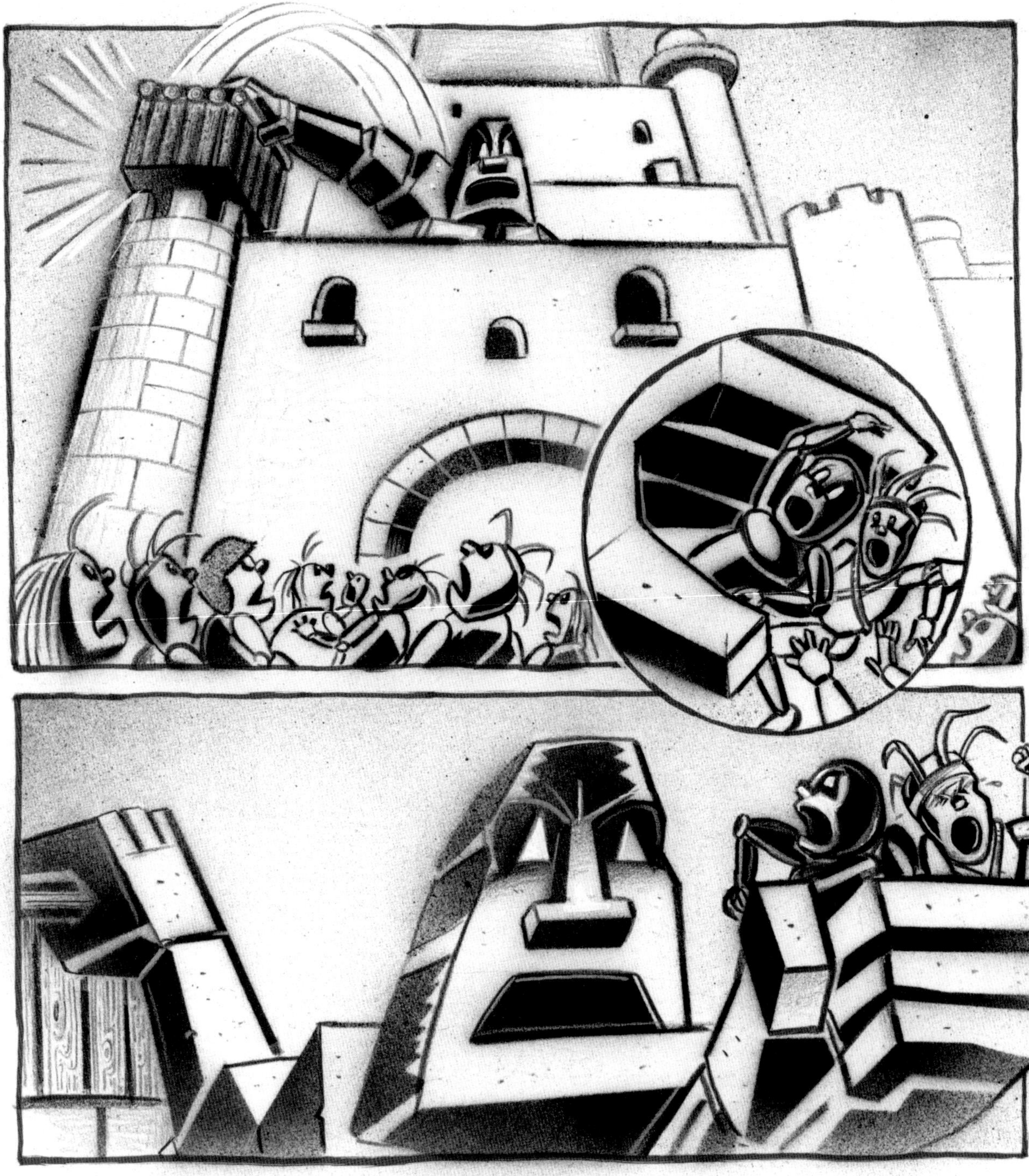

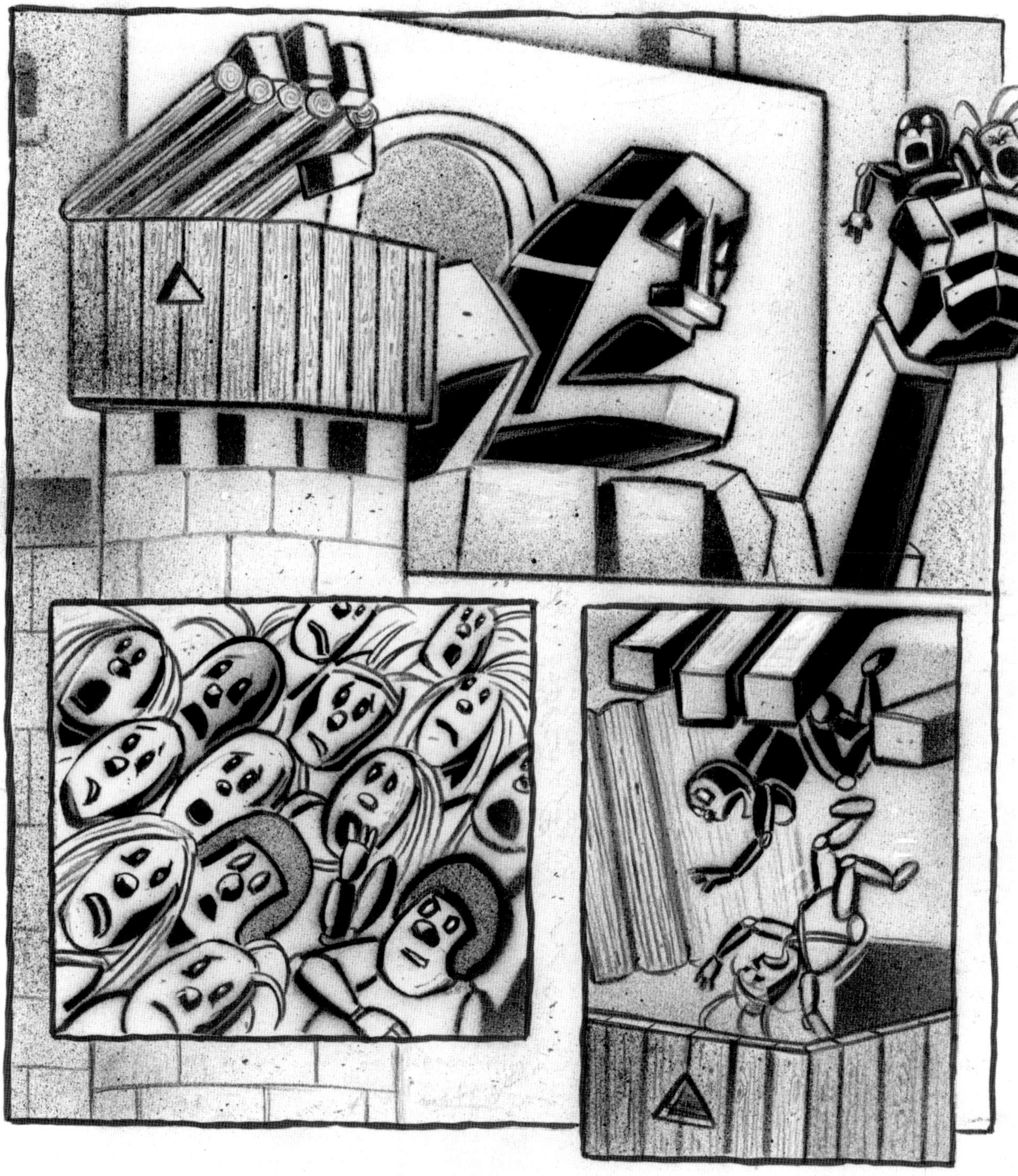

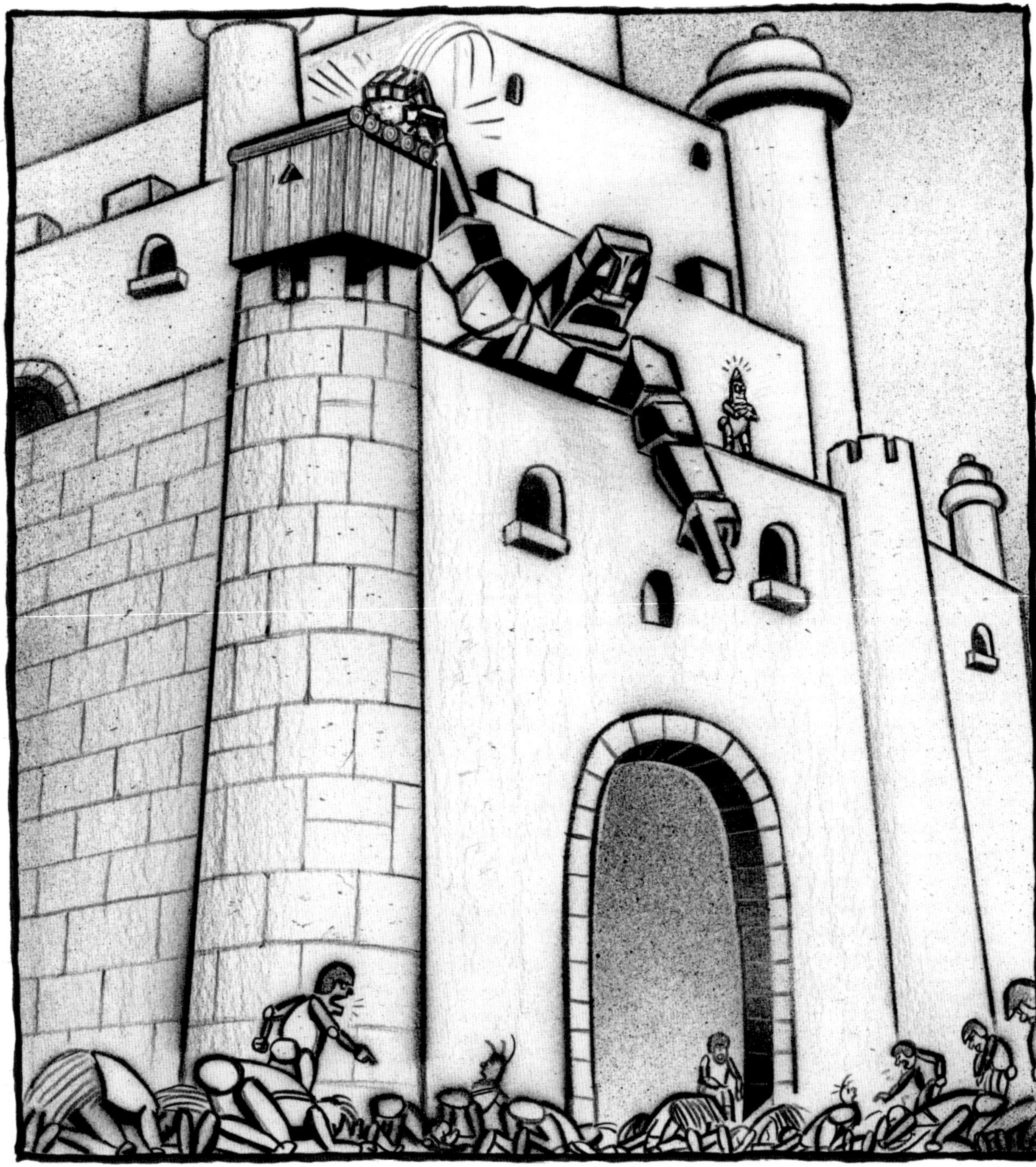

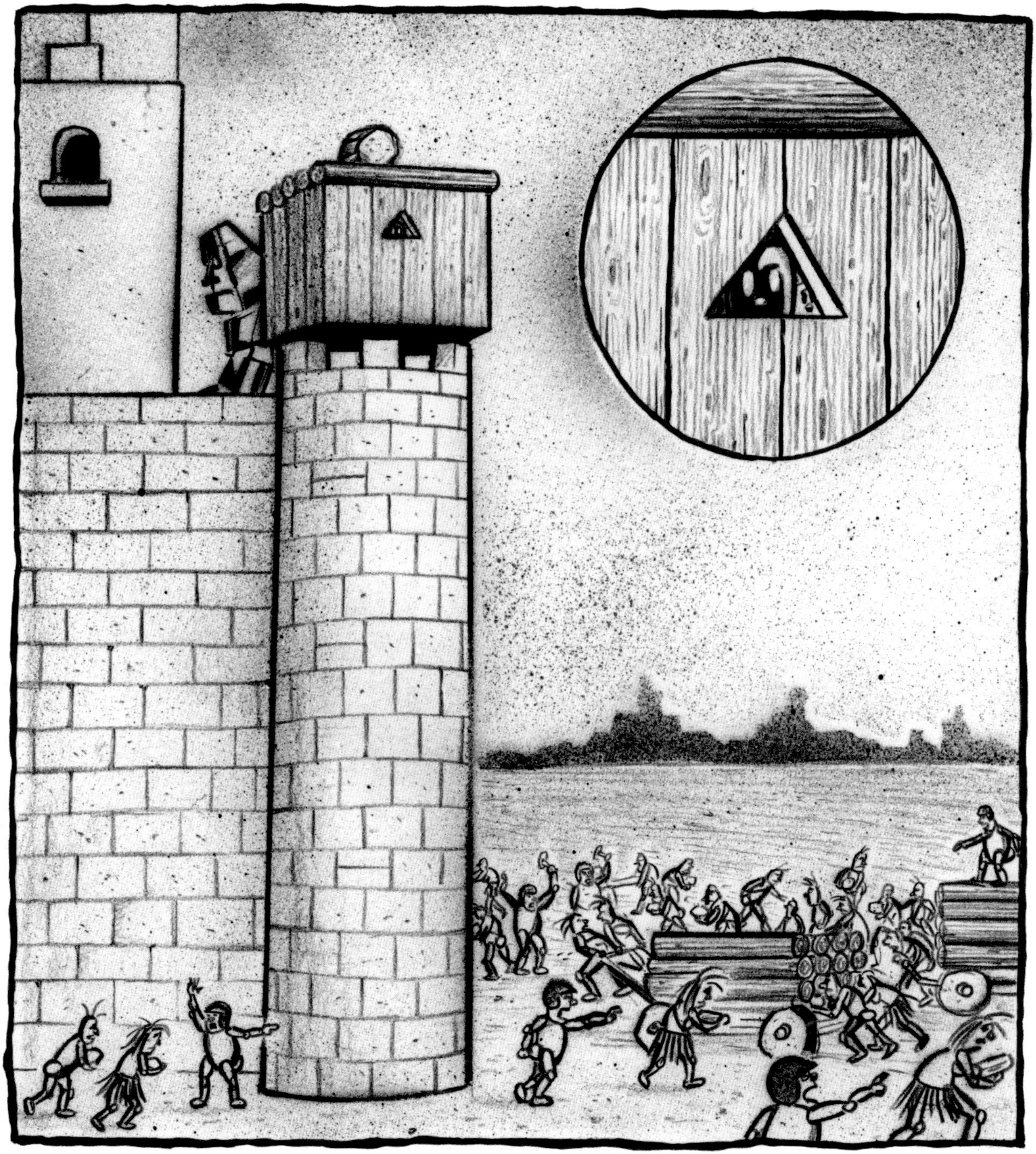

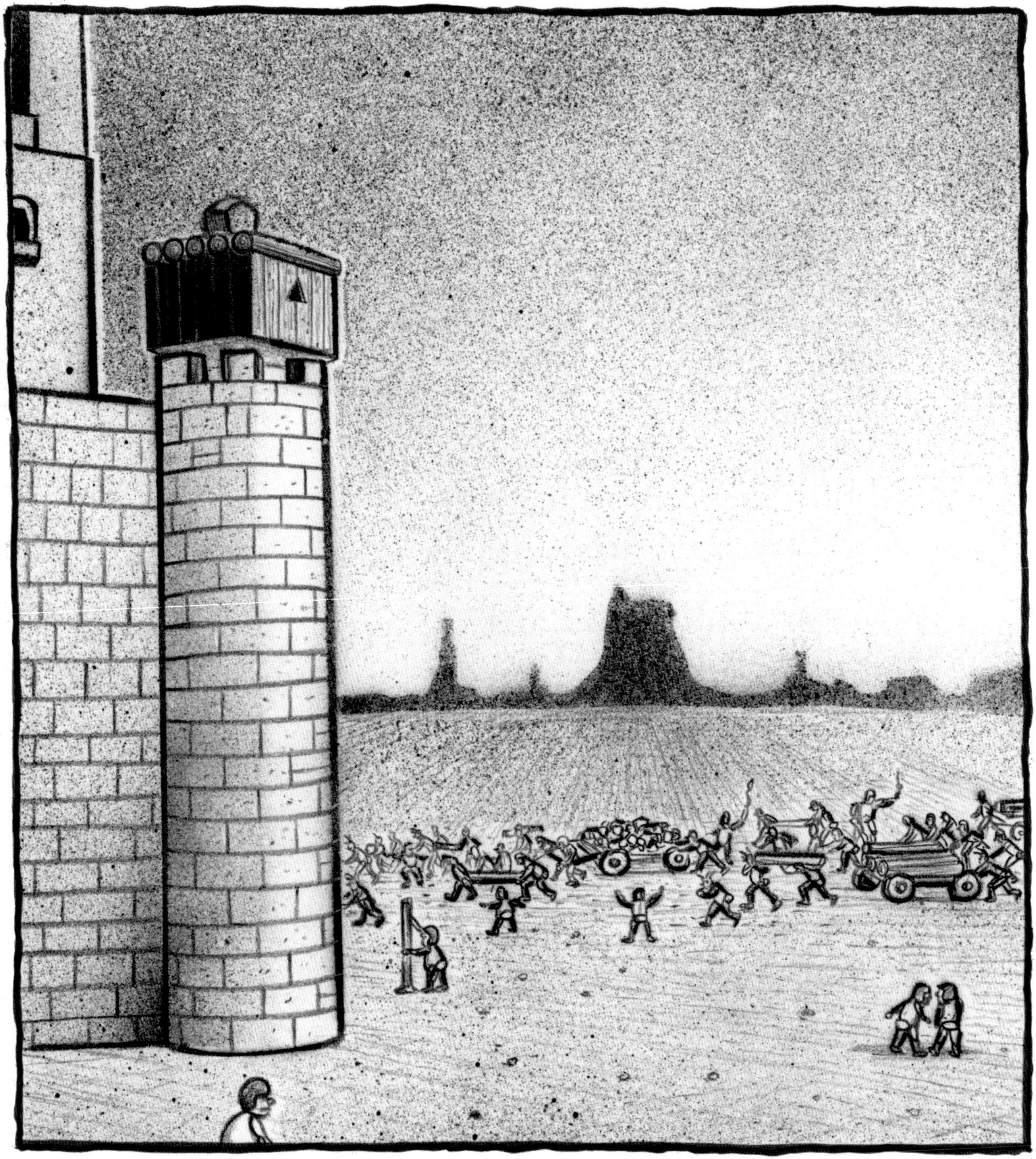

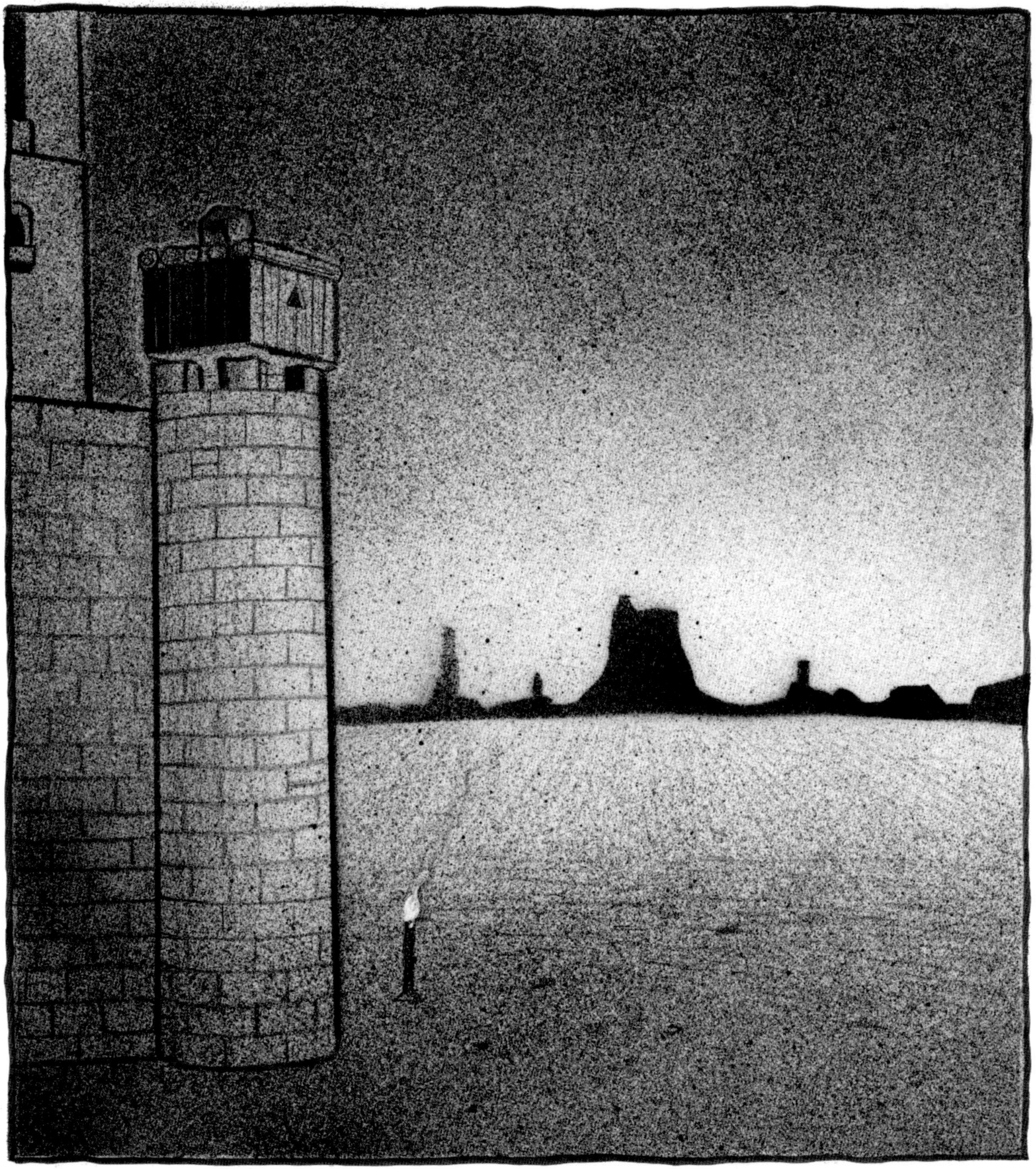

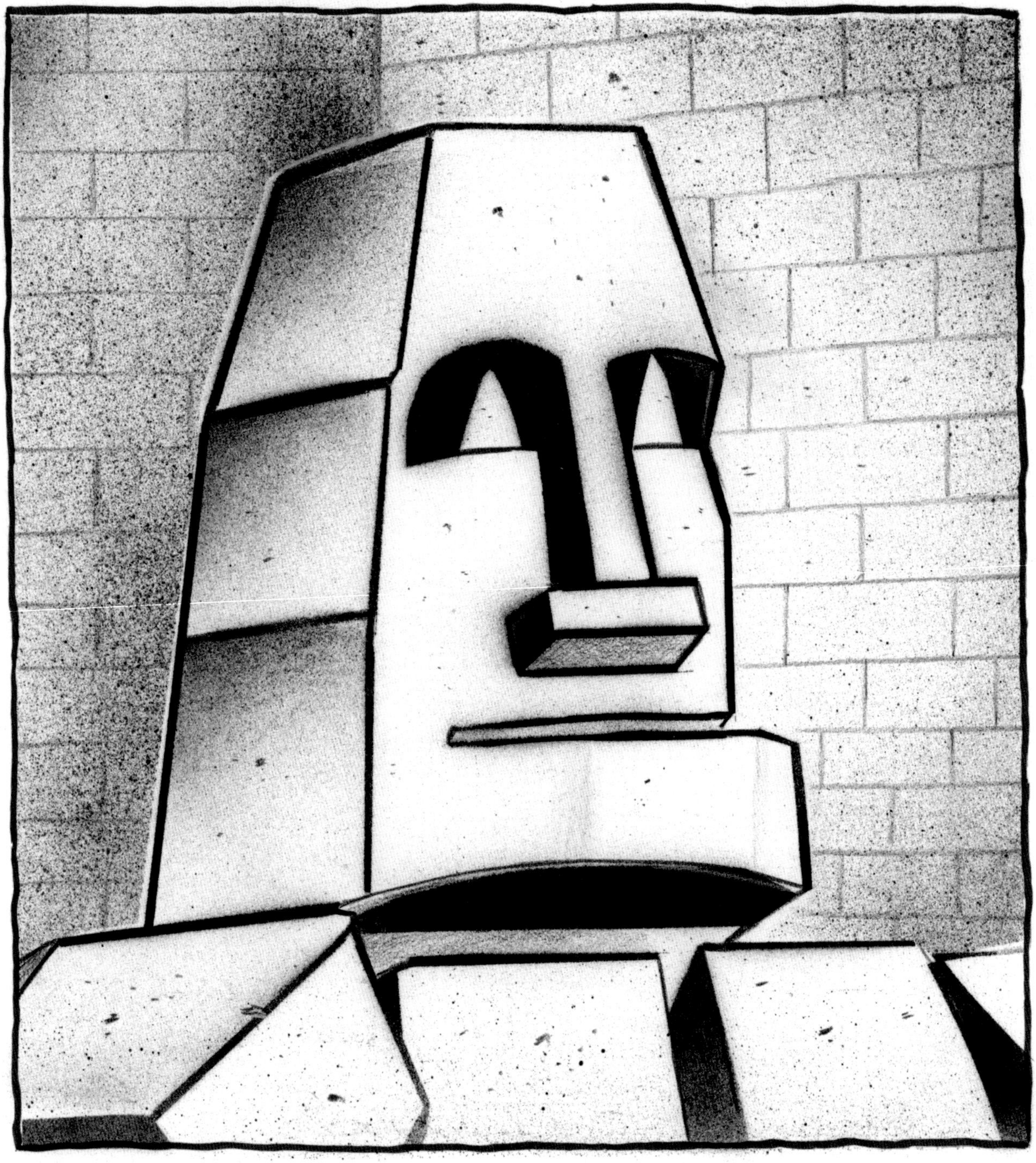

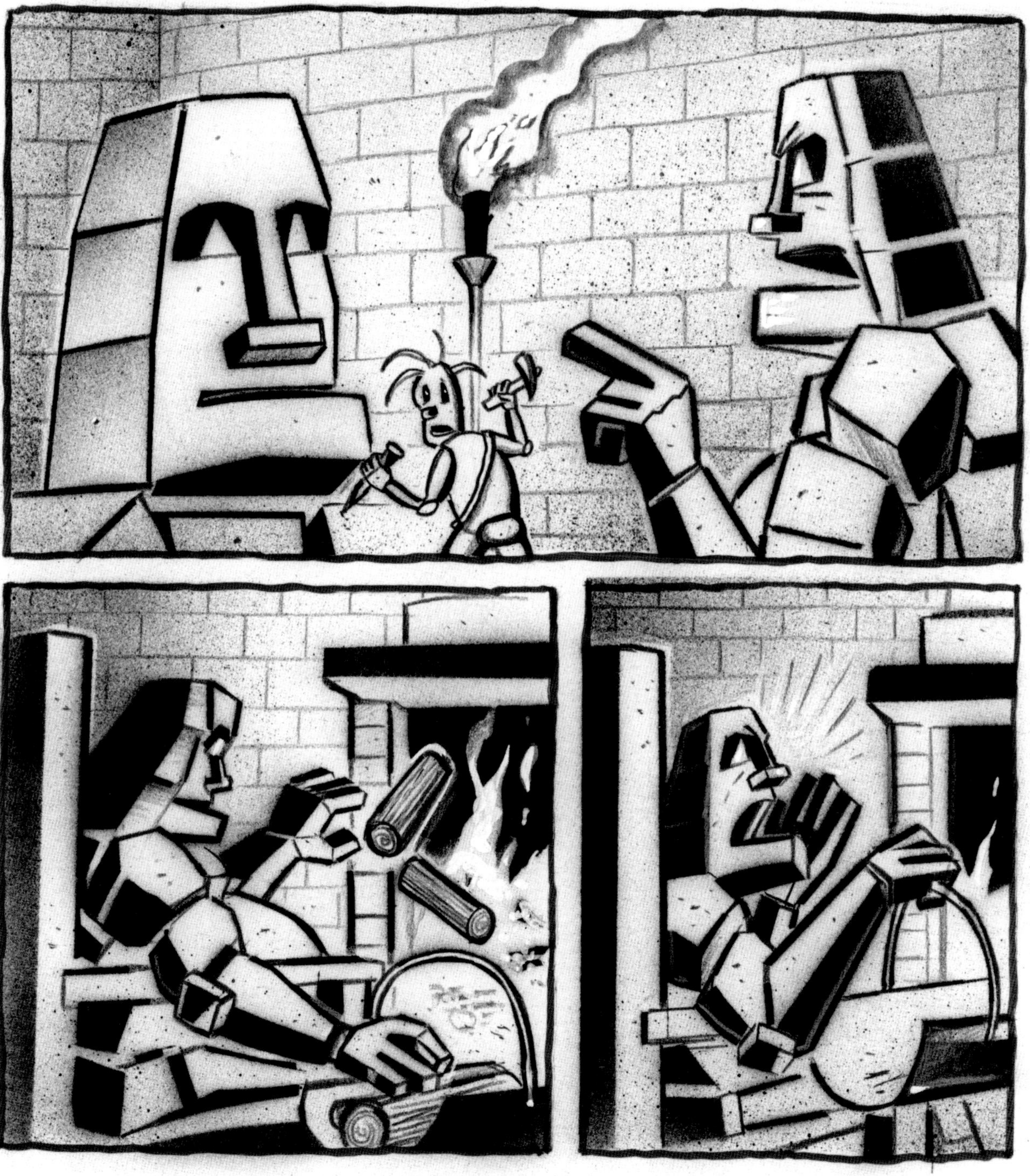

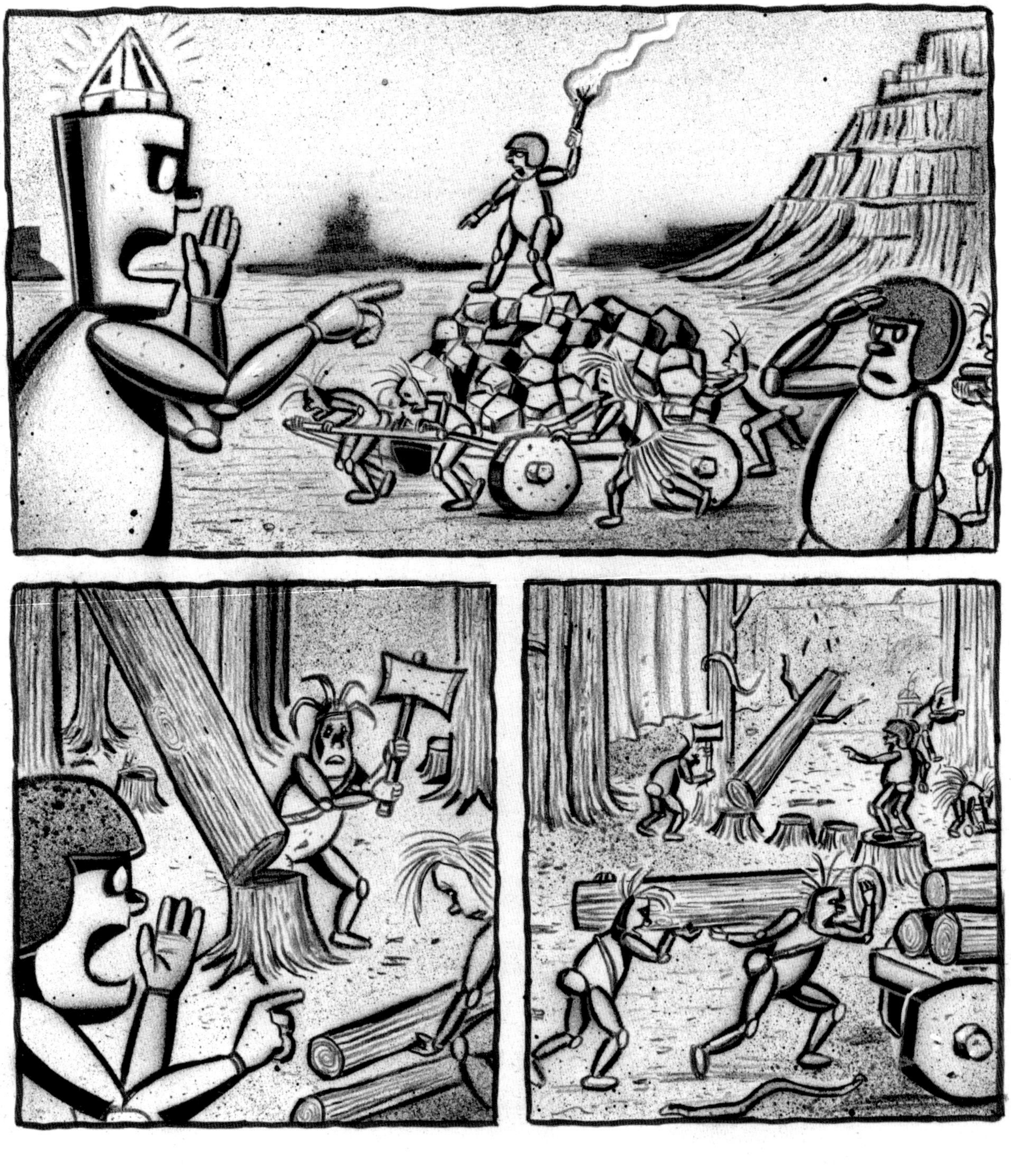

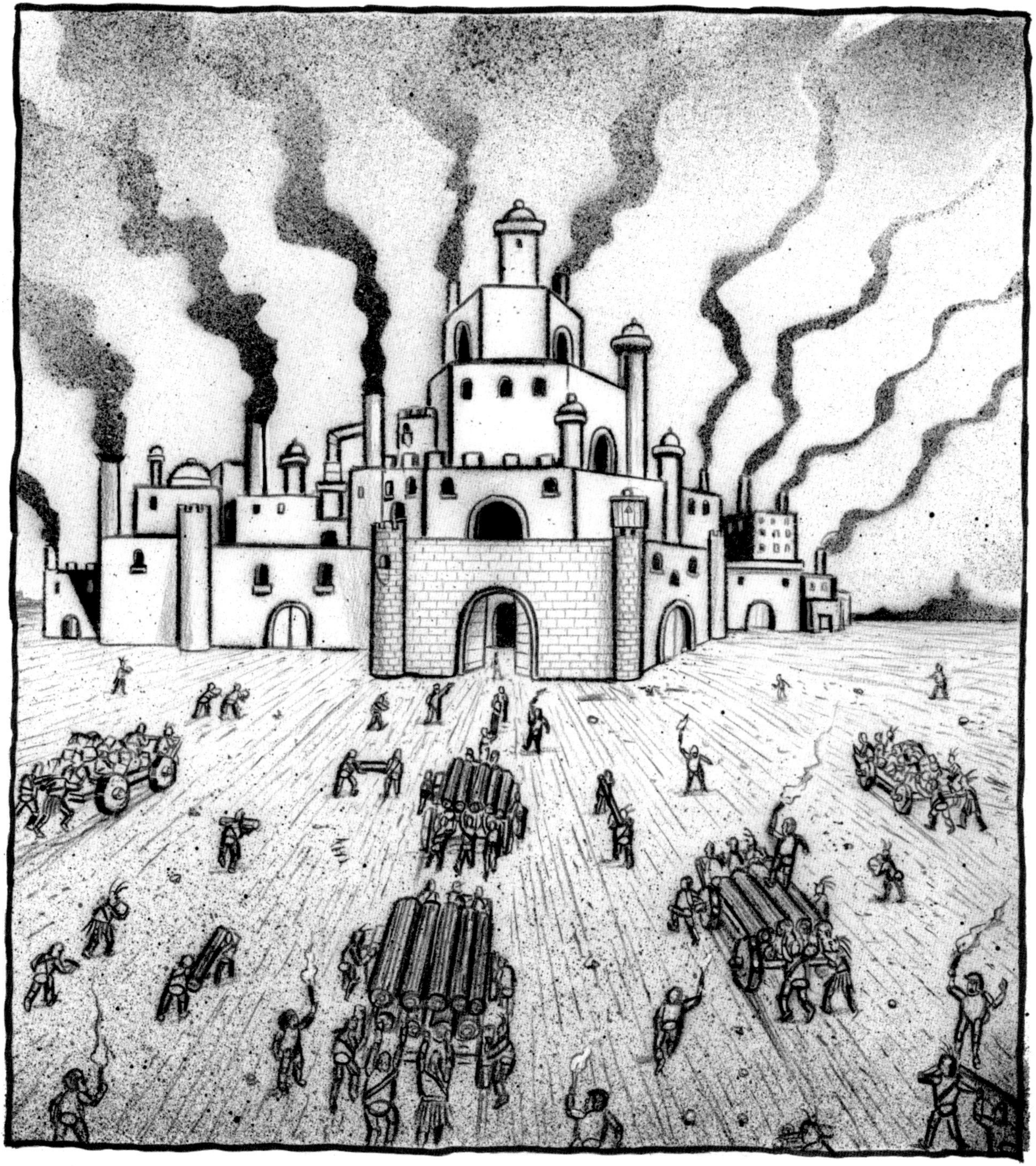

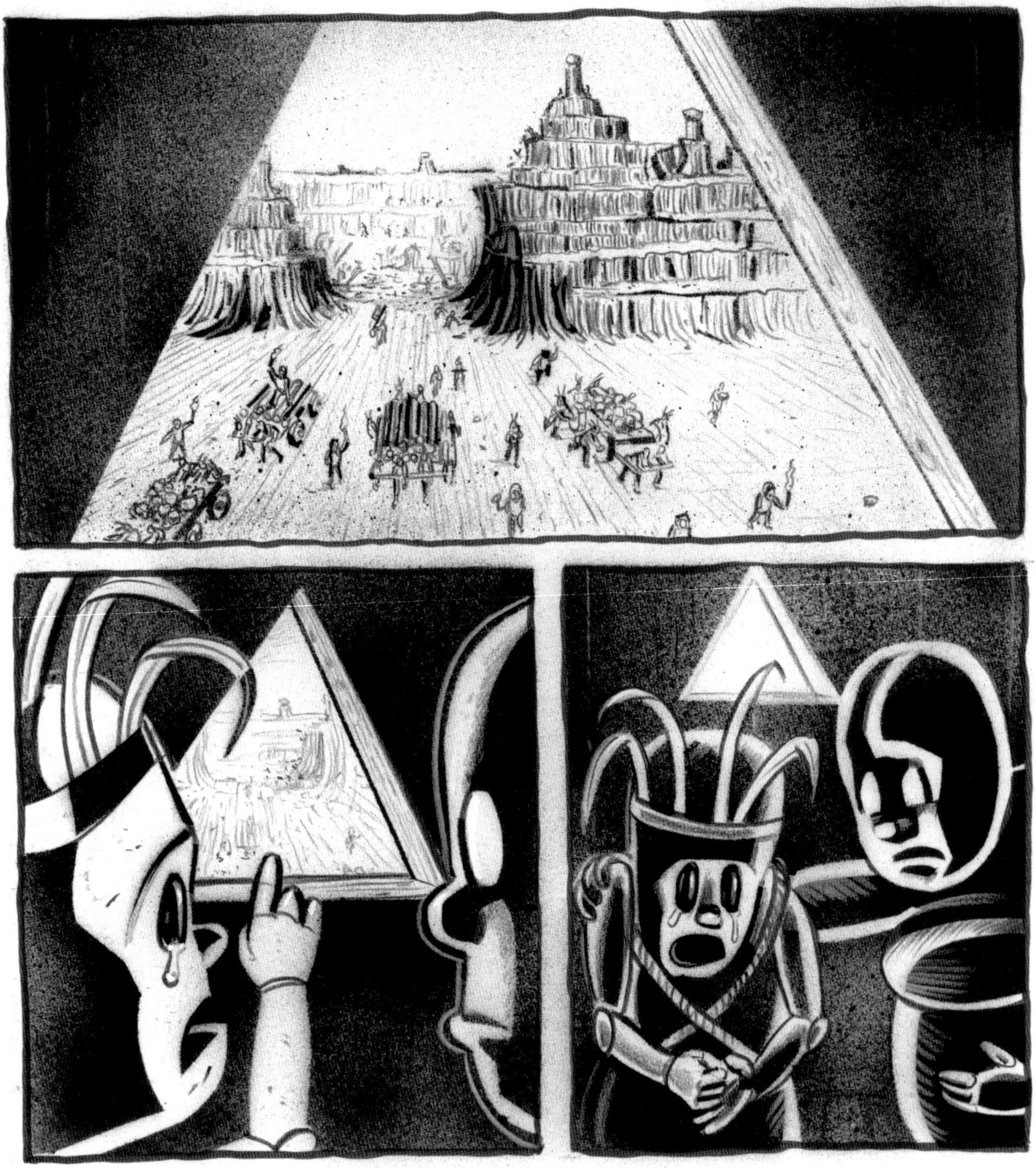

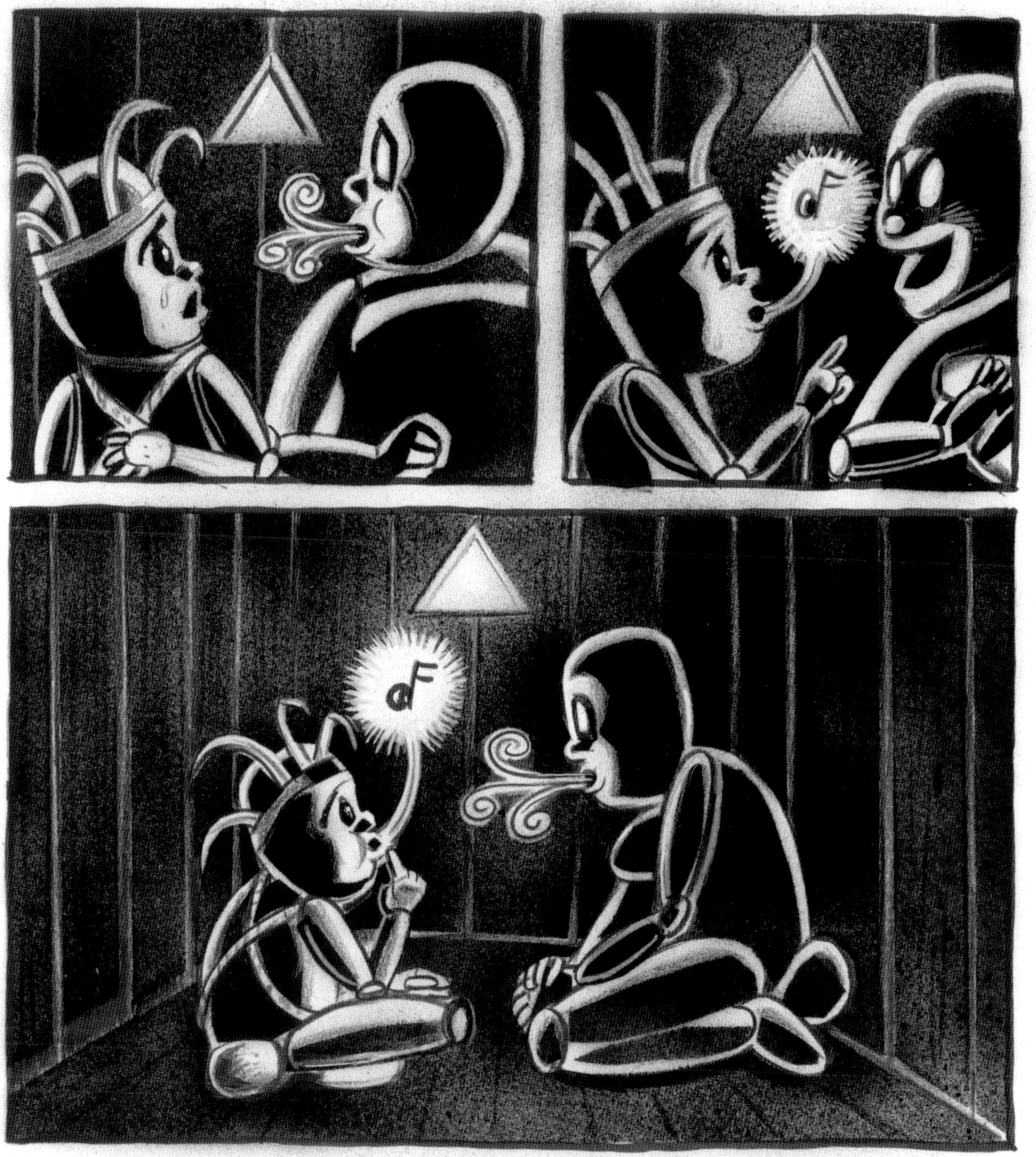

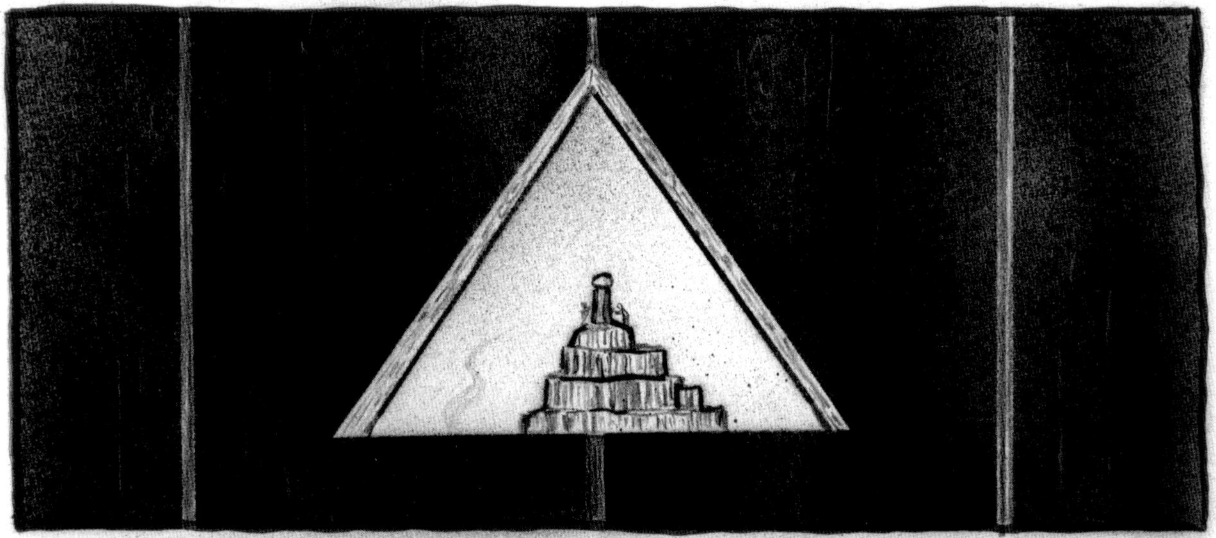
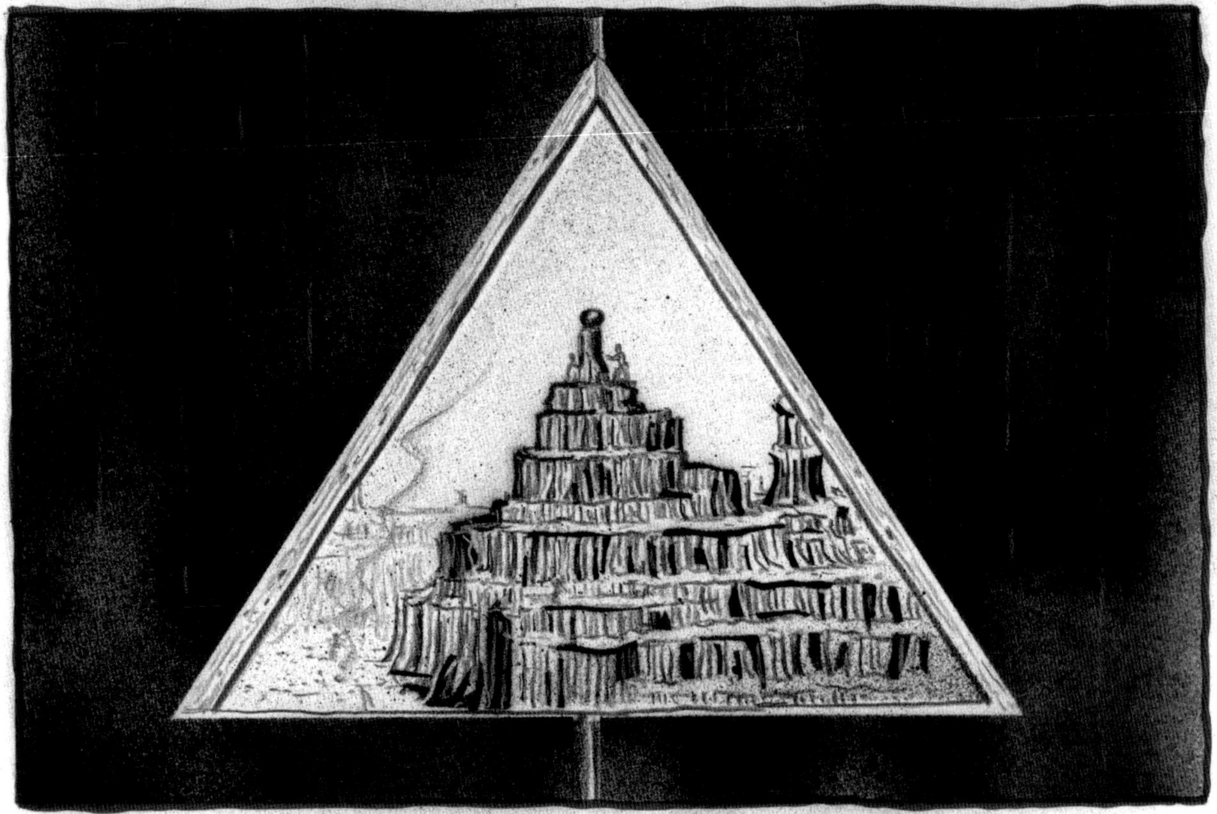

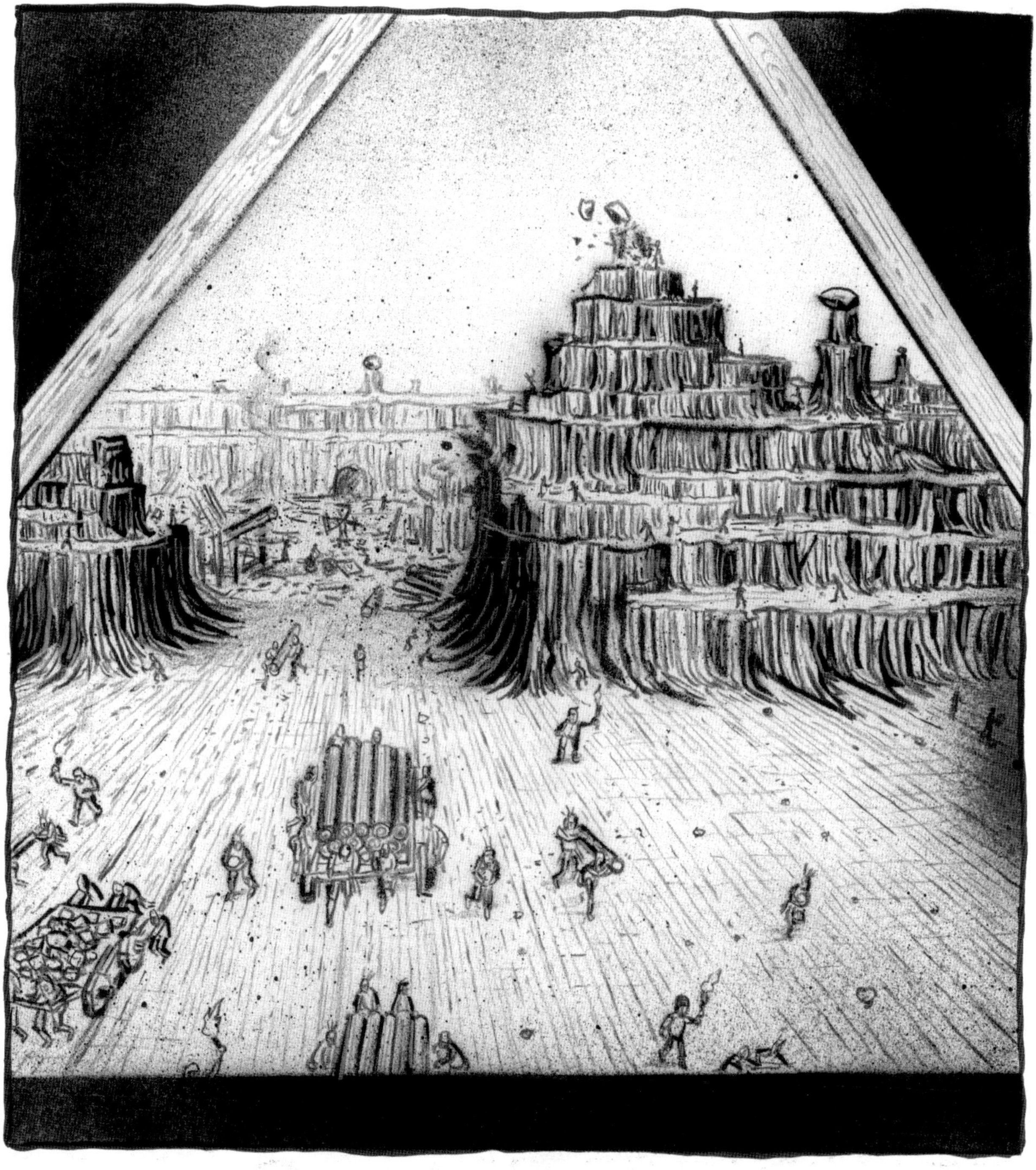

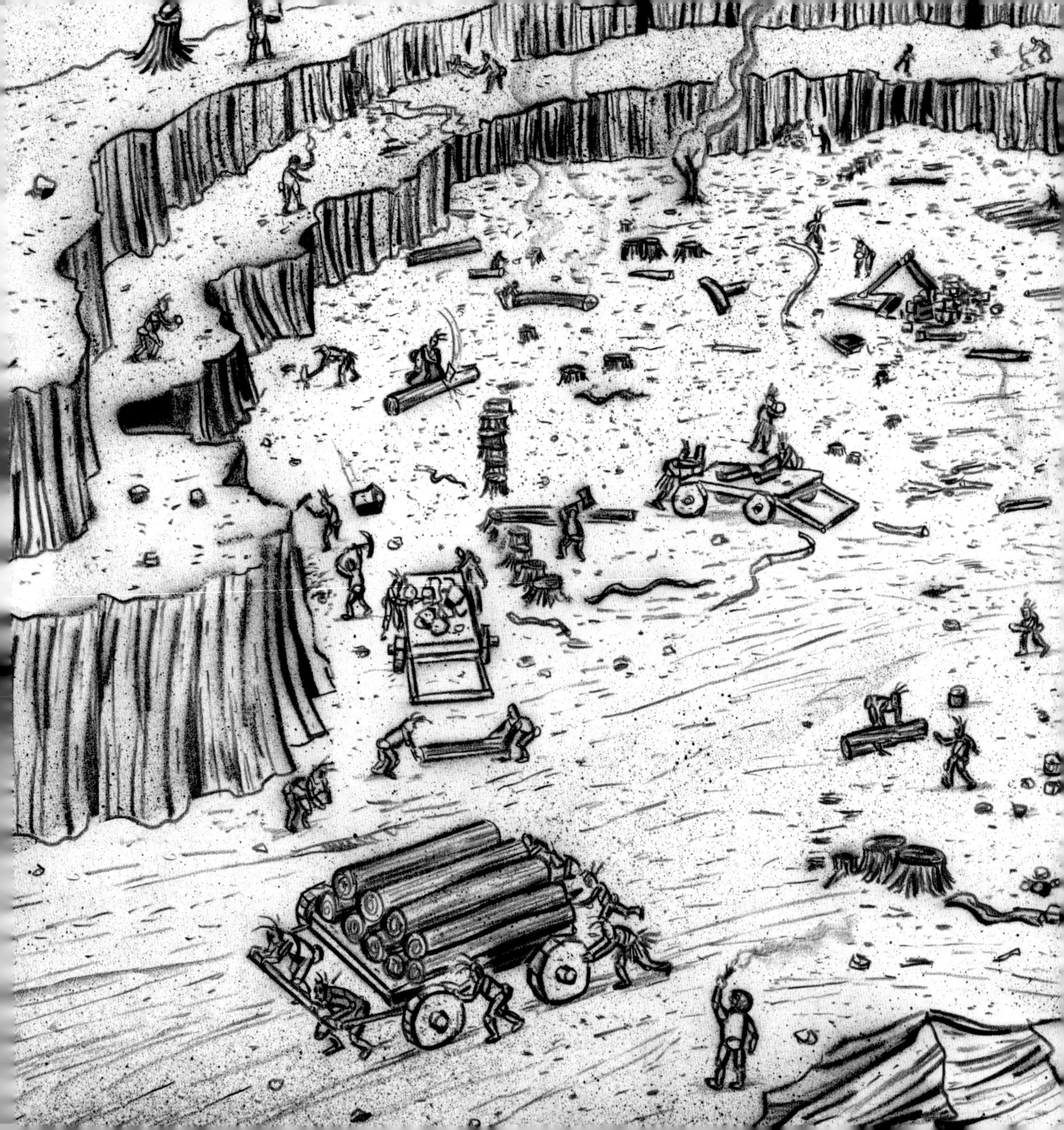

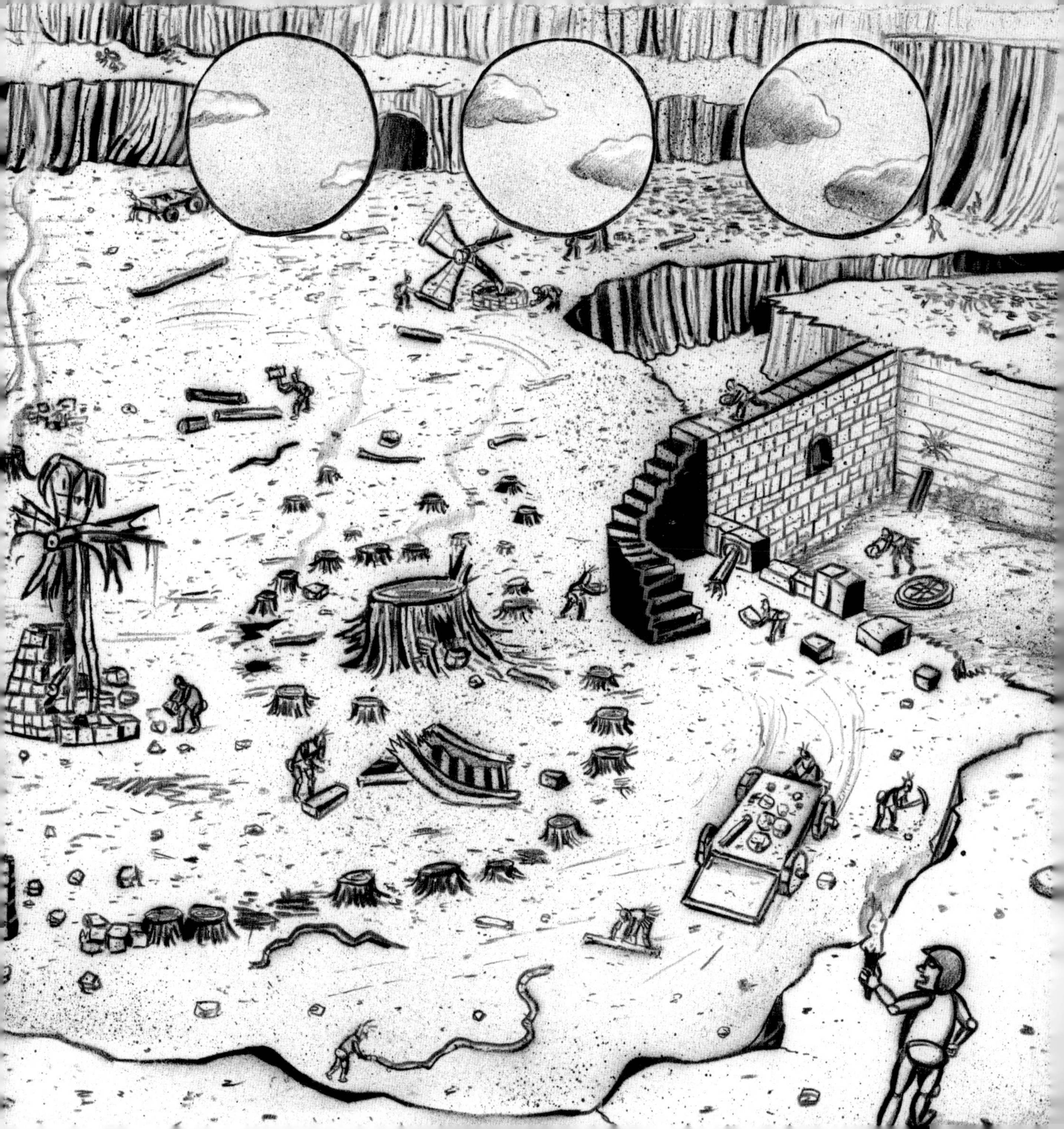

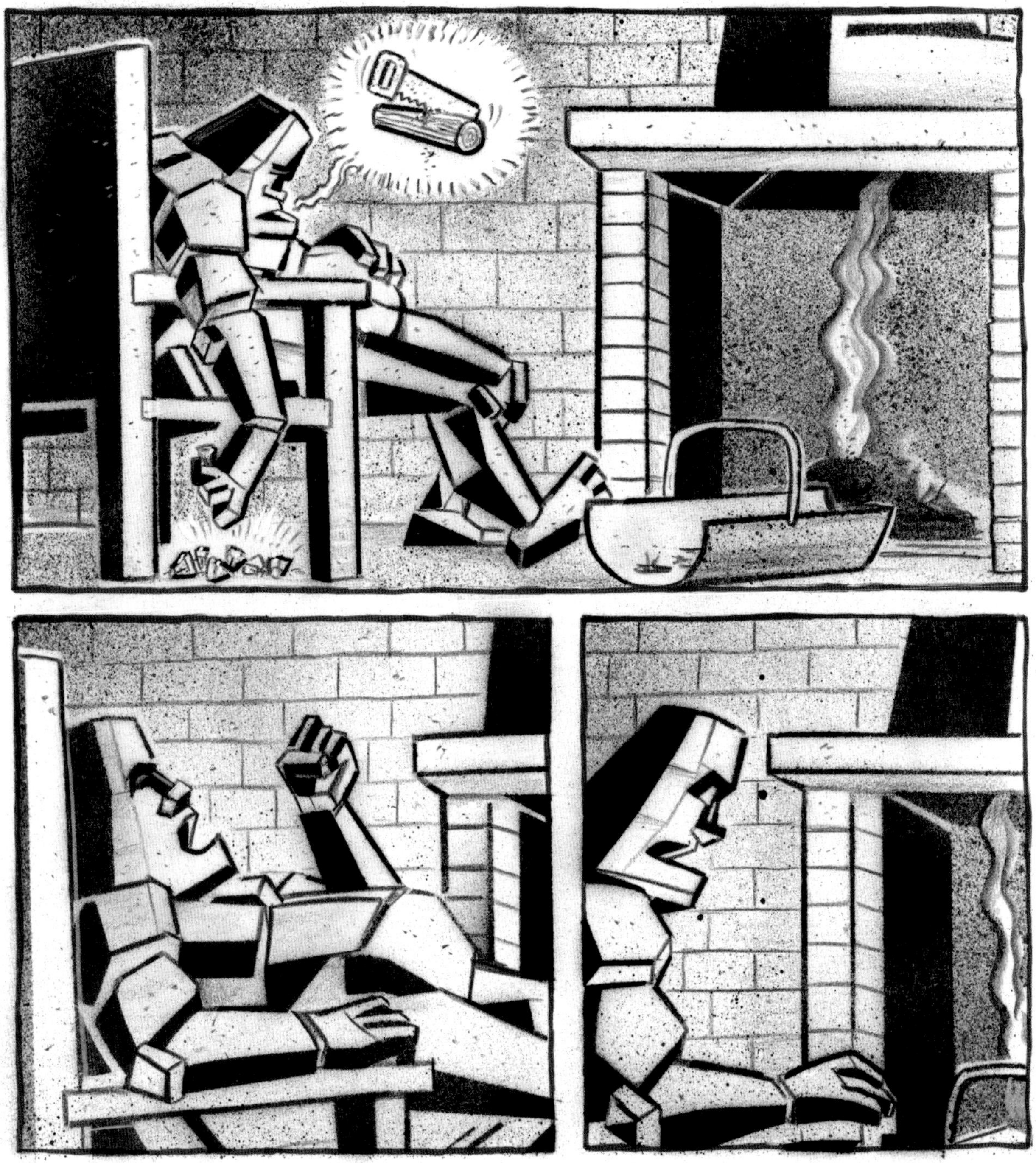

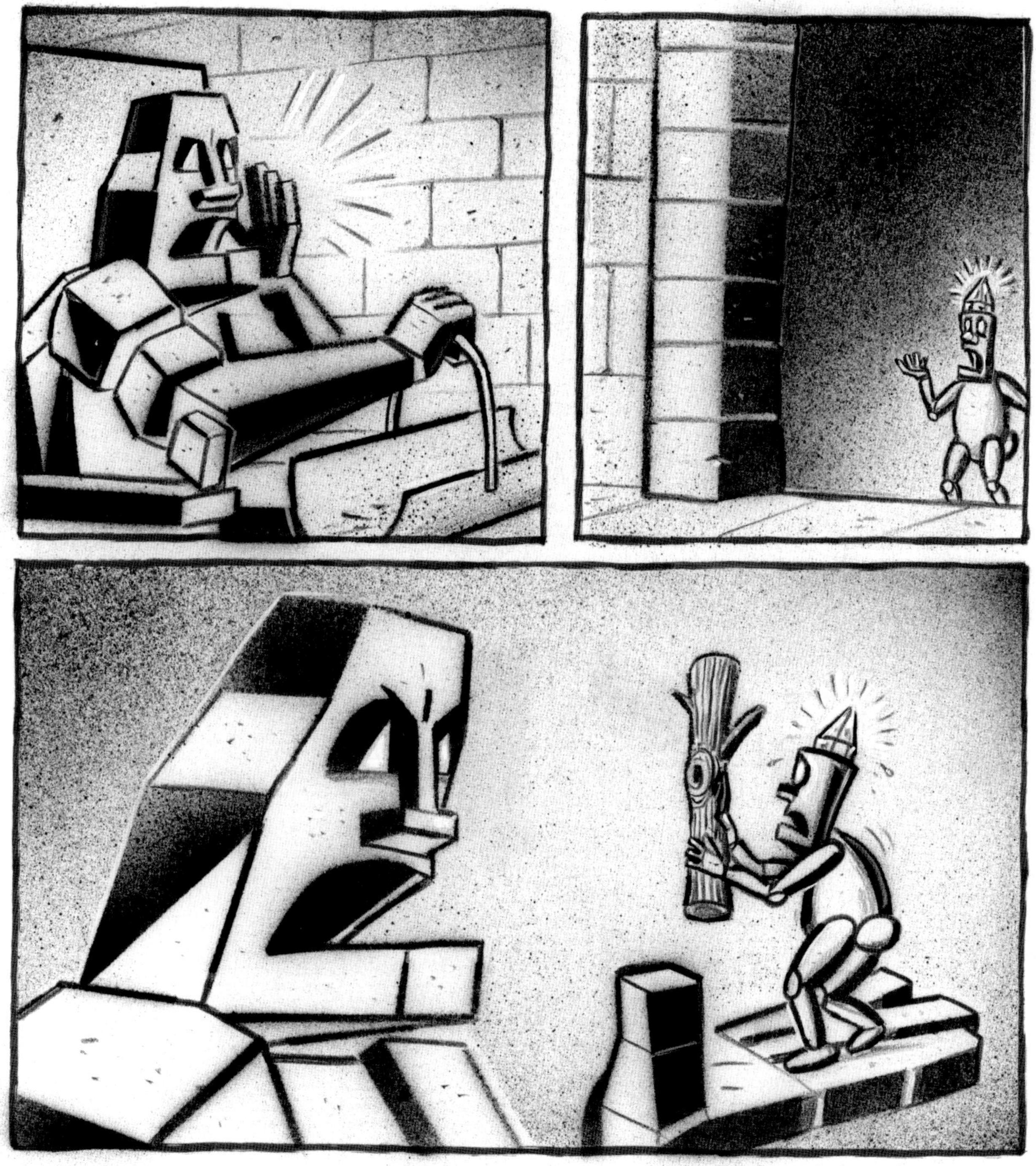

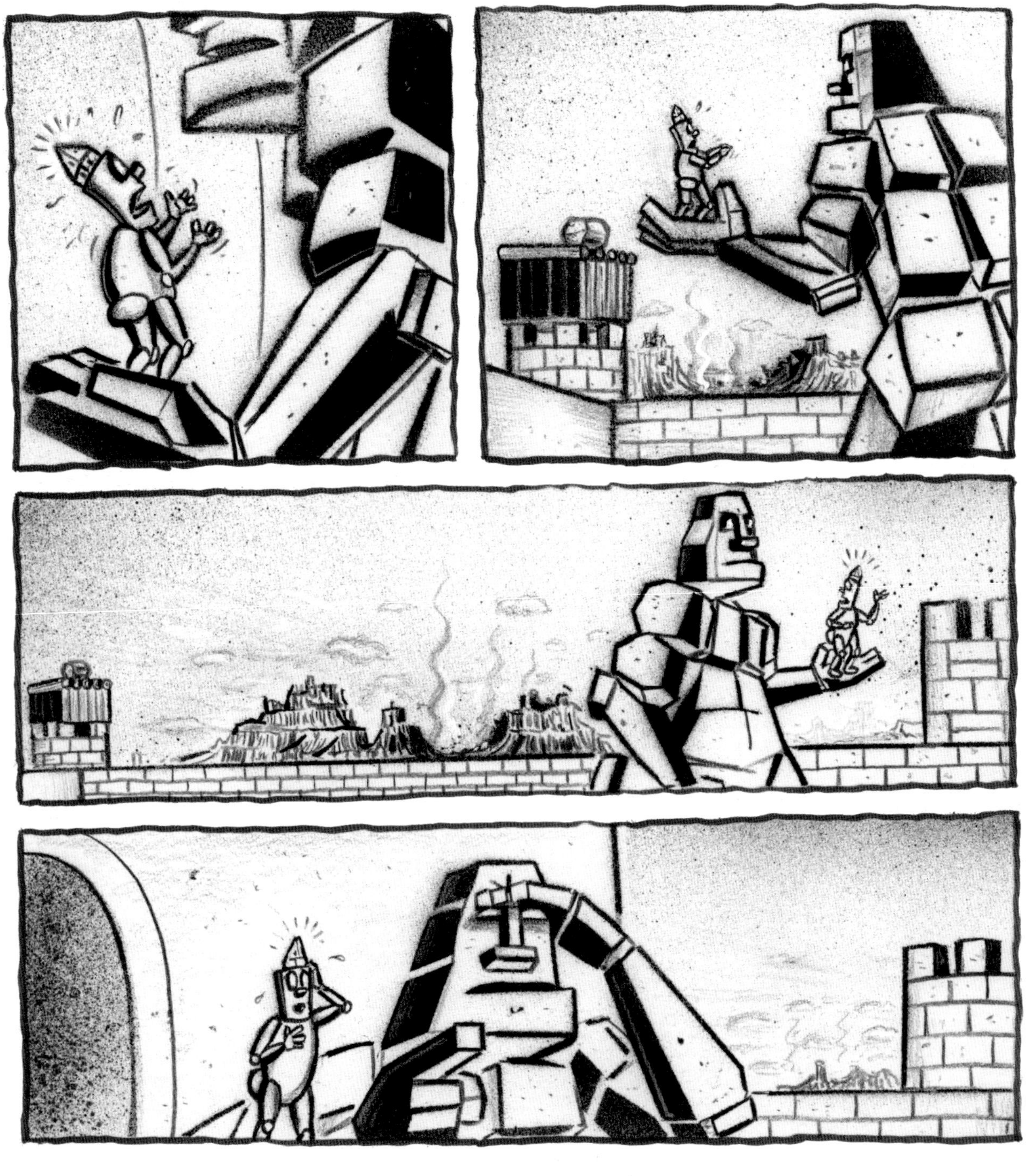

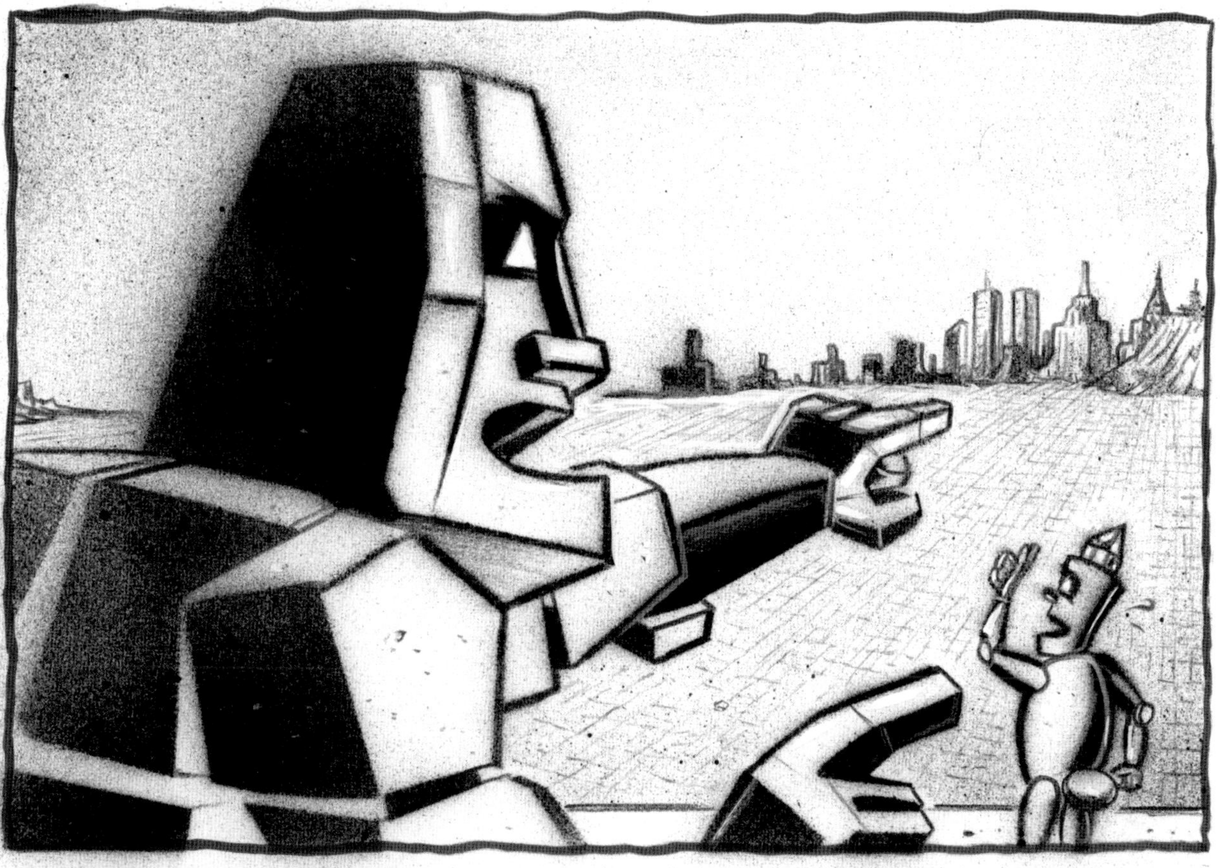
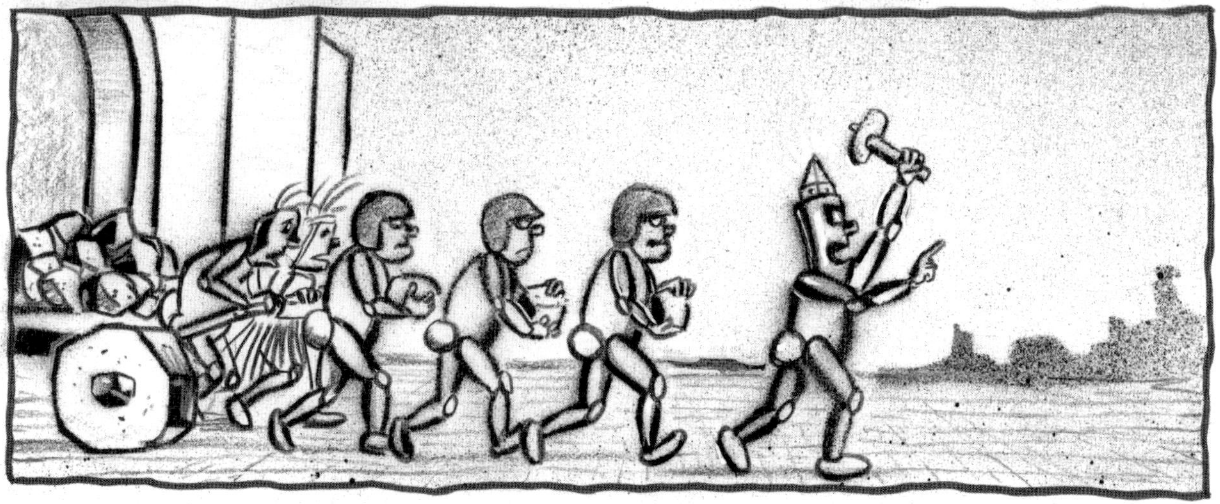

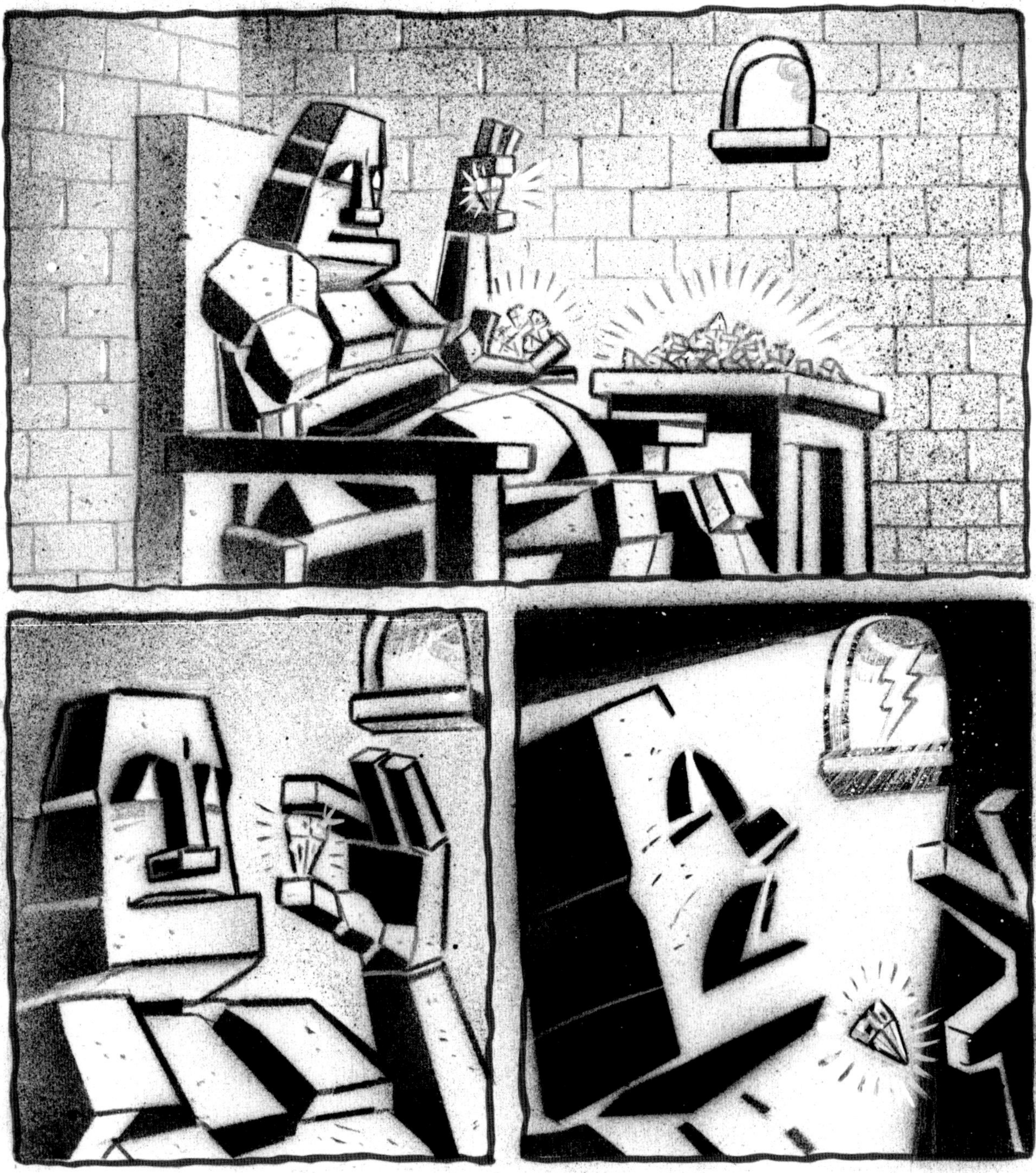

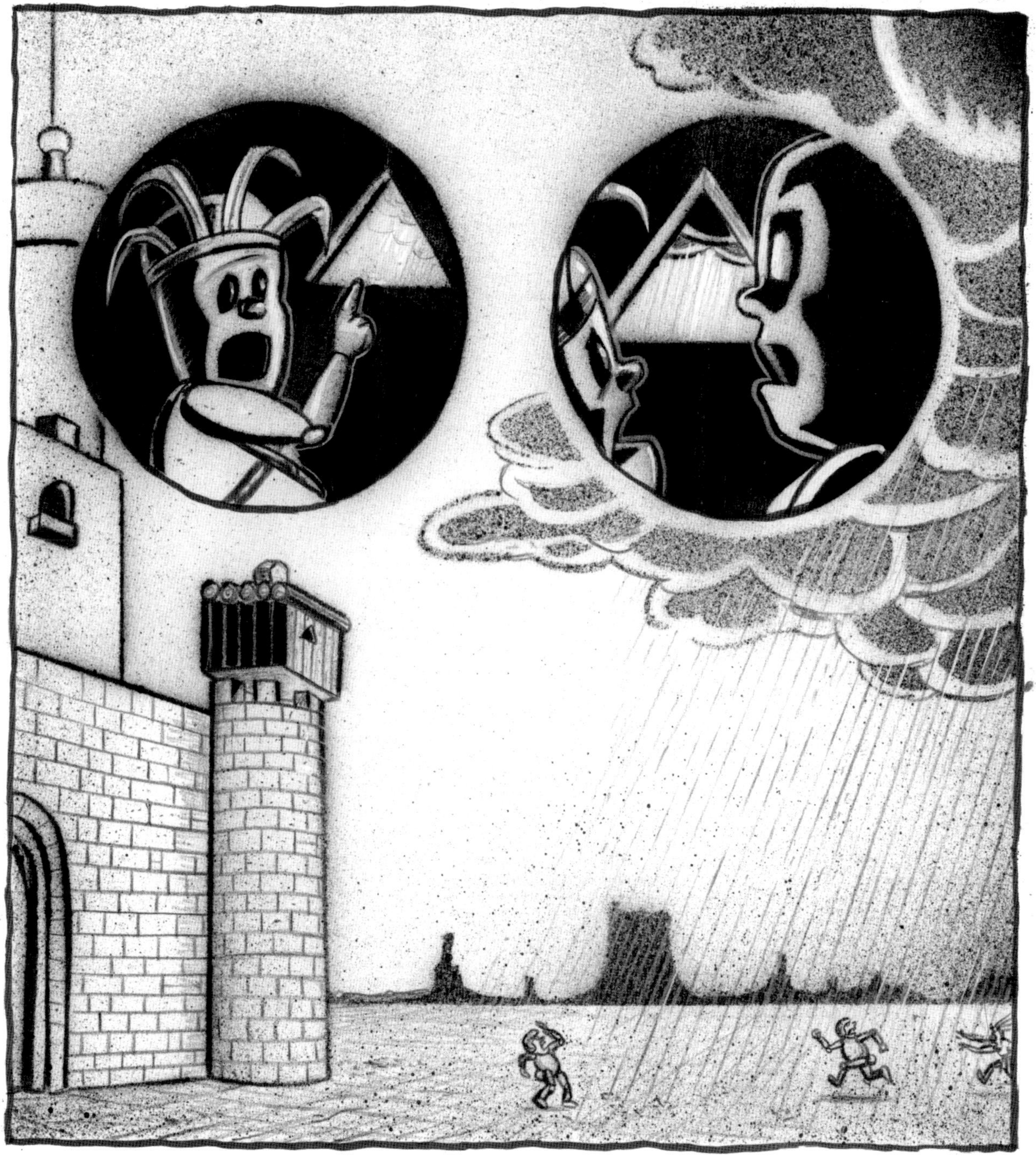

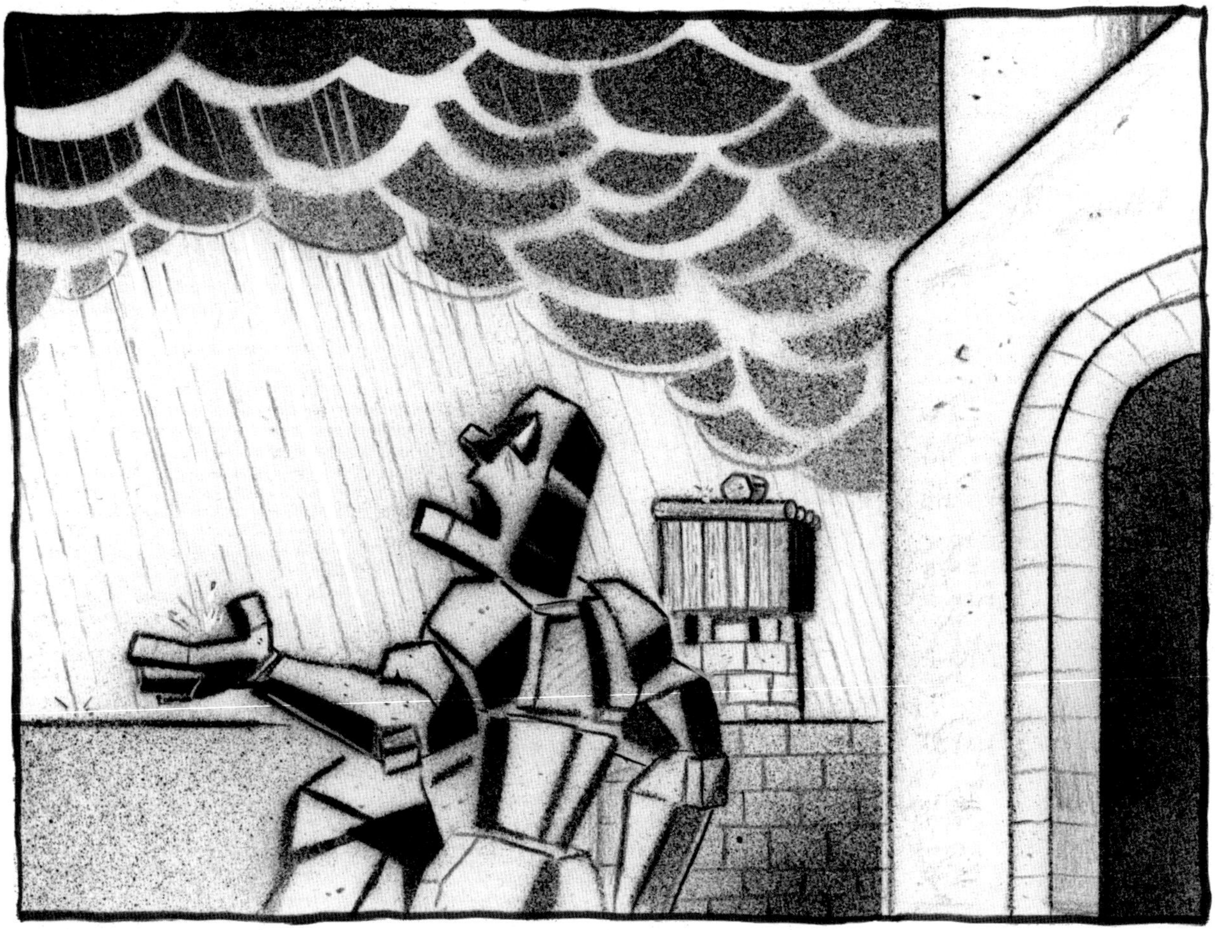
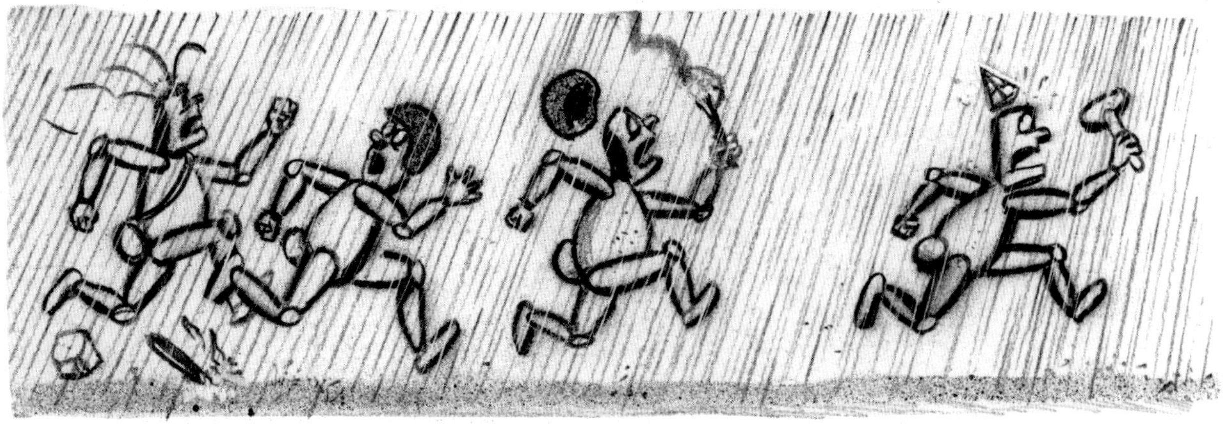

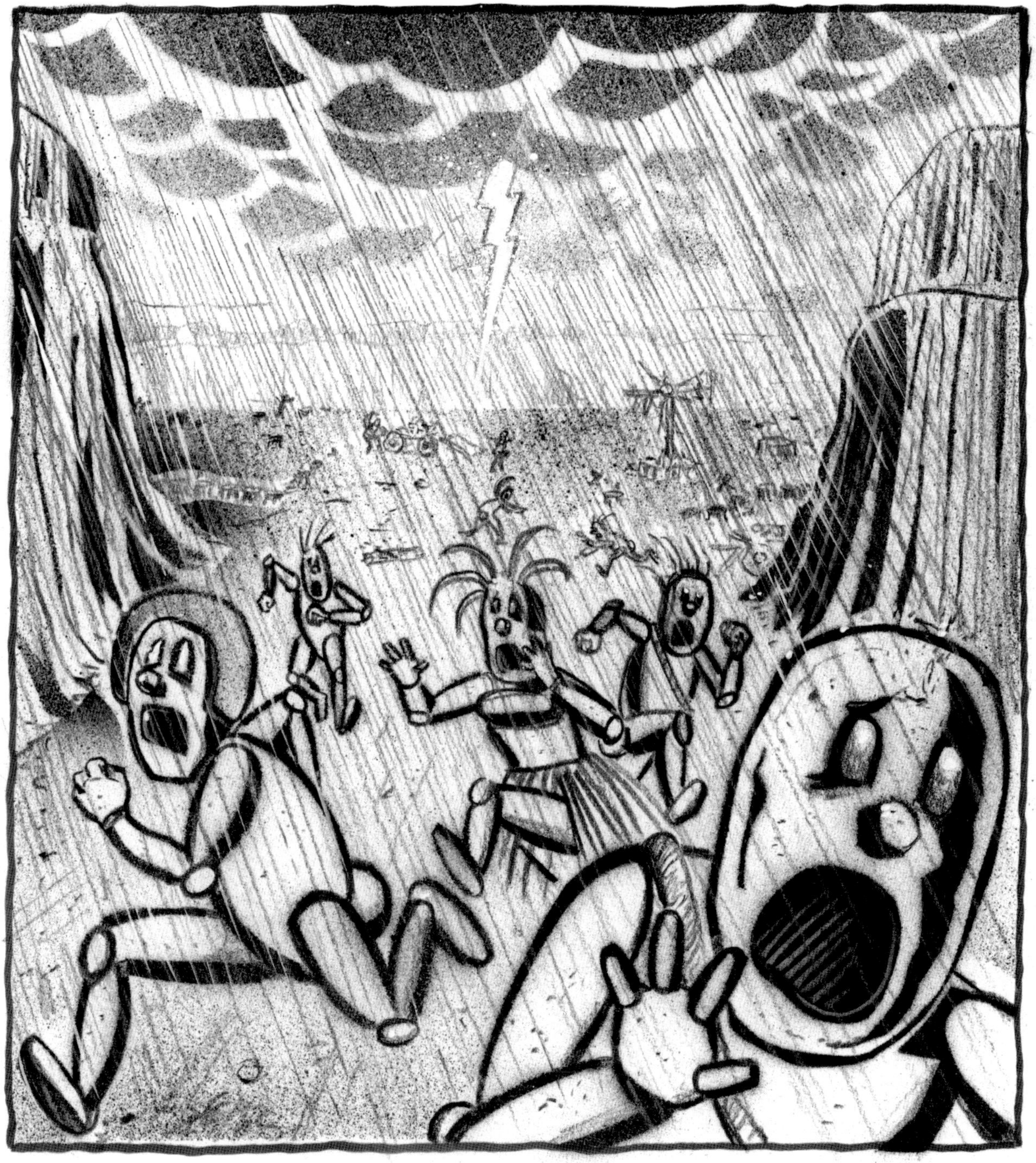

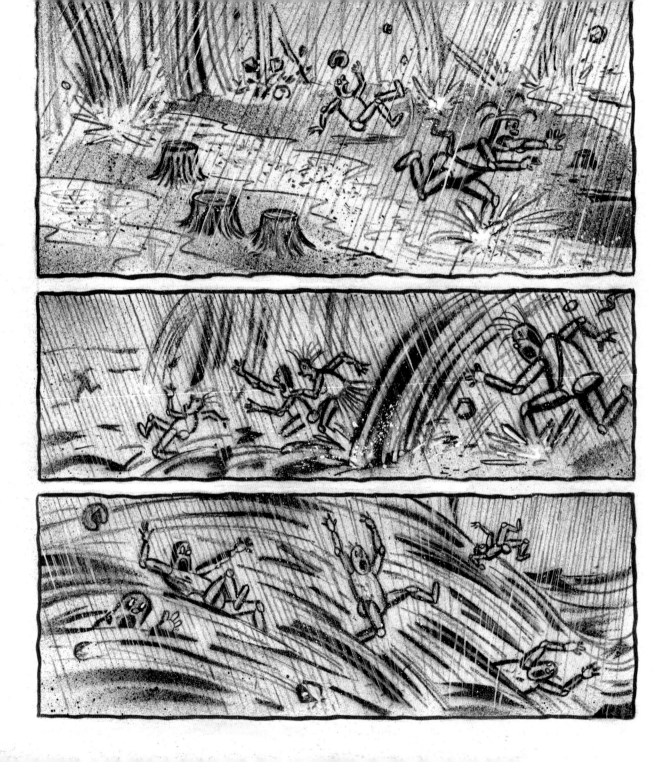

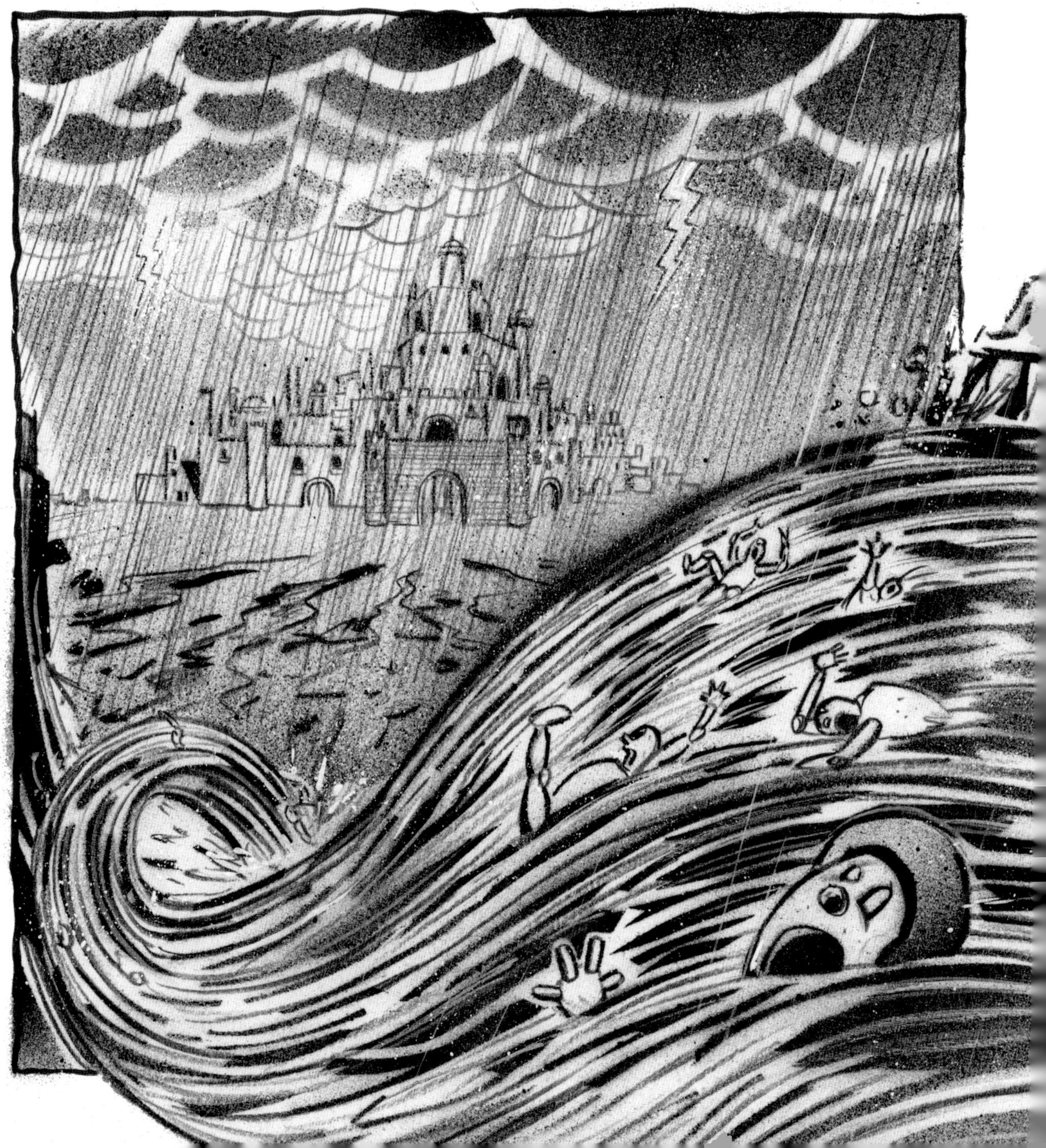

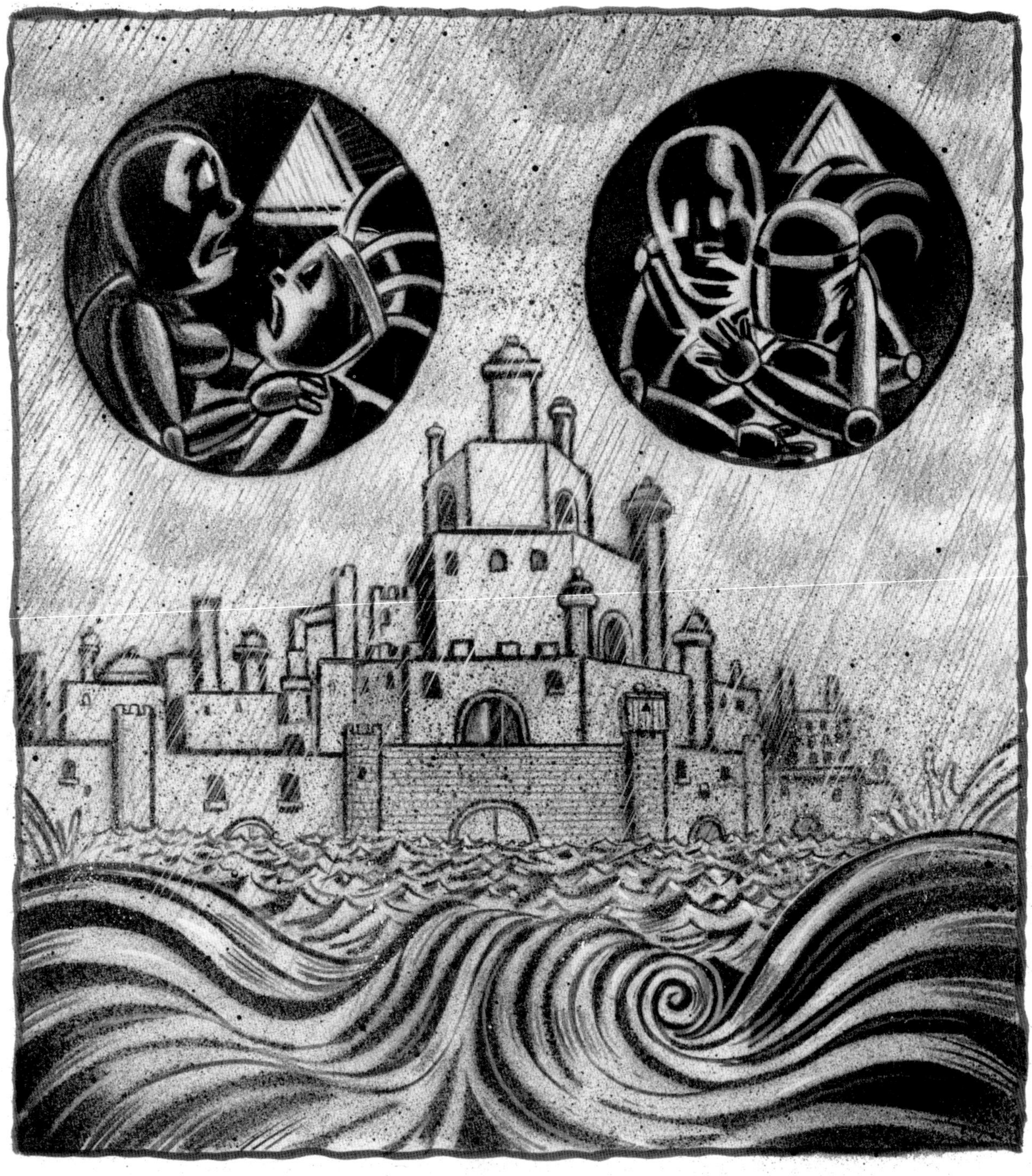

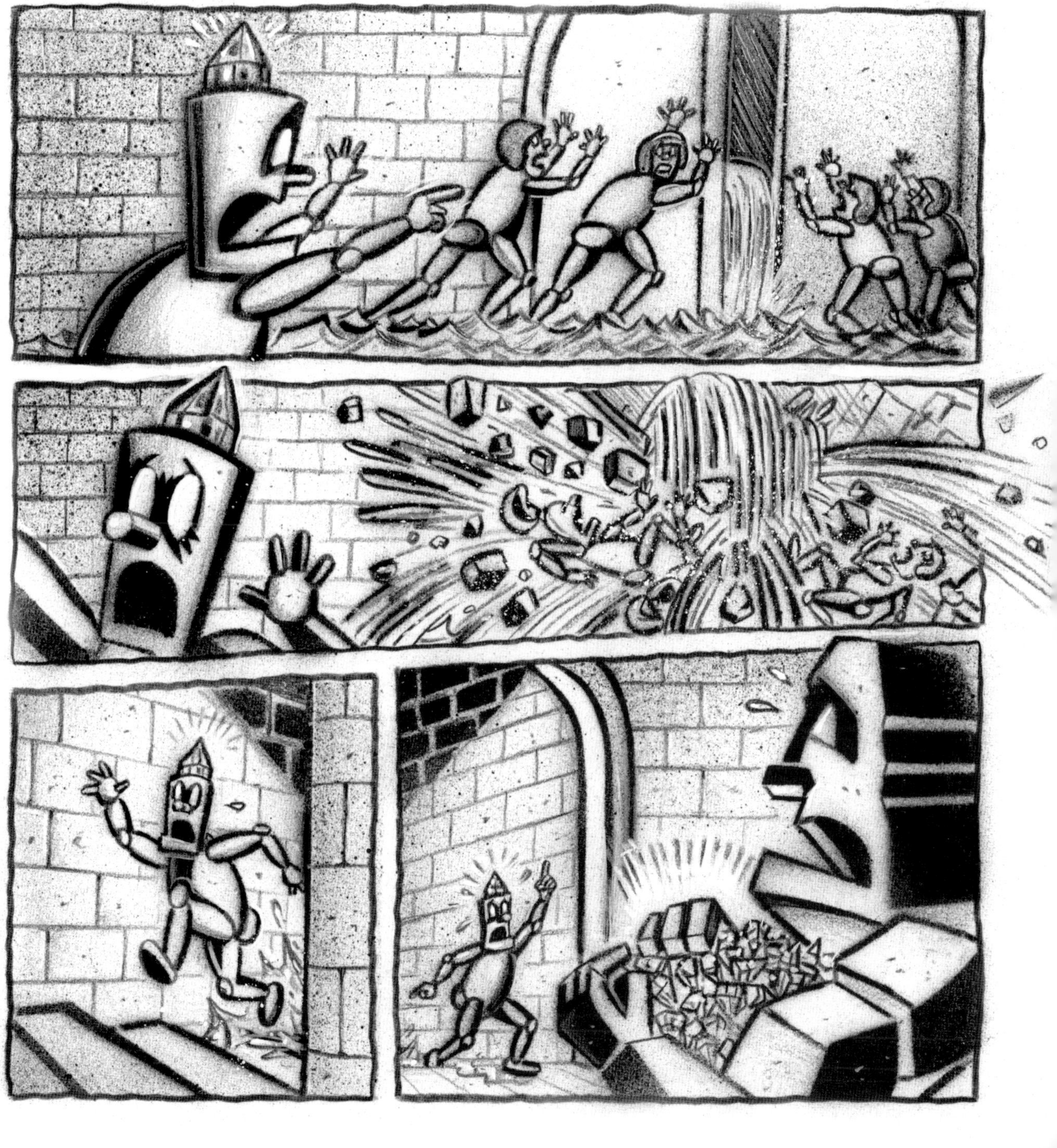

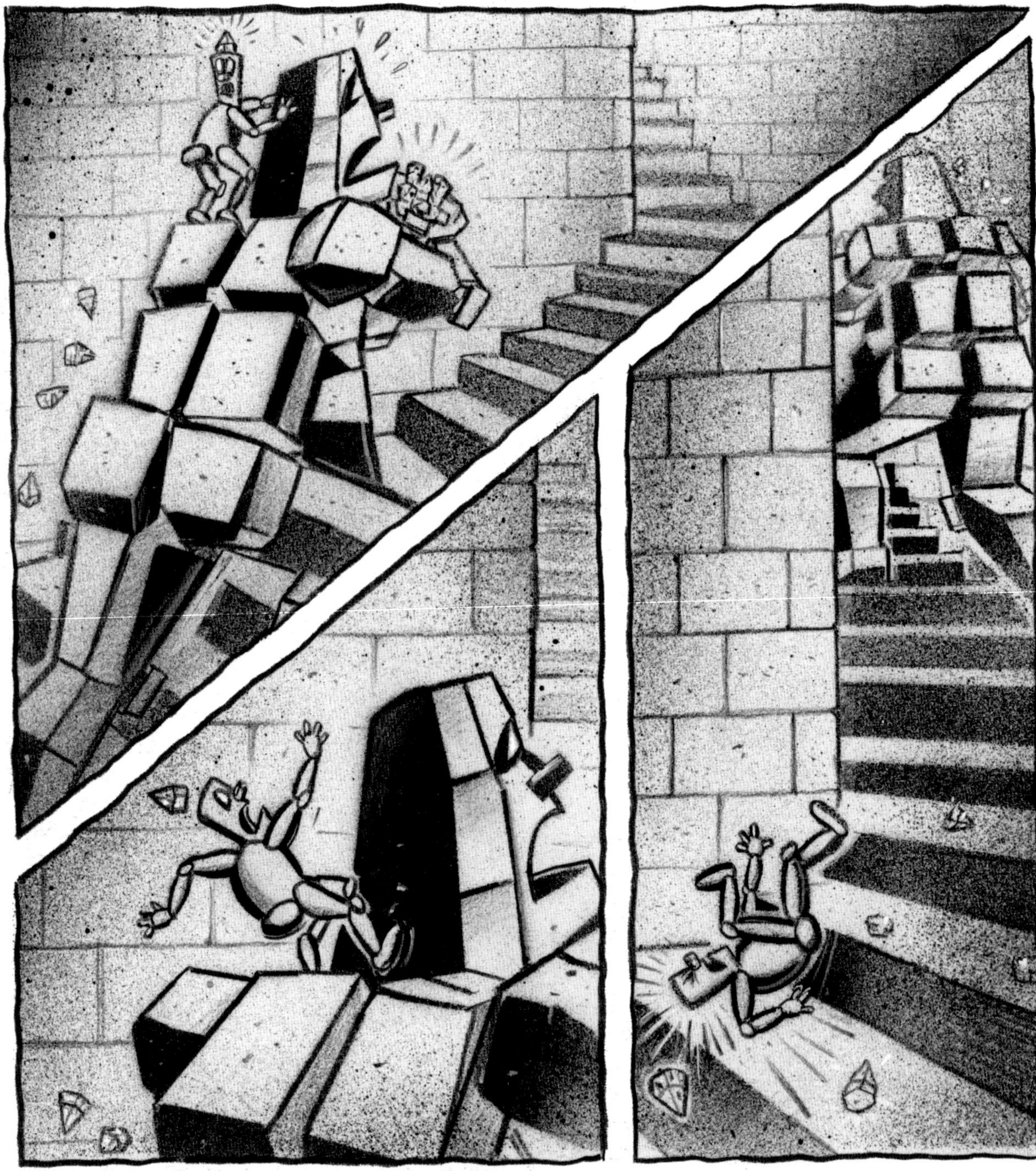

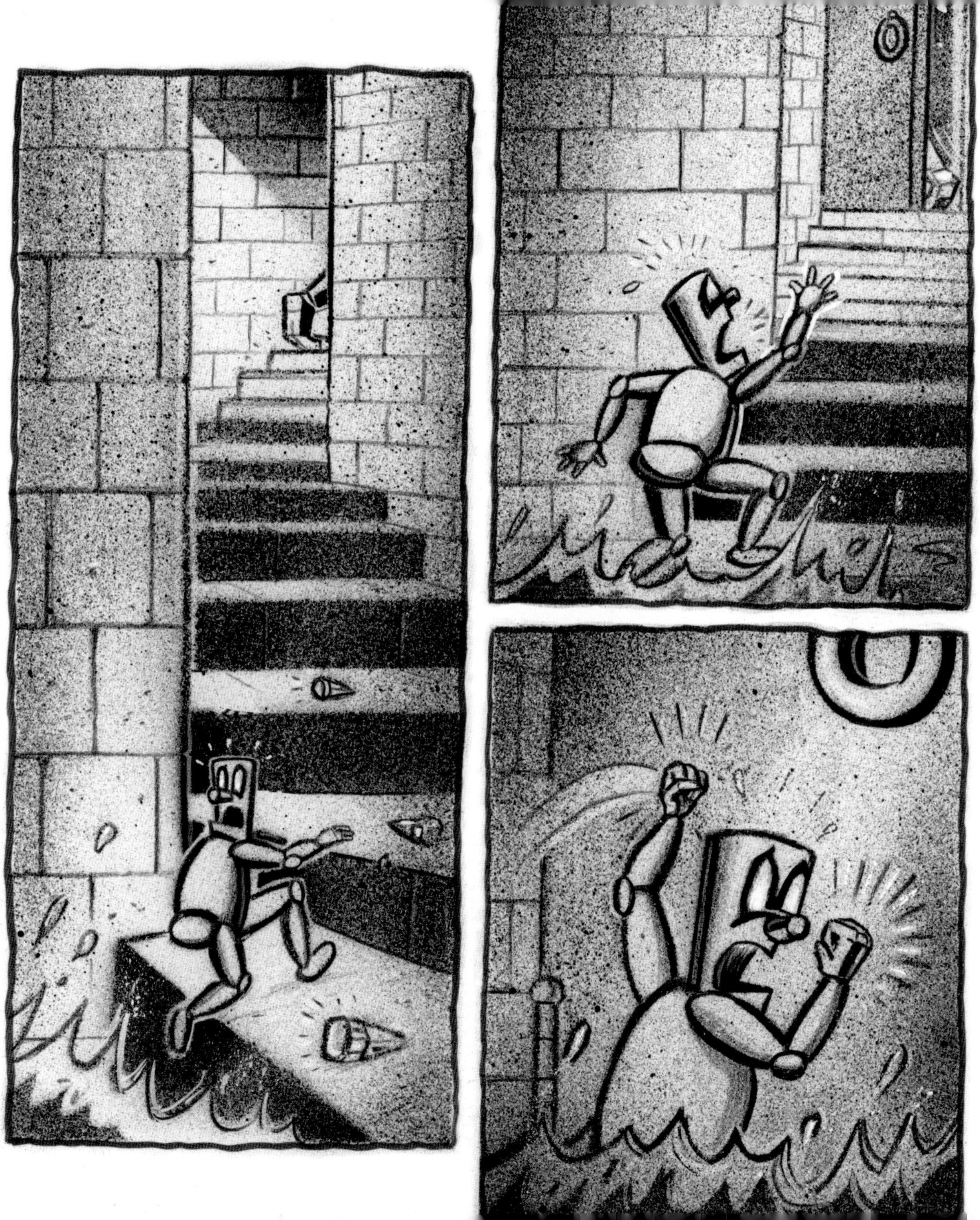

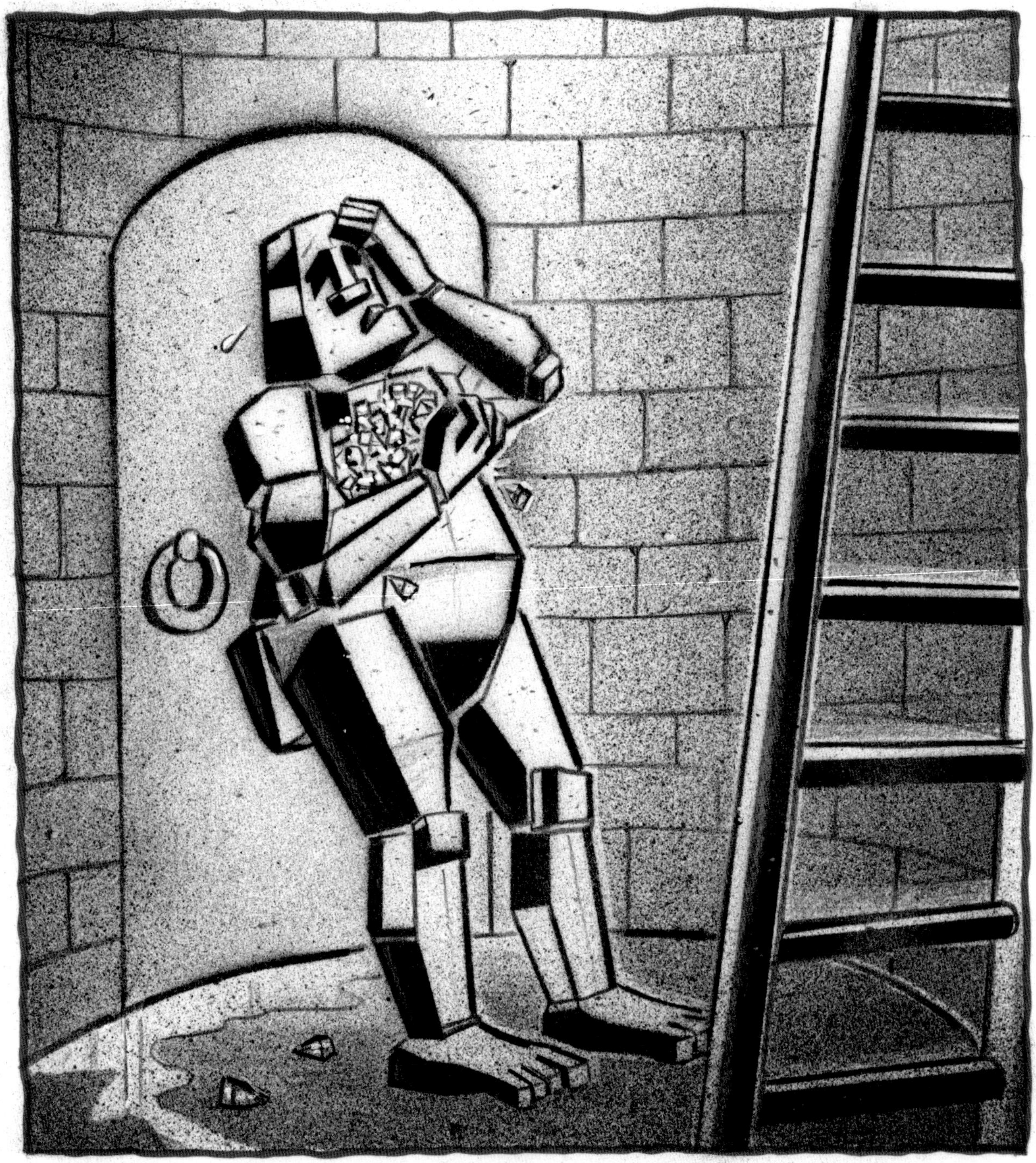

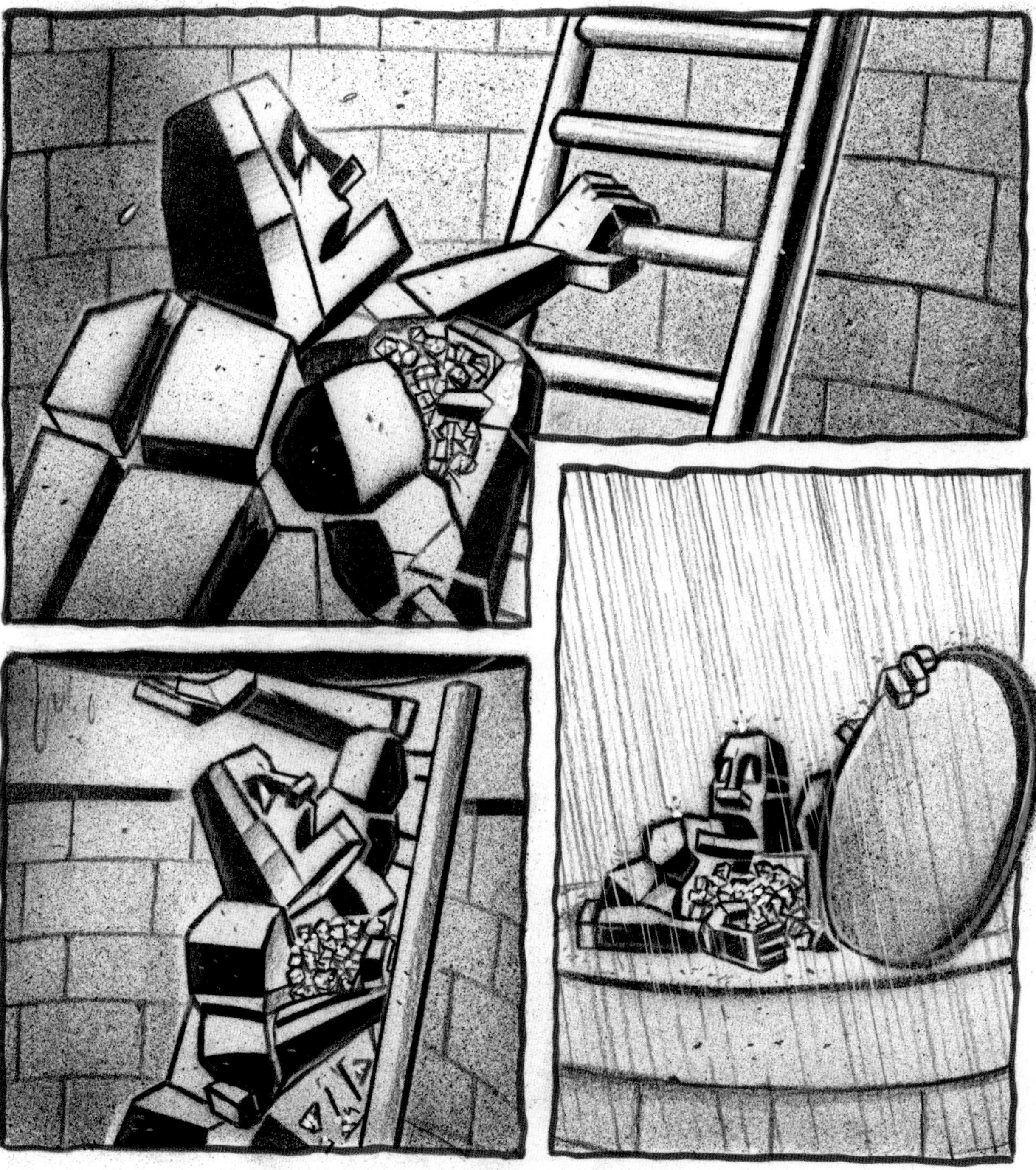

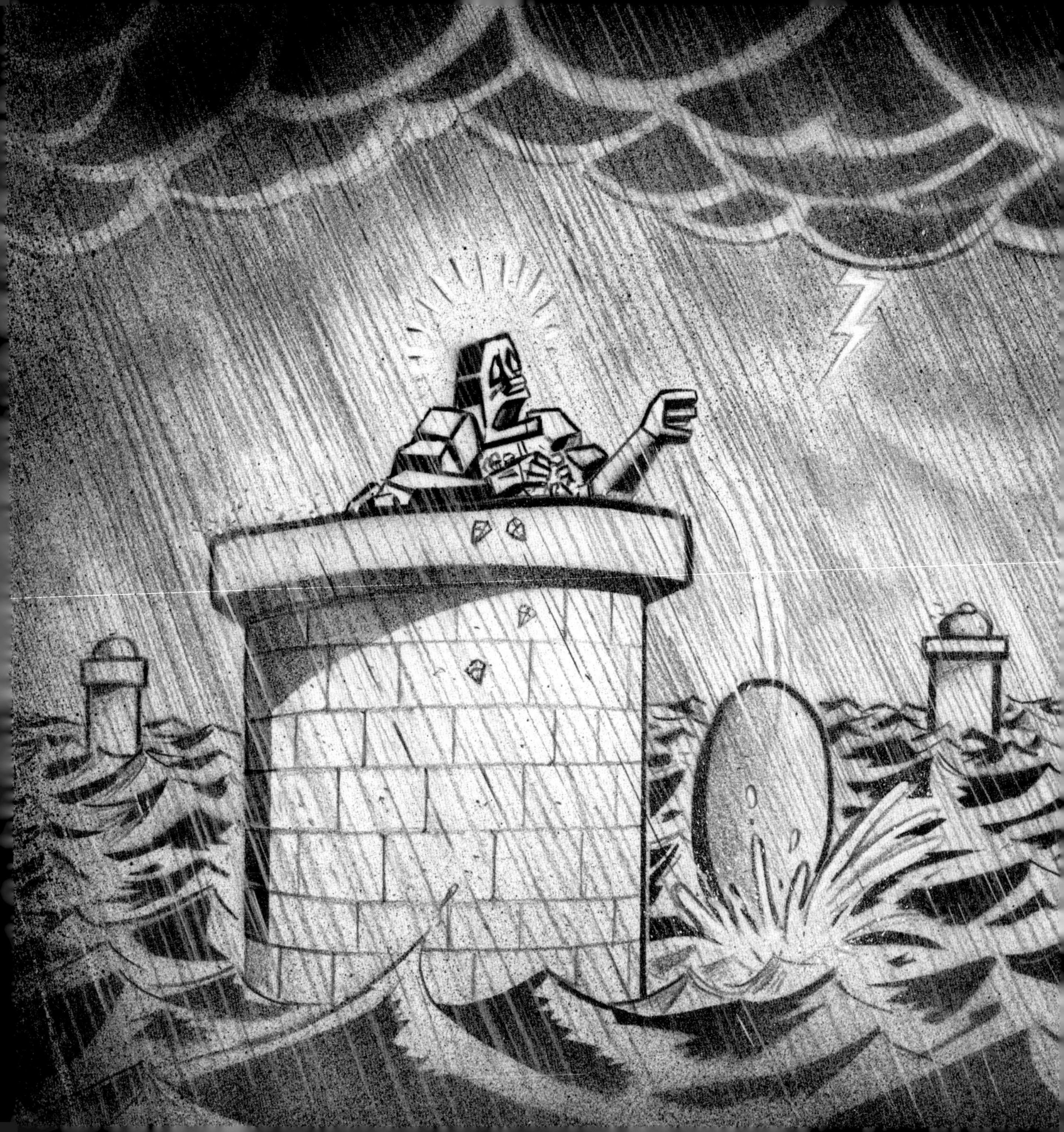

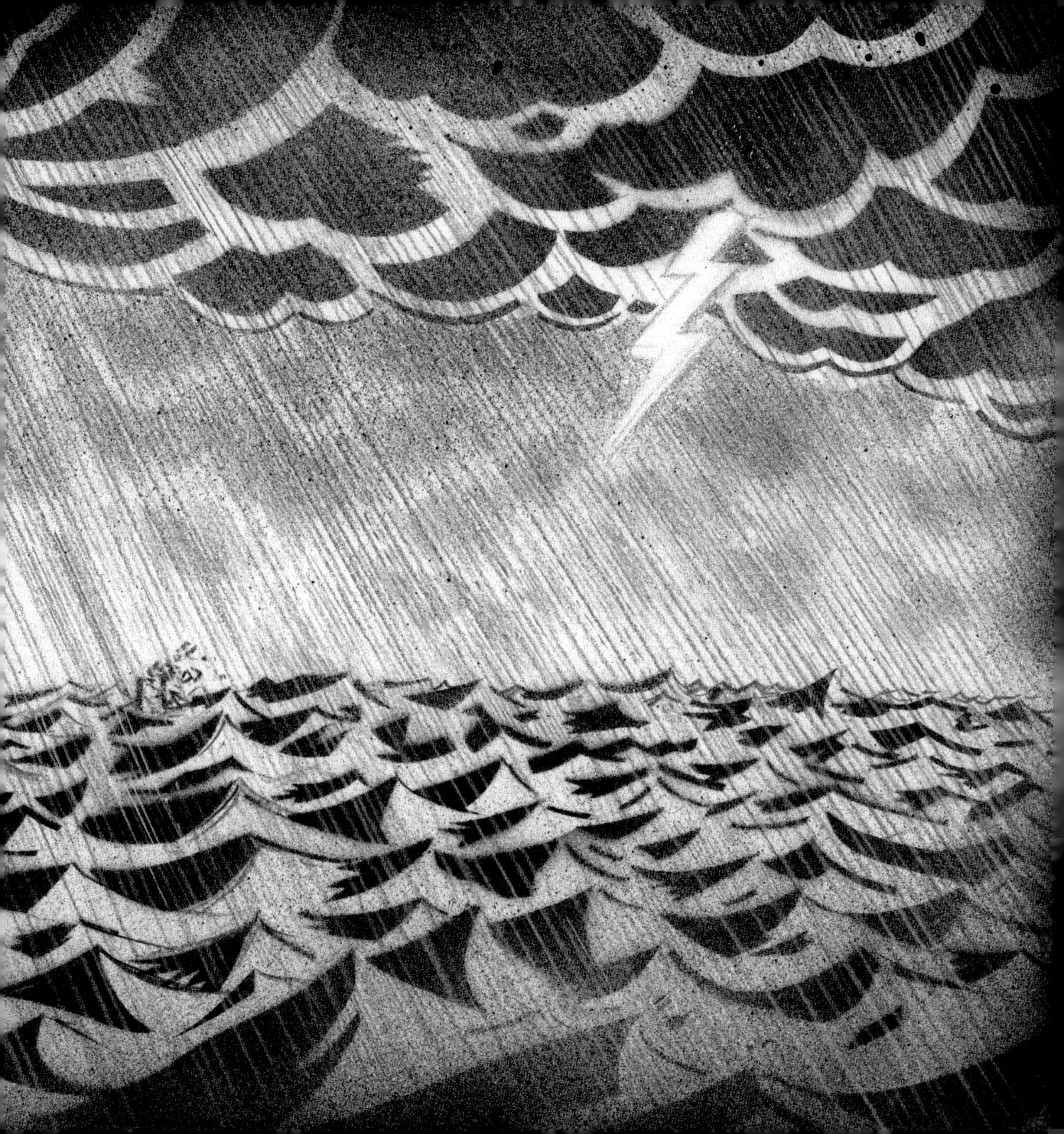

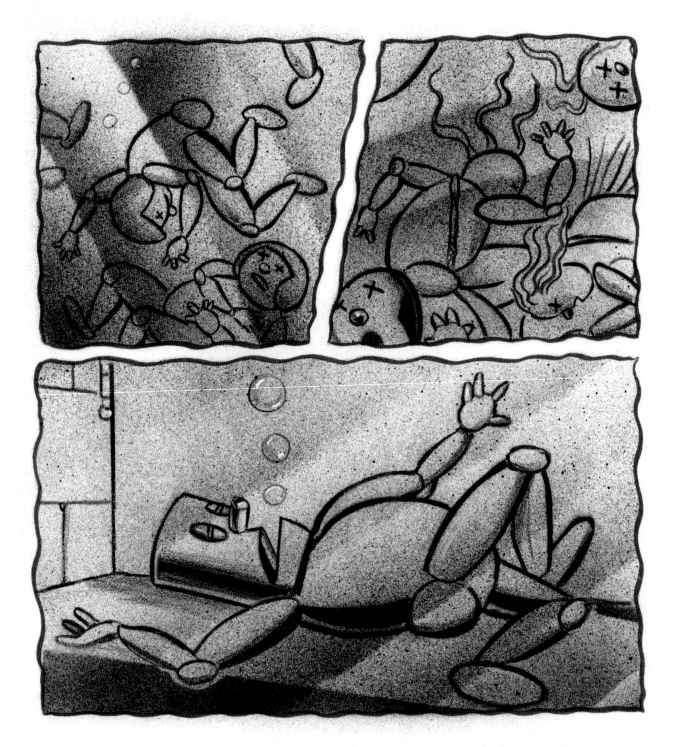

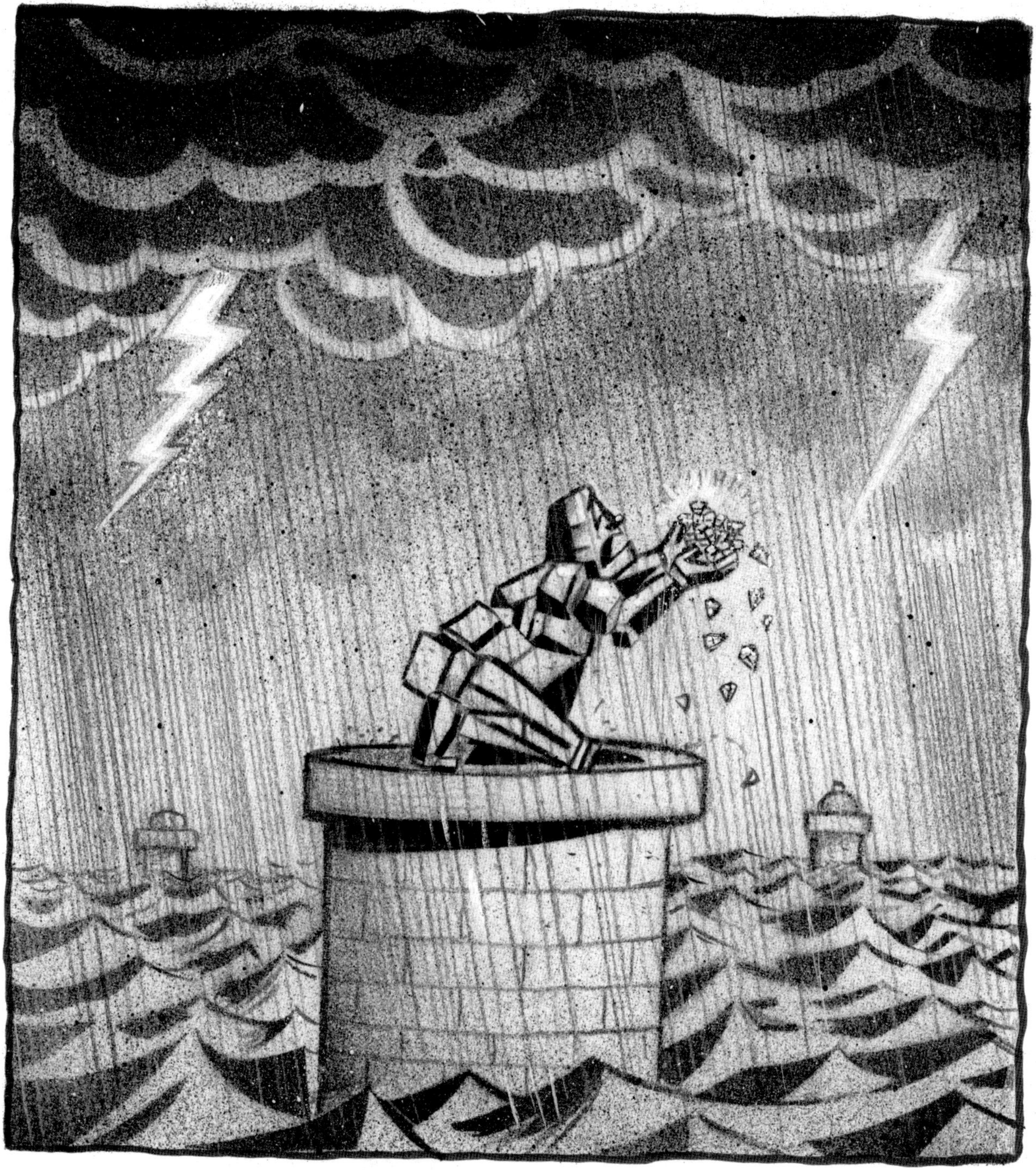

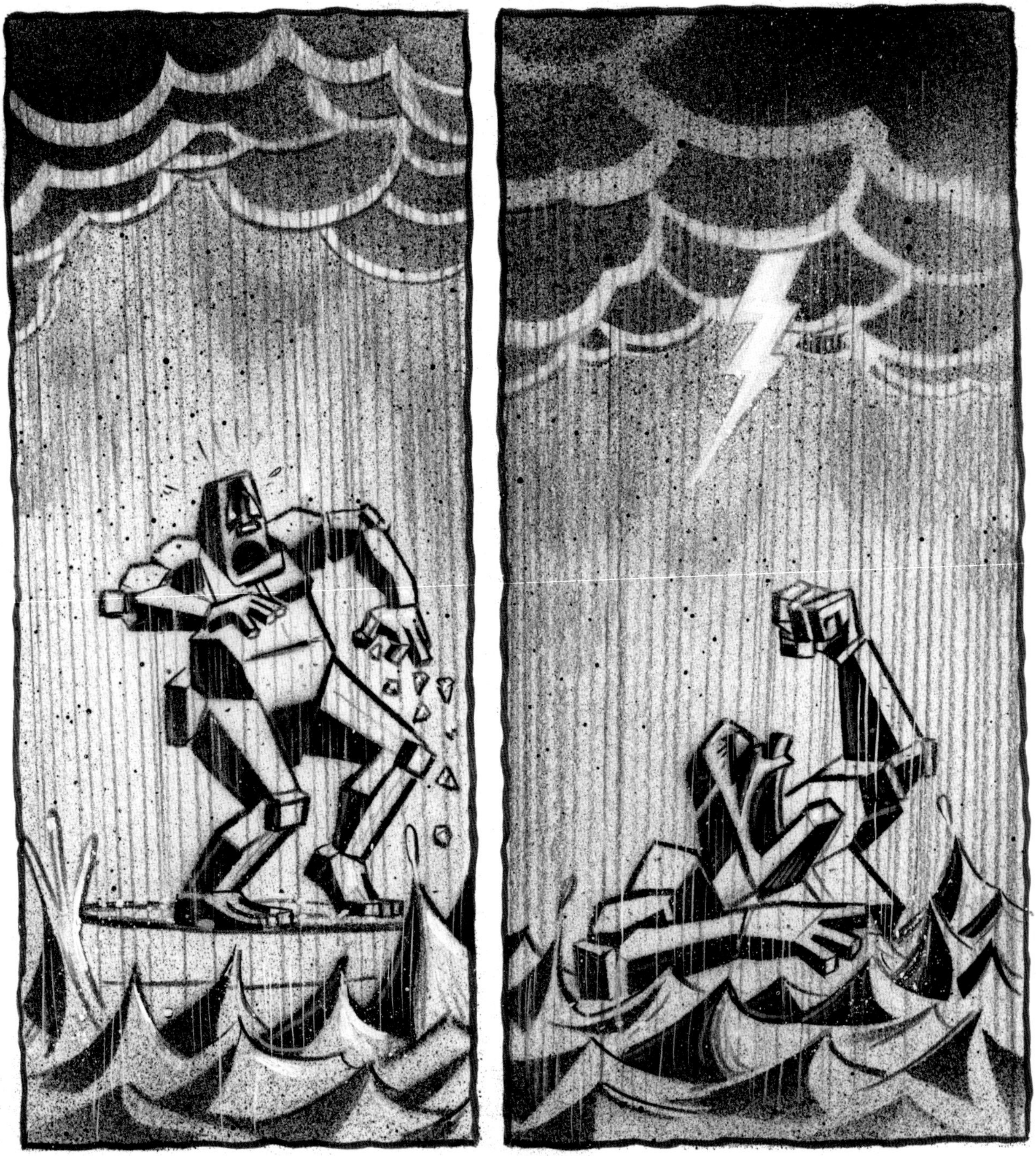

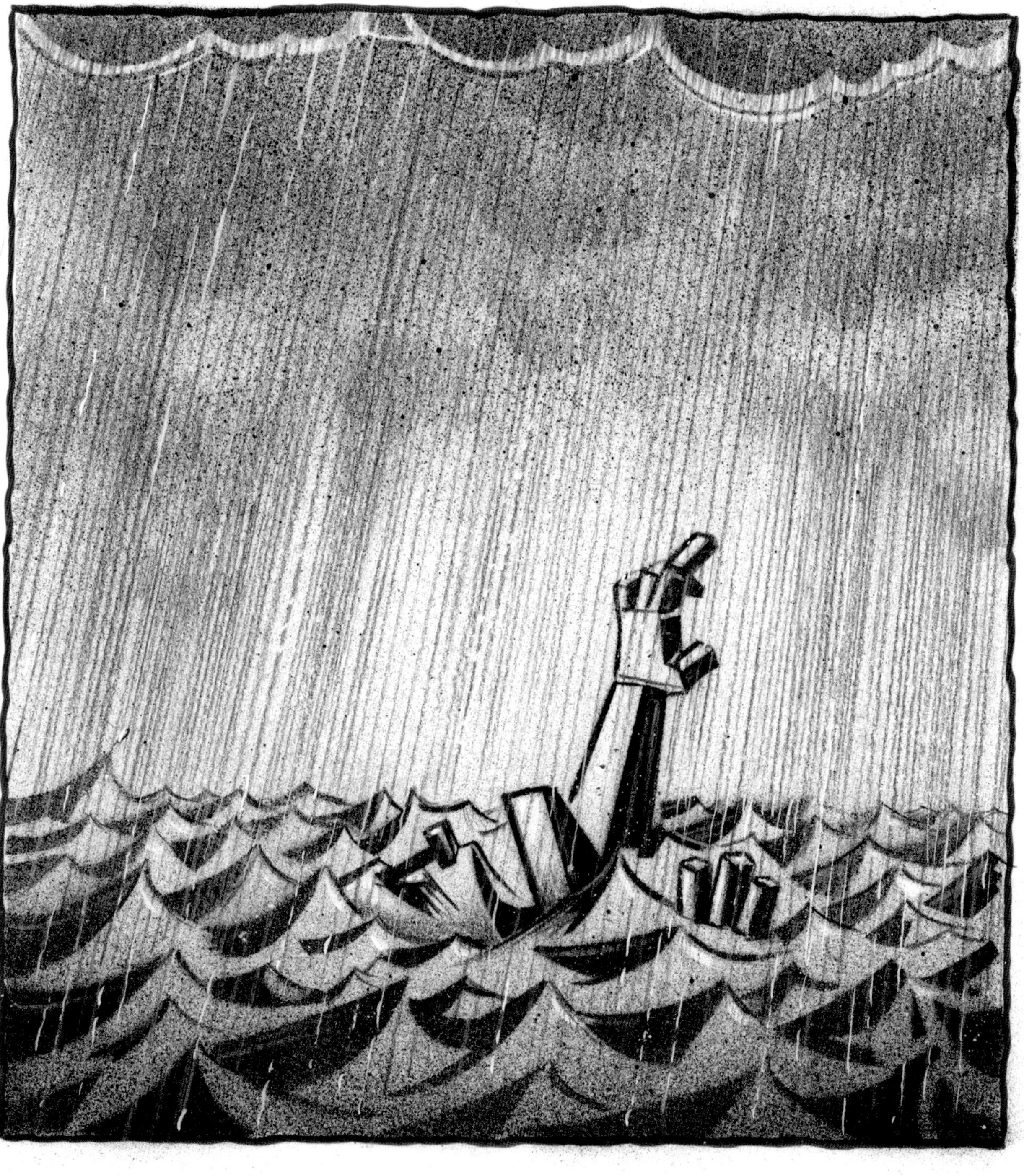

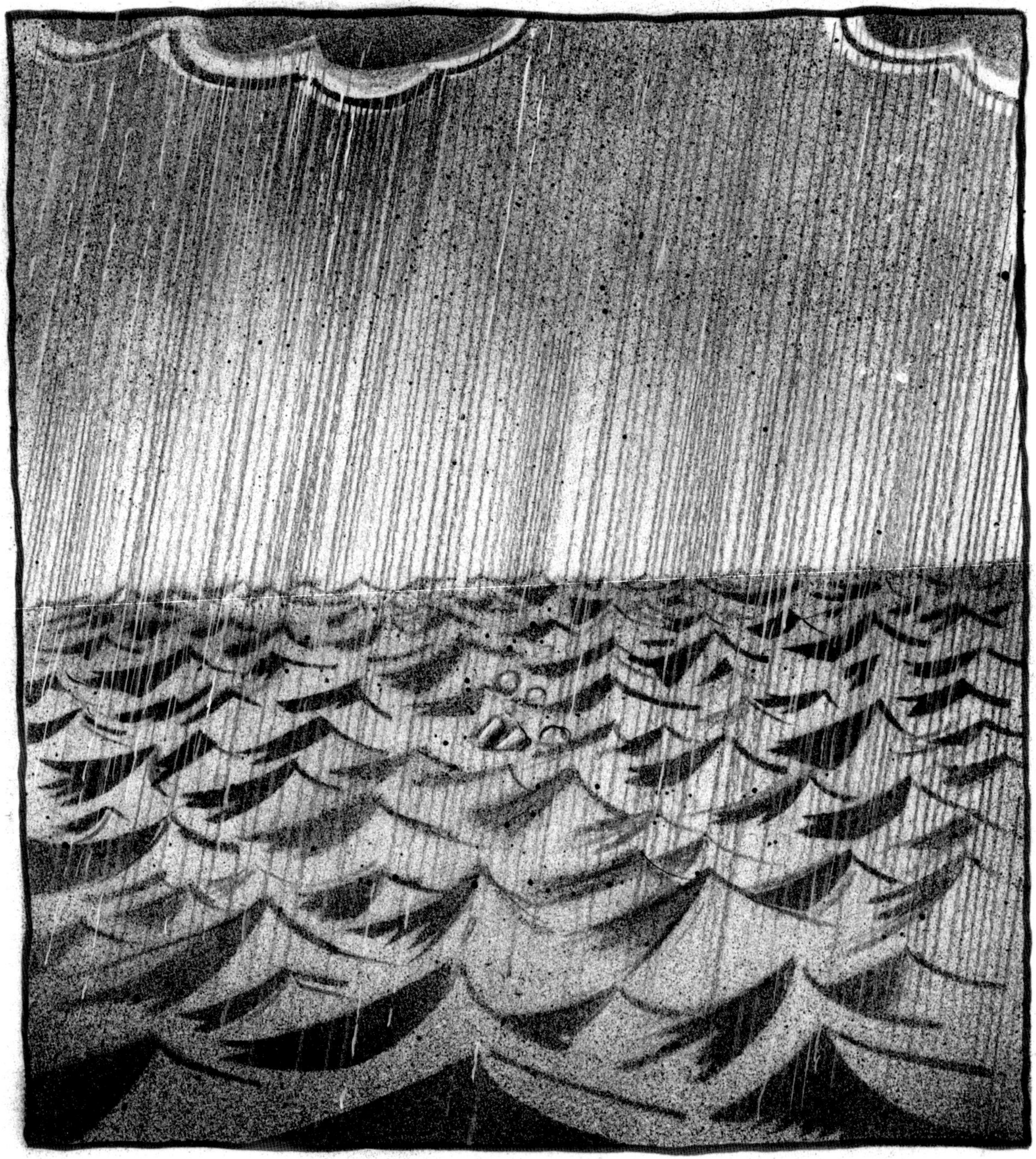

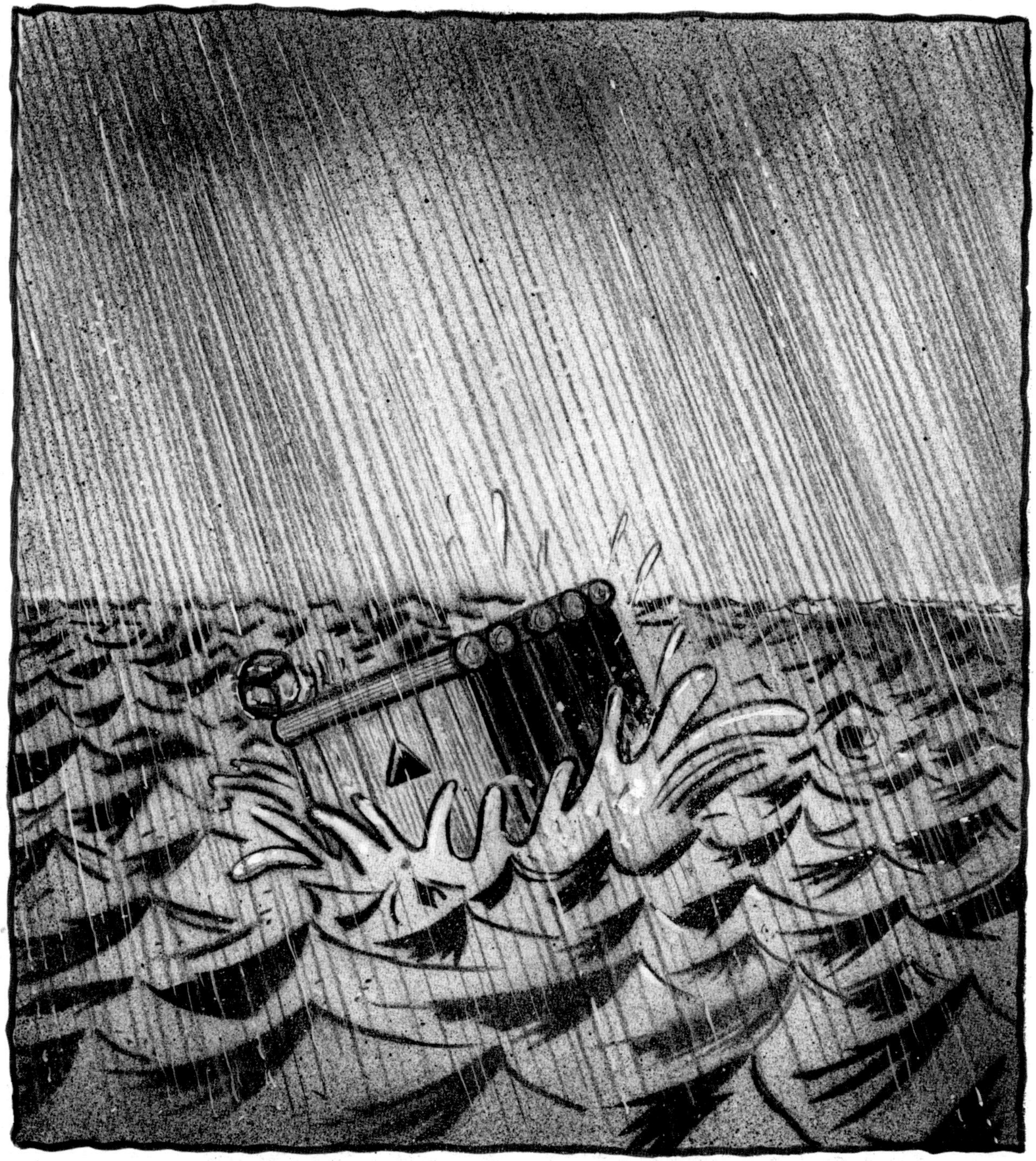

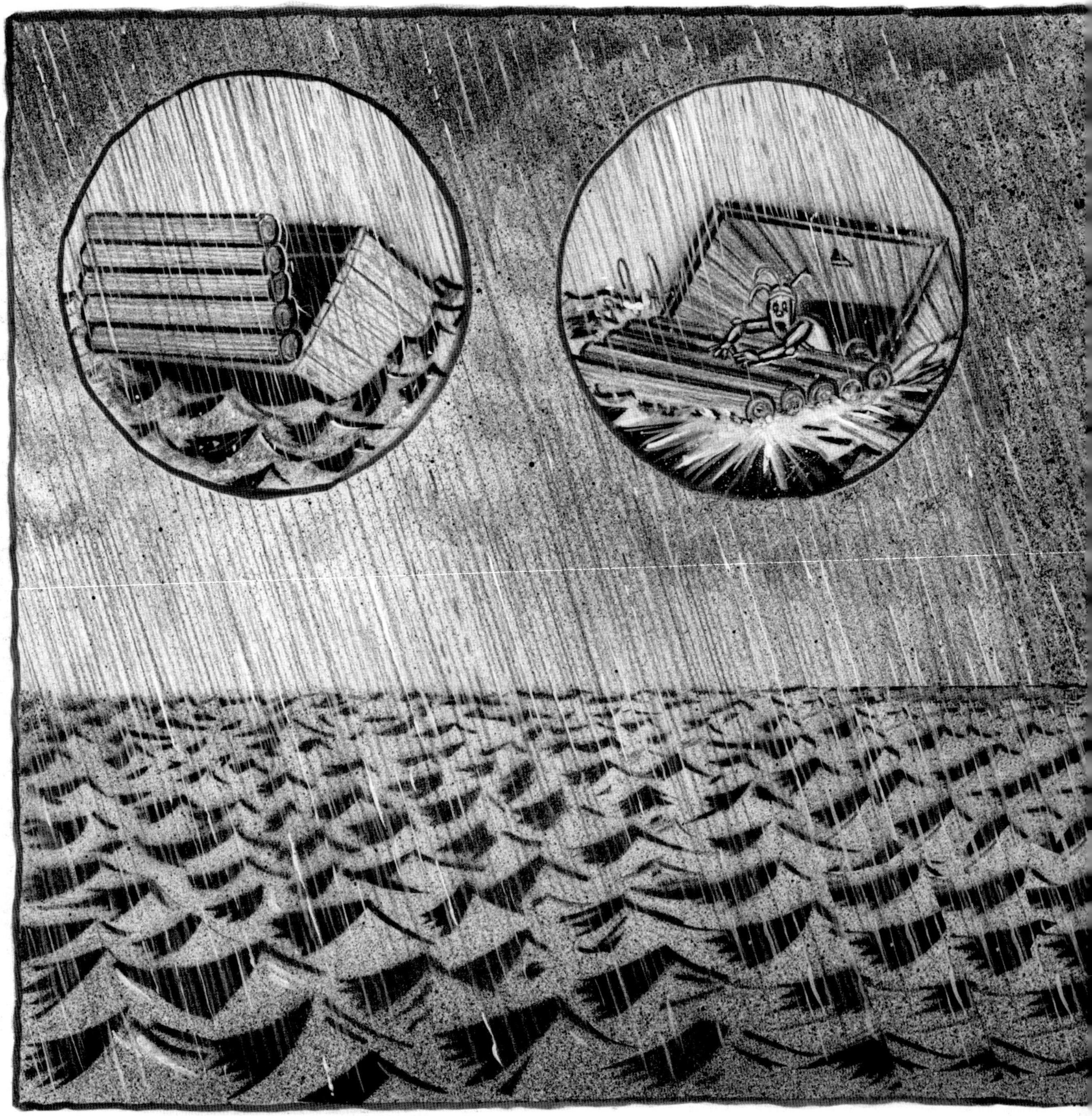

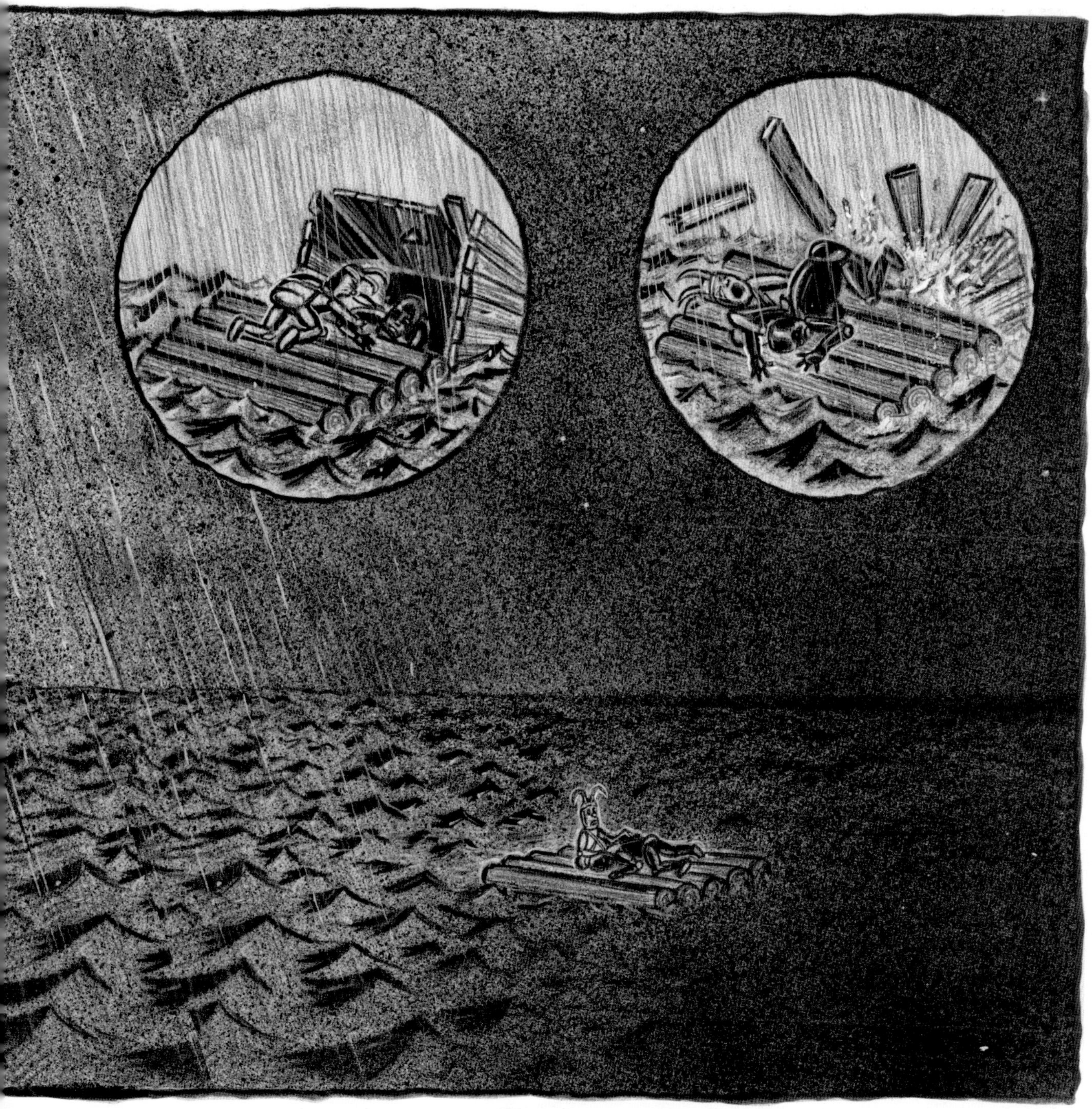

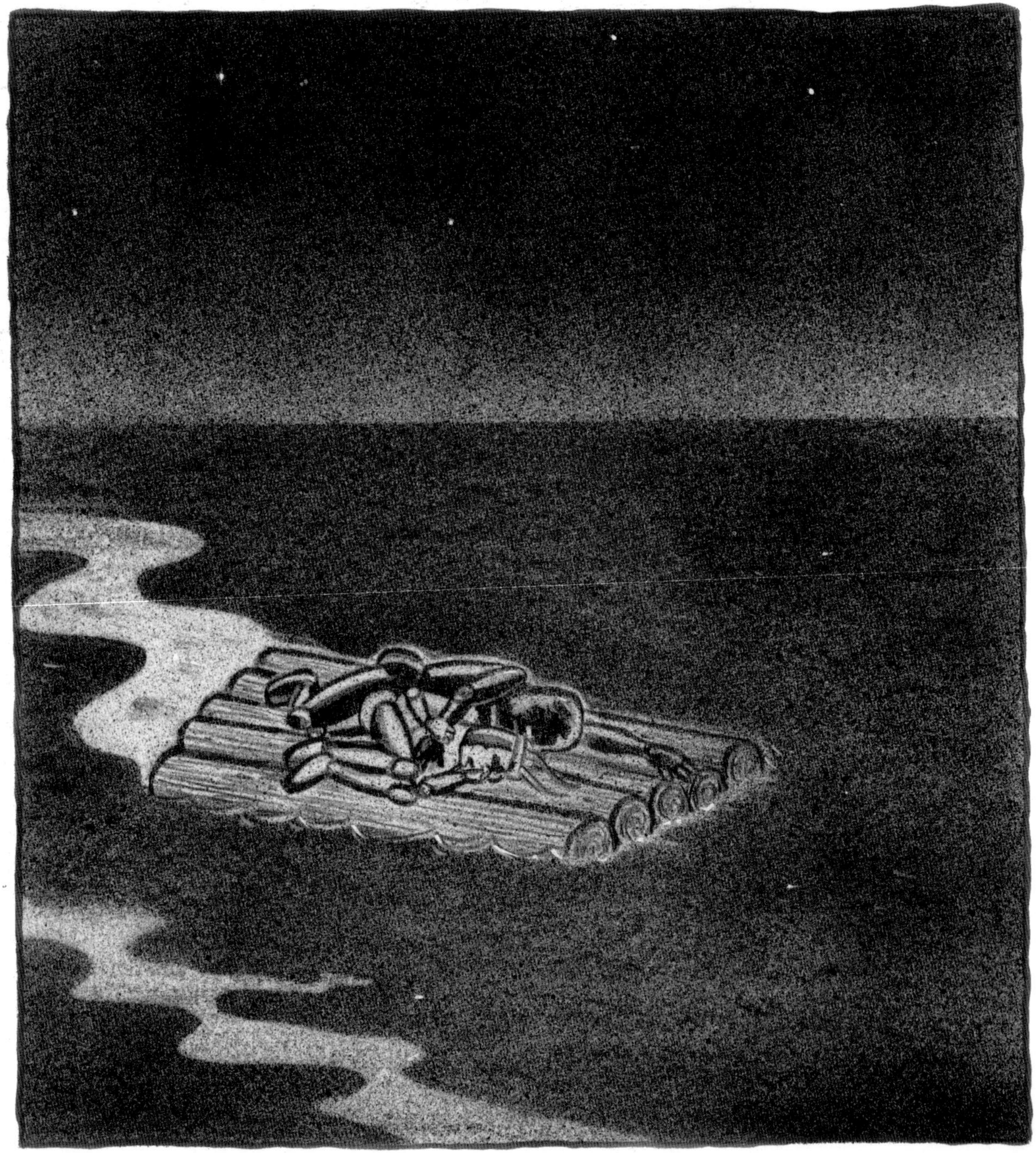

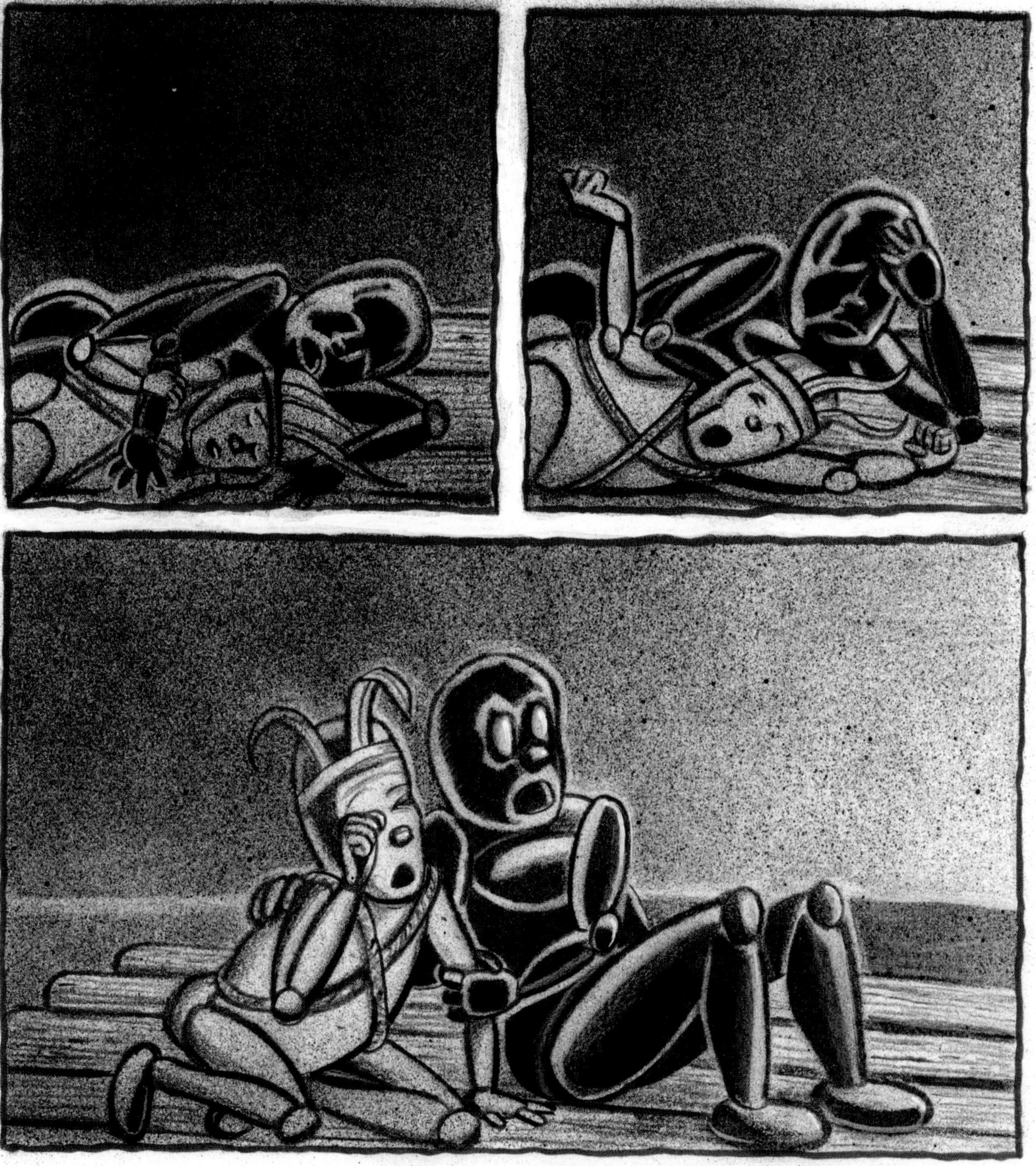

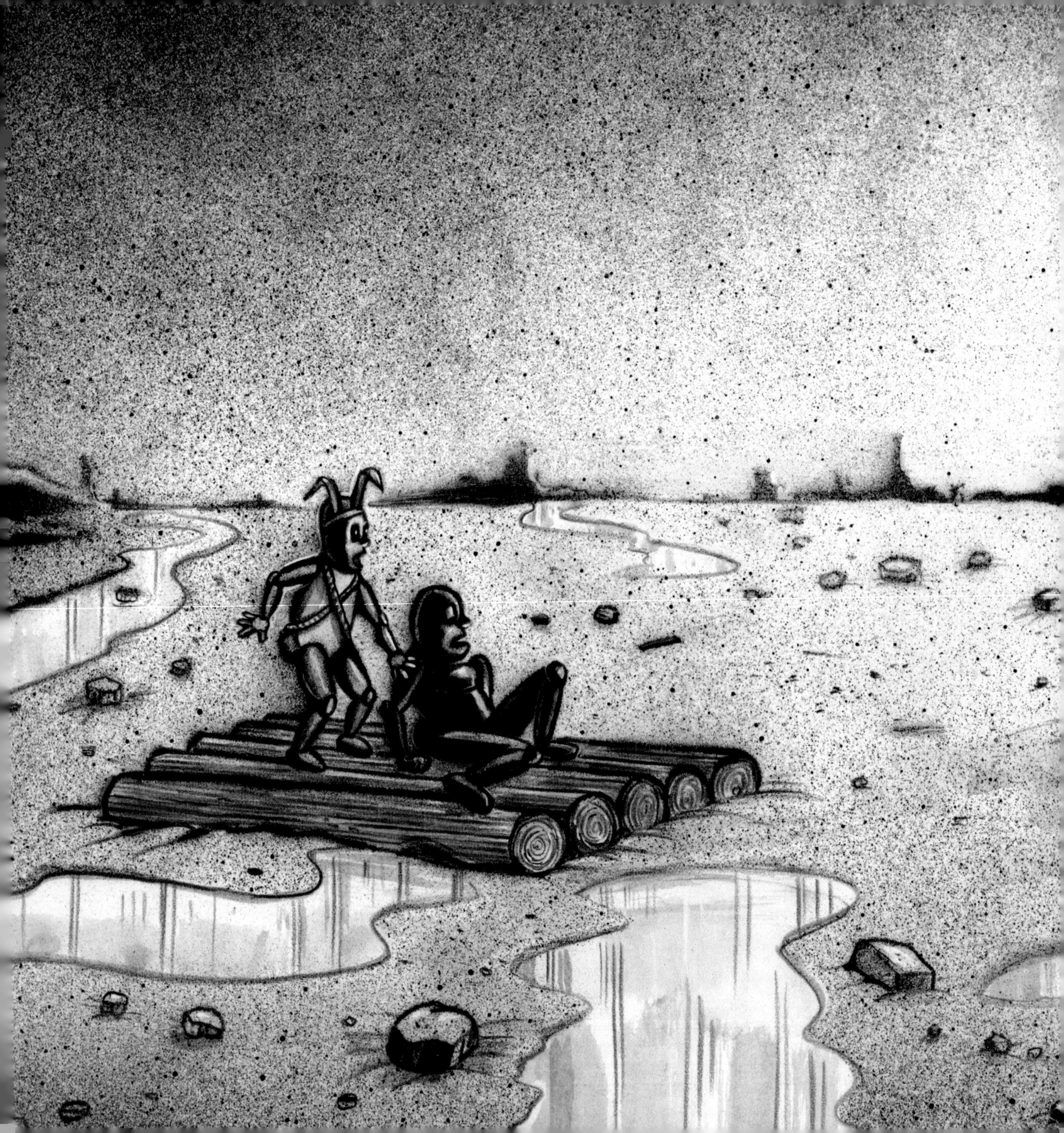

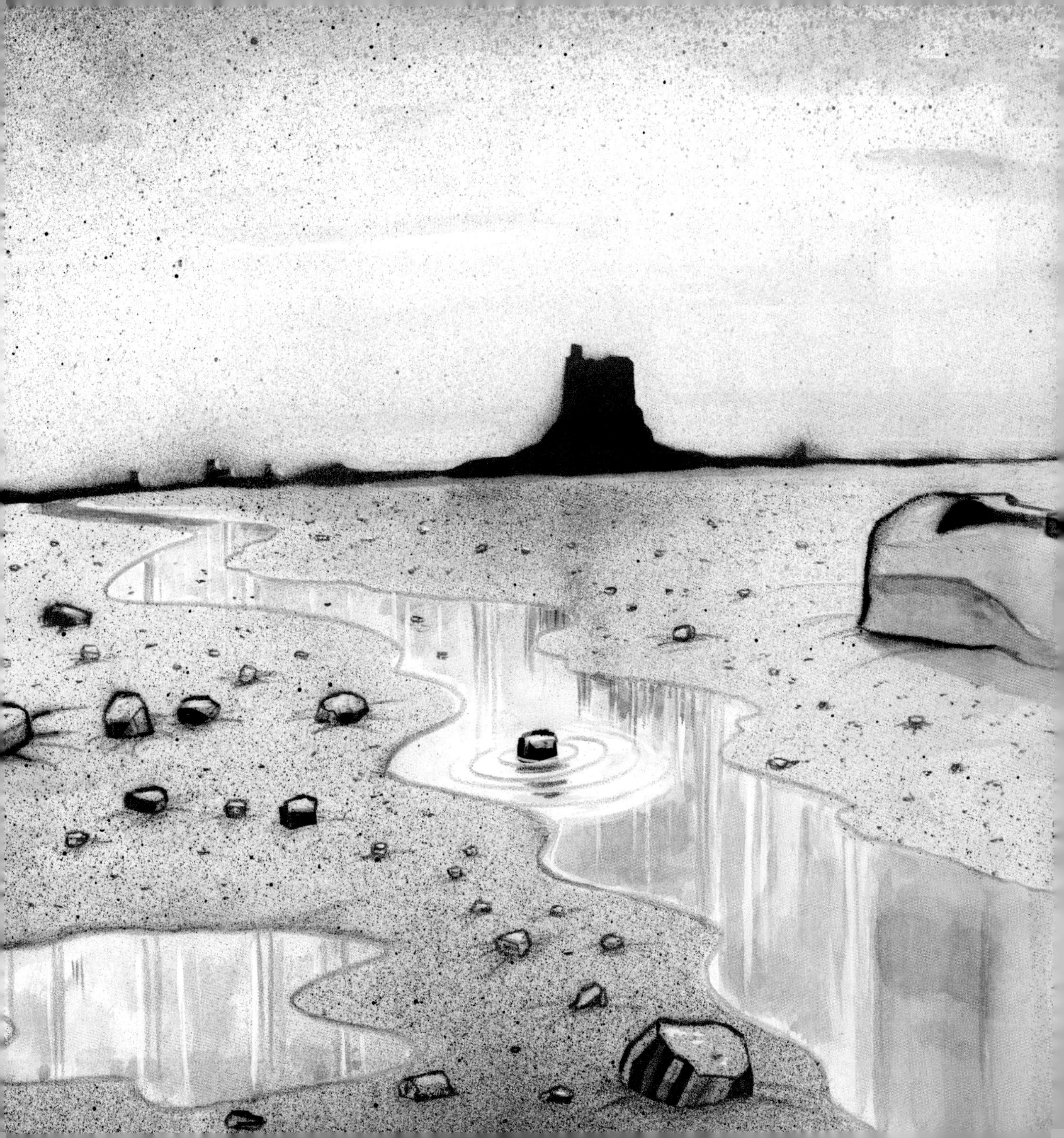

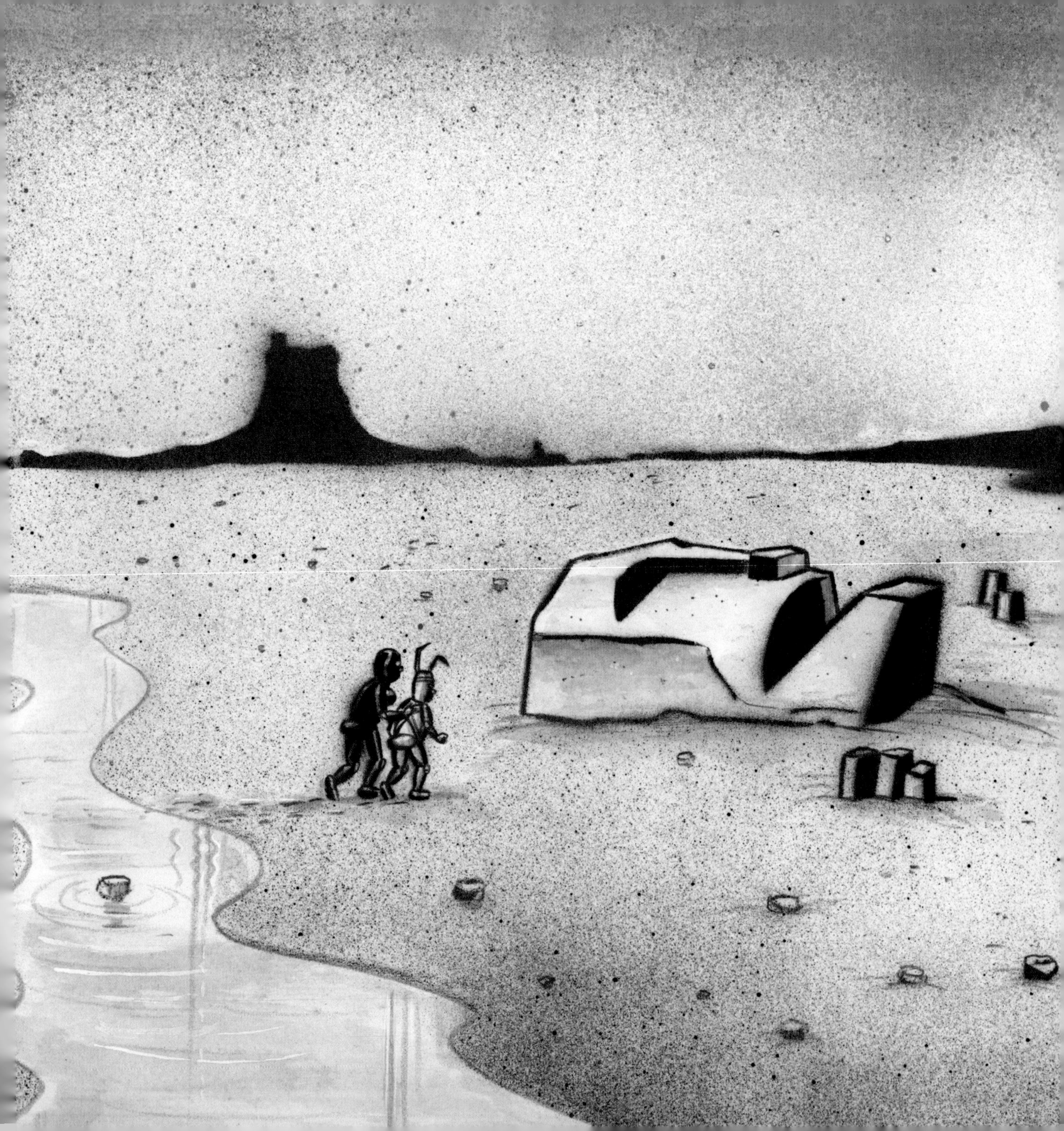

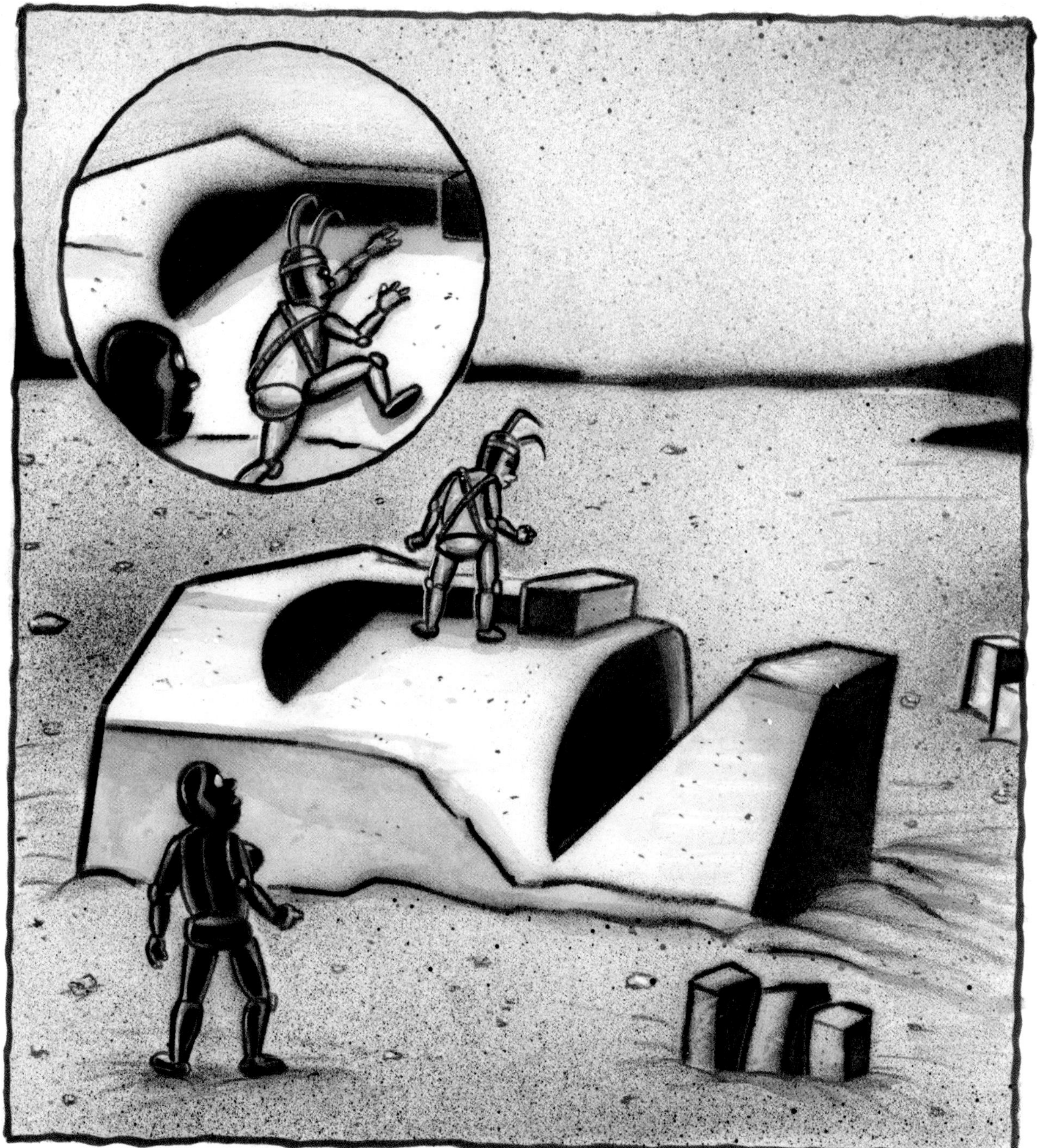

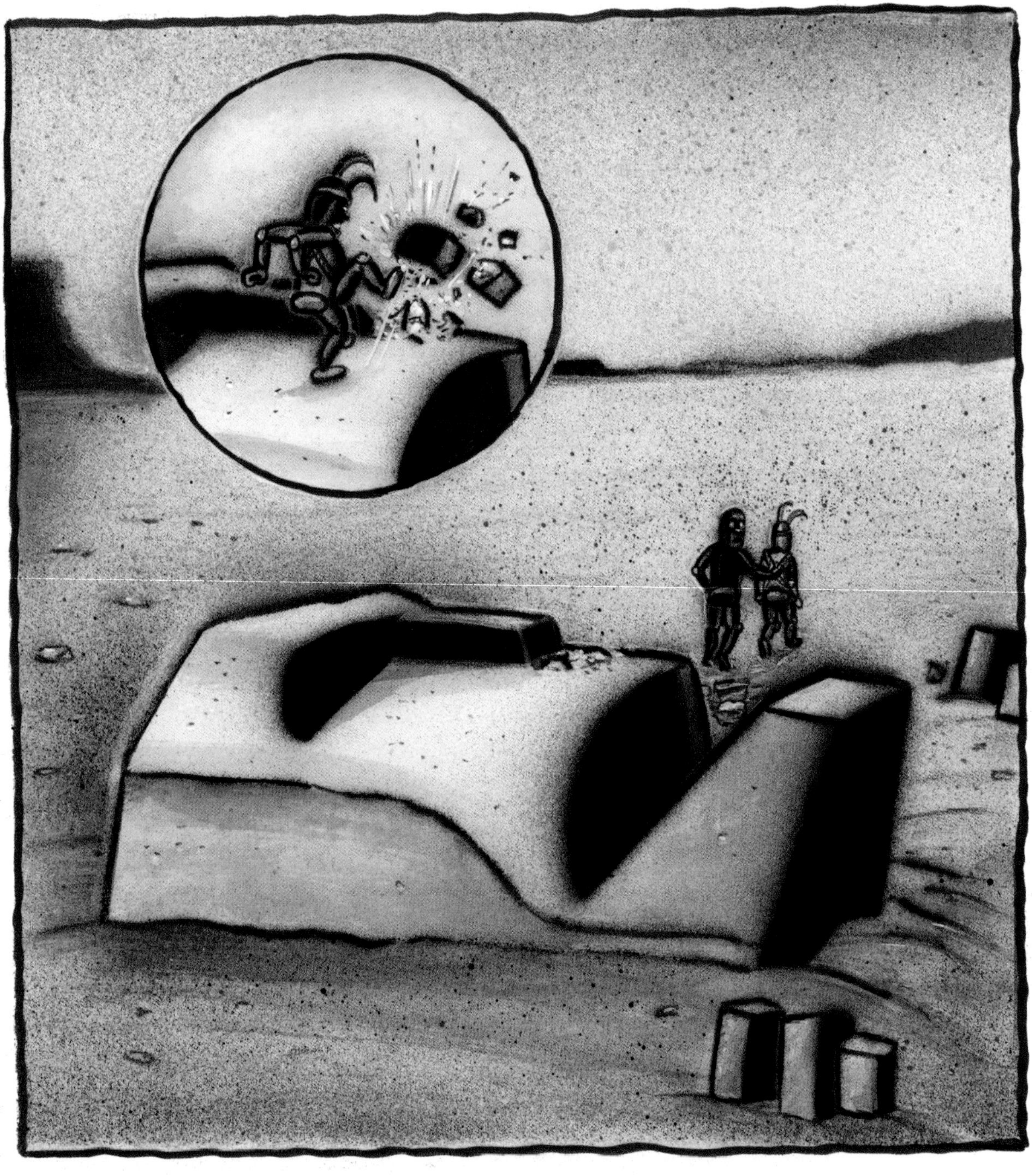

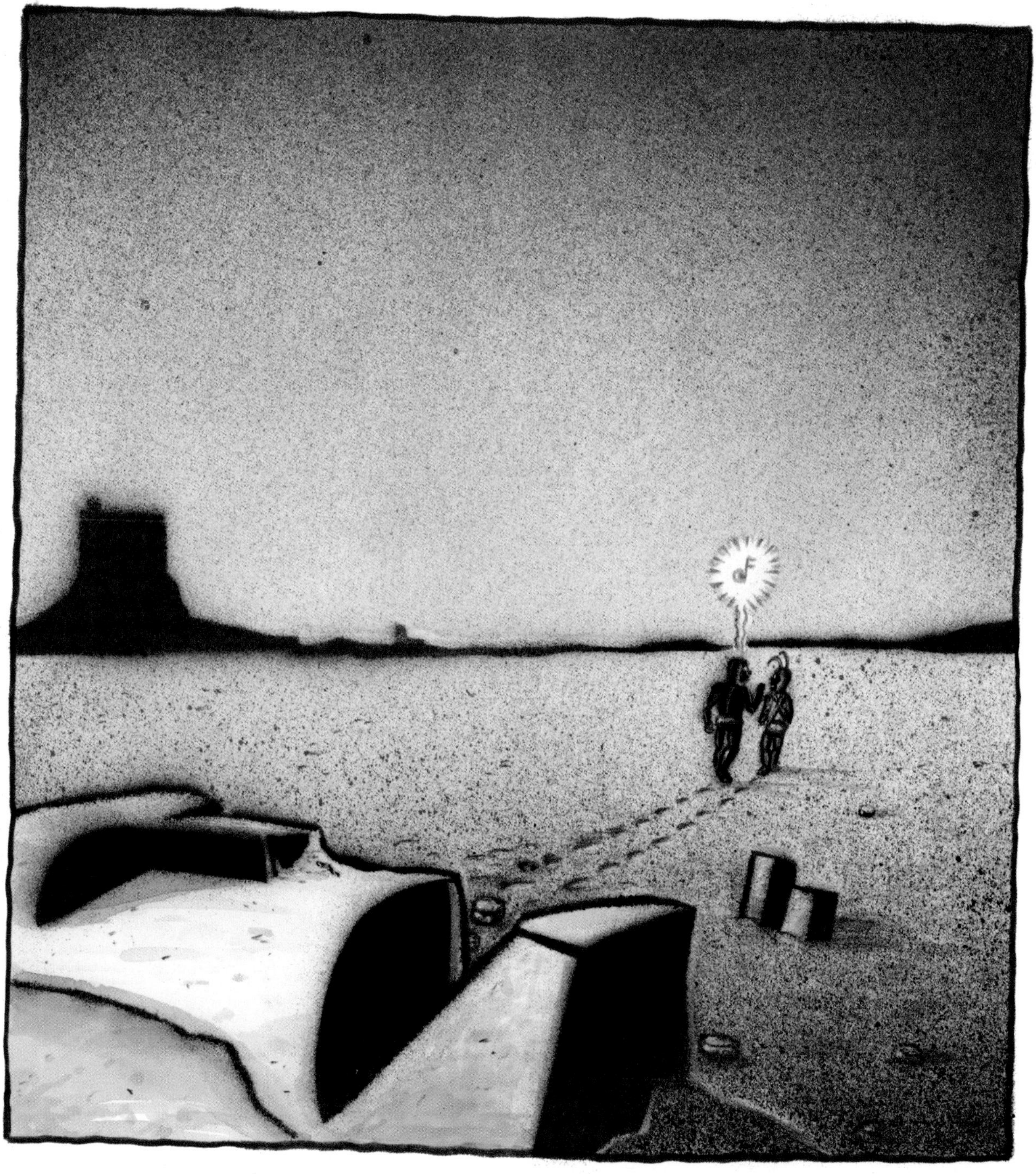

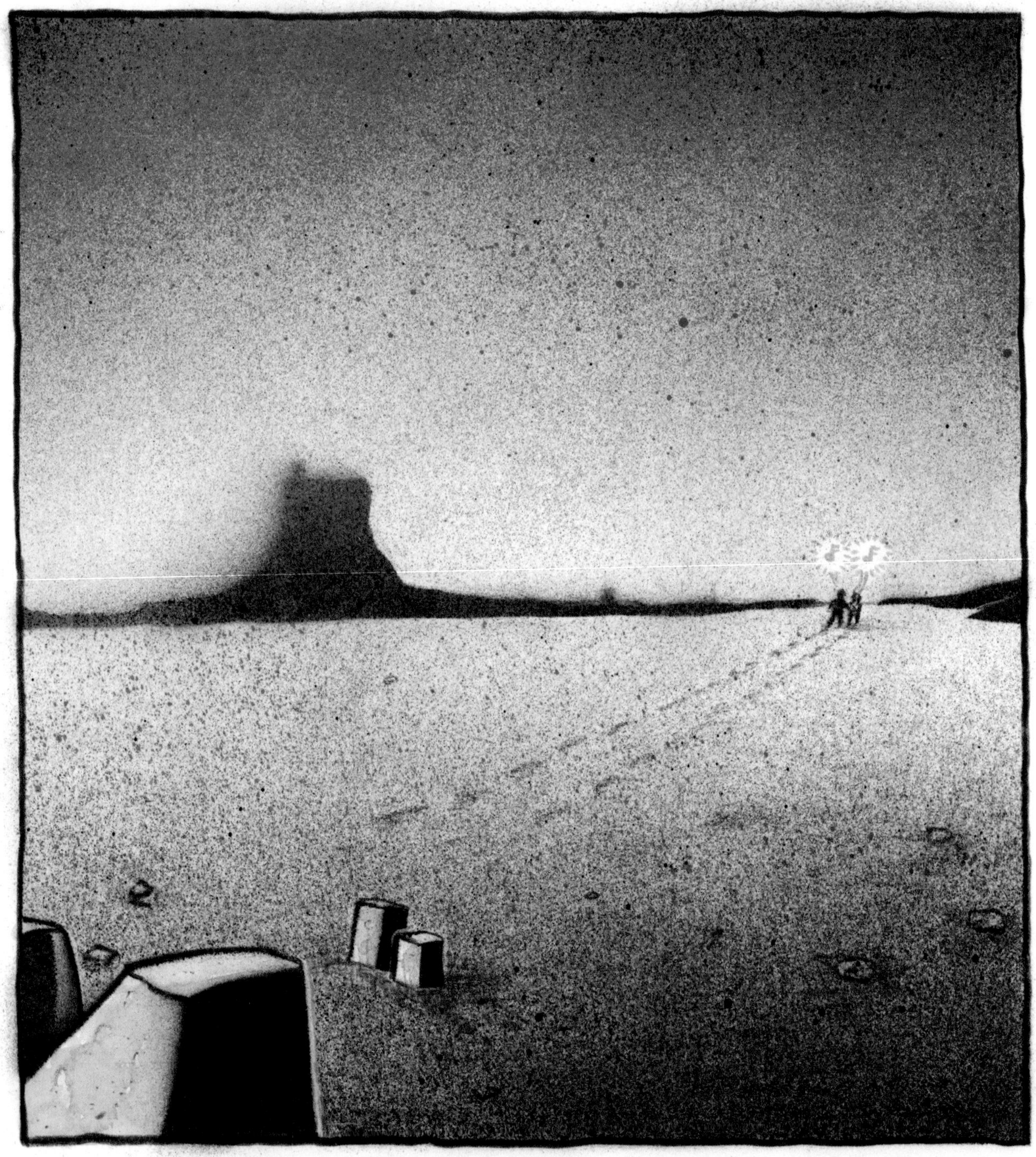

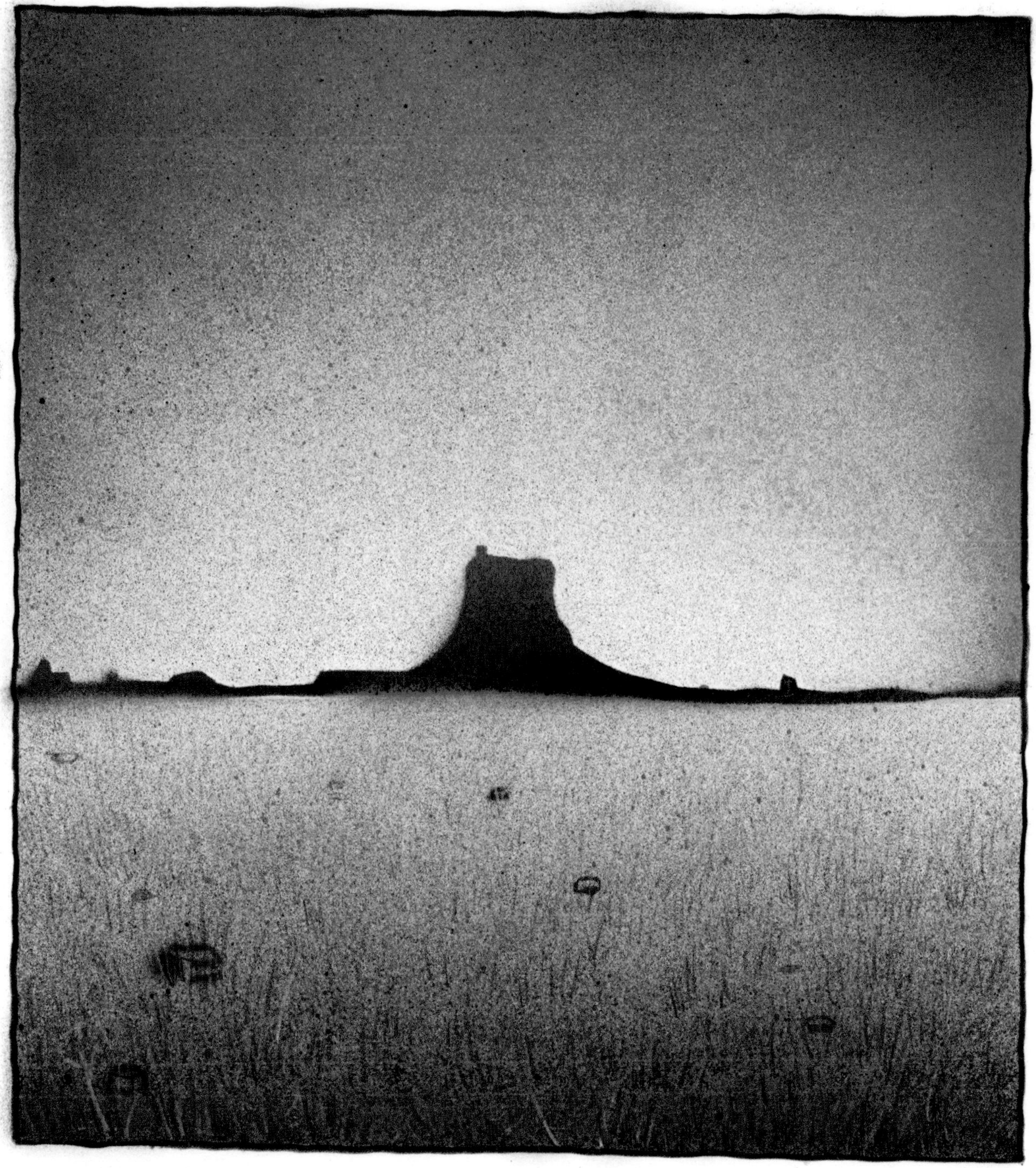

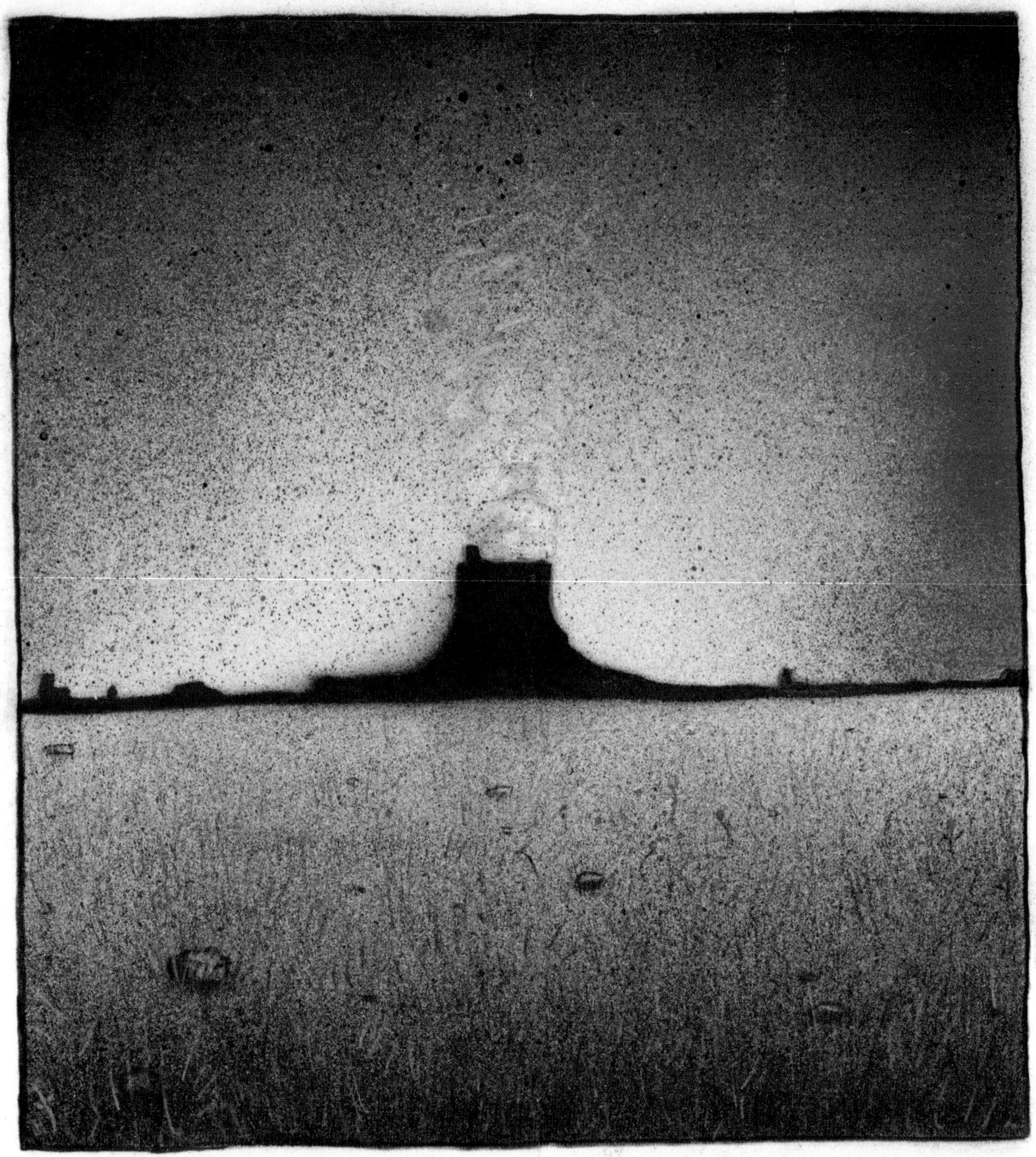